Talk Is Cheap

DATE DUE	
GAYLORD	PRINTED IN U.S.A.

Talk Is Cheap

Sarcasm, Alienation,
and the Evolution of Language

JOHN HAIMAN

Oxford University Press

Oxford   New York
Athens   Auckland   Bangkok   Bogota   Bombay   Buenos Aires
Calcutta   Cape Town   Dar es Salaam   Delhi   Florence   Hong Kong
Istanbul   Karachi   Kuala Lumpur   Madras   Madrid   Melbourne
Mexico City   Nairobi   Paris   Singapore   Taipei   Tokyo   Toronto   Warsaw

and associated companies in
Berlin   Ibadan

Published by Oxford University Press, Inc.
198 Madison Avenue, New York, New York 10016

Oxford is a registered trademark of Oxford University Press.

Library of Congress Cataloging-in-Publication Data
Haiman, John.
Talk is cheap : sarcasm, alienation, and the evolution of language
/ John Haiman.
    p.   cm.
Includes bibliographical references and index.
ISBN 0-19-511524-4; ISBN 0-19-511525-2 (pbk.)
1. Language and languages—Philosophy.   2. Semantics.
3. Pragmatics.   4. Irony.   I. Title.
P106.H2885   1997
401—dc21   96-40140

9 8 7 6 5 4 3 2 1

Printed in the United States of America
on acid-free paper

For Claire and Nina
with sweet memories, fond hopes,
and lots of love

Acknowledgments

I would like to thank the John Simon Guggenheim Foundation for having "validated" the unconventional project of a study of sarcasm with a fellowship in 1989; and Joan Bybee, director of the Linguistic Society of America Linguistic Institute in Albuquerque, for having invited me to present the ideas which arose in the course of pursuing this project in the summer of 1995. My thanks to Joan, the late Dwight Bolinger (philosopher, linguist, poet), Penelope Brown, Arthur Danto, Ellis Dye, Michele Emanatian, Suzanne Fleischman, Ivan Fonagy, Paul Friedrich, Talmy Givon, Bernd Heine, Dell Hymes, Ronald Langacker, Rachel May, Jeff Nash, Alan Rumsey, Frederick Schauer, Satoko Suzuki, Sandra A. Thompson, Anna Wierzbicka, and H. C. Wolfart for having done me the honor of reading and responding to earlier versions of portions of this work. I owe particular gratitude to Noam Chomsky for the ultimate professional courtesy of responding to portions of this manuscript which are critical of his theories, thereby engaging with ideas he vehemently disagrees with and could very easily ignore. I wish to acknowledge as well a number of lively and stimulating discussions with students and colleagues at the institute. For beautiful data on sarcasm in Mandarin, my thanks to Xiao Hong and Cheng Luo, formerly of the University of Manitoba, for as yet unpublished work; for data on sarcasm in German and Japanese, thanks to Anders Jonsson and Takanori Adachi, for two wonderful honors theses at Macalester College; for data on the ritualization of stress in English, thanks to LeAnn Sipple for a beautifully thought out and elegant independent project, also at Macalester.

Finally, I would like to personally acknowledge the influence of three deep thinkers who are already cited massively in the references but who merit more recognition here for the impact they have had on me. Ivan Fonagy has for decades been investigating the relationship between culture and personality in human language. His profound and suggestive studies on the phonetics of irony and cliché, on creative repetition, and on the iconicity of style represent only the most visible portion of a lifetime devoted to the study of the very subject matter of this book. Jorge Luis Borges is for my money the greatest philosopher of language—I suppose I should say "since Plato"—but since this is a personal and idiosyncratic tribute, I will say simply: Borges is the greatest philosopher of language that I know. Dave Barry is as brilliant and perceptive a social critic and philosopher as any of the American "public intellectuals" whose demise Russell Jacoby so eloquently and myopically mourns in his recent book *The Last Intellectuals*: he belongs (for me) in the company of Dwight MacDonald, Philip Rahv, Erving Goffman, and Susan Sontag—and my great countryman, Frigyes Karinthy.

St. Paul, Minnesota   J. H.
November 1996

Contents

Talk Is Cheap

Introduction

The Cheapness of Talk

> The essence of language is its creativity. This sentence, for example, has never been uttered before in the history of the human race. (popular linguistic proverb of the 1960s)

Language is replete with clichés and commonplaces: we recycle. In fact, it is appropriate that a book like this one, devoted as it is to recycled speech (both my own and that of others), should be creaking under the weight of other people's memorable quotations, and that it should begin with a quotation in order to justify the apparent flippancy of my title (itself, of course, a familiar slogan): "The world of human aspirations is . . . a symbolic-behavioral world *removed from the boundedness of the present moment, from the immediate stimuli which enslave all lower organisms*" (Becker 1971:139; emphasis added). The symbolic world, being removed from the here-and-now, is therefore *inconsequential* in the real objective world. With all due respect for human speech, then, and in this technical—even laudatory—sense of "cheap" which I have emphasized in the passage above, I contend that what is true of the symbolic world of human aspirations is quintessentially true of the medium within which almost all of these aspirations are expressed: Talk *is* cheap, and actions *do* speak louder than words. That is why we can even consider allowing ourselves such luxuries as the First Amendment; in fact, a forceful defense of the principle of free speech is based on exactly this property of symbolic behavior (see F.S. Haiman 1972). Granted, much of what we do in our lives is talk. Granted, also, that almost everything we actually physically do is a response to, and is organized by, some kind of talk. Granted, finally, that our "fictions are not super-

3

fluous creations that could be 'put aside' so that the 'more serious' business of life could continue" (Becker 1971:139).

Still there is a profound difference between *just doing it* and *"merely" saying it* (at least for human beings; cf. Dawkins 1982:60–64 for the case of animal communication). On the one hand, there are honest-to-God *manipulative* actions like changing a diaper, washing the dishes (or uttering magic spells like "Shazam" or, for that matter, saying "Aaaa" for the doctor), or running a computer program (replete with ordinary English words like "begin," "if," and "do"). Dawkins (ibid.) argues that all "animal communication" belongs with manipulative activities of this type. On the other hand, there are ordinary *communicative* speech acts like those of informing, commanding, cajoling, persuading, inciting, titillating, excommunicating, or insulting our fellow human beings.

As the partial list of examples given above makes clear, the difference between acts of manipulation and acts of communication is functional rather than purely formal. To utter a magic spell like "Shazam" (and thereby turn oneself into Captain Marvel) is purely instrumental behavior, like flicking a switch. To "send the message" in these cases is to directly effect a change in the physical world. Ordinary human language isn't like this. It is symbolic, not instrumental. Even the most seemingly instrumental "performative" speech act—from an omnipotent employer saying "You're fired," to Caligula giving the thumbs down over a fallen gladiator, to producing a work of pornography so effective that it will cause any male who picks it up to experience an instant erection (cf. Schauer 1982, who argues for limits on free speech on the grounds that some pornography is purely instrumental in this way), all the way to the most brilliant and subliminal propaganda ever designed to make us buy Coca Cola or vote for Ronald Reagan—requires social mediation and psychological interpretation in ways that magical speech acts, chemical messengers, and computer programs do not. It is only after the message is interpreted and voluntarily obeyed that the physical and social transformations which it "performs" are effected in the real world. For example, before he or she acts, it is (at least) necessary for the employee/gladiator to hear the boss's words, understand them, accept the boss's authority, acknowledge the uselessness of resistance, and decide not to put up an argument in the hope of changing his or her mind.

Unlike physical action, then, talk is *displaced* or removed from the world. As I have indicated, it is displaced by the acts of interpretation and voluntary acquiescence that go on in the *hearer's mind*. As the contrast between "Shazam" and "You're fired" should illustrate, the hearer's will plays a critical role in connecting what is spoken with what he or she then proceeds to do. Even the most abject slave or the most thoroughly brainwashed Praetorian guardsman, whose cooperation may be axiomatic, must first understand and inwardly agree. And until he or she does, even the emperor's speech is inconsequential—nothing but hot air.

But talk is displaced from the world from the *speaker's* point of view as well. There is an abyss between sweating profusely in the heat or screaming with pain, on the one hand, and saying "It's hot" (or "Whew!") or "That hurts" (or "Ouch!"), on the other, and this abyss is no less deep than the one between uttering "Shazam" and "You're fired." We may have no control over the tell-tale symptoms of our physical states (pain, cold, fatigue, or sexual desire), but we do control our linguistic signs: in any human language, we can utter fictions, whose prototype is the outright lie. Here, it is the speaker's will which mediates between what is going on in the world and what is said. And even the most fanatical I-am-a-camera truth-teller, whose honesty may be axiomatic, must miss a lot, must necessarily adopt a biased perspective on what he or she relates, and, in any case, may often remain silent. There is no necessary connection between the reality in the speaker's mind (let alone the reality of the outside world) and the image of it which the speaker presents to the hearer in human language. To say this is merely to reiterate the almost universally accepted dogma of the intentionality of meaning (cf. Grice 1957): human language means what it does because human speakers want it to. As speakers of a language, we have choices that symptomatic communicators do not have, including, of course, the choice of lying (Sapir 1921:15).

Guarantors of Sincerity

> As one judge said to the other "Be just, but if you can't be just, be arbitrary."
> (Burroughs 1968:22)

It is so axiomatic that any interested speaker who exercises personal volition will be dishonest or at least hopelessly biased that a surprisingly large number of social institutions have been erected with the express purpose of performing some kind of end-run around the speaker's free agency: mooring the hot air of his or her utterances to the ground of reality, and producing ostensibly disinterested "meaning without intention." DuBois has devoted important studies (1986, 1993) to an ethnographic examination of two of these institutions in local societies: ritual language and the language of divination. In ritual language, the actual proximate speaker establishes disinterestedness by uttering a script which is attributed to the Culture, the Deity, or some other impartial and superorganic source. In oracular utterances, an aleatory mechanism such as a throw of the dice or the unpredictable number of petals on a daisy guarantees the honesty of a natural divinely uttered "symptom" for choices which are expressed, but not made by, the speaker.

In the modern person's imagination, ritual formulas such as the liturgy and divinatory utterances based on coin tosses or the like may seem to be unimportant vestiges of an obsolete and superstitious worldview. I would agree with this commonsense view, but that is not to say that there are no functional equivalents to the tribal guarantors of impartiality in the megalopolis. In fact, I would argue that *most of the bureaucratic machinery in large-scale secular societies is devoted to achieving precisely the same ends that ritual language and alea-*

tory mechanisms allegedly achieve in local communities. Secular analogs to
fortune telling include unbiased merit evaluations (calls by umpires and refer-
ees; school and college grades; SAT, GRE, and I.Q. scores; civil service ex-
aminations) and personality assessments (e.g., MMPI, Briggs-Myers personality tests) based on objective criteria; impersonal and abstract legal codes
(whose greatest boast is that "the law is no respecter of persons"); verdicts
uttered by disinterested strangers; and democratic elections (vox populi, vox
dei). They include the institution of our major symbolic system for mediating
social relationships, the institution of money itself. To pay for anything with
money is, in effect, to make a promise. When this promise is "uttered"—apt
word—by the disinterested mint, it is legal tender, but when uttered by the
individual, it is at best a personal IOU, and at worst, counterfeiting or forgery,
a criminal act.

Marxists, critical legal scholars, and others are of course correct in pointing
out the bias and the class interest which are built into all of these allegedly
impartial mechanisms, but the fact that they find it necessary to attack the
appearance of impartiality is exactly my point. The ostensible purpose of the
disinterested institution is to achieve truth and justice by bleaching out the individual speaker and separating meaning from that speaker's personal intention.

The appearance of disinterest ("justice," or failing justice, arbitrariness) is
what acts as a guarantor of sincerity, assuring that social discourse achieves
meaning without the intervening obfuscations and distortions of the speaker's
will. But there is a crucial difference between the sincerity of a private personal symptom (as manifested in one's signature or the reading on a lie detec-
tor) and the impartiality of legal discourse in a large-scale society. The private
symptom is iconic: the legal decision is essentially arbitrary, as is the social
image. And this very arbitrariness is what acts as a second-best guarantor of
justice, as Burroughs's junky points out.

The idea that the image of himself or herself or others—in other words, the
message—which the interested speaker presents can be free-floating, decoupled
from its original context, and unmoored in reality is, it seems to me, one of the
"novel discoveries" of postmodernism. In his brilliant survey of this sensibility, Ewen (1988:25) pays tribute to Oliver Wendell Holmes, an unacknowl-
edged precursor of Walter Benjamin and Daniel Boorstin, for his "prescient
understanding"—in 1859—that photography could give "substance to the idea
that images could be the conclusive expression of reality on the one hand, and
exist autonomous of that reality on the other."

But this insight, of which Ewen perhaps imagines he is unearthing one of
the earliest known expressions, is only a slightly reworded restatement of one
of the oldest chestnuts of linguistics, the doctrine of the arbitrariness of names,
labels, and linguistic signs in general. Even as a truism, this goes back not to
Saussure's famous *Cours de linguistique générale* ([1916] 1966), or to Shakespeare's "What's in a name?," or even to the Stoics (pace Jakobson 1965), but
at least to Plato's *Cratylus*: "How realities are to be learned or discovered is
perhaps too great a question for you or me to determine; but it is worth while
to have reached even this conclusion, that they are to be learned and sought

for, not from names, but much better through themselves than through names" (1926:187). What is novel in the observations of Holmes, Benjamin, and Boorstin is not the fundamental (and far from trivial) insight that *words are not (just) things*. Rather, it is that the photographic image is still thought at least to *originate* as an icon of its referent (and is meant to be interpreted as one), while the verbal image does not.

Guarantors of Consequentiality

> How do you think the Egyptians built the Sphinx? Surely, you don't think that a bunch of common Egyptians just got together one day and said: "Hey, why don't we build a Sphinx!" Of course not. Left to their own devices, the common Egyptians would have spent their time growing food. To get some real *culture*, to get the *Sphinx*, the Egyptians needed a government authority, someone with vision, someone with taste, someone with whips and spears. (Barry 1987:164)

The hook which anchors words in reality from the point of view of the free agent-hearer is the one which ensures consequentiality for the speaker's words. And—at least in a society of strangers, where personal charisma and moral authority are not an inducement to obedience and the threat of ostracism is not a deterrent to disobedience—this enforcing device is simply one of two kinds of physical power:

1. The power of the speaker to back up his or her words by political or economic coercion. Without this power, mere words are not attended to. United Nations General Assembly resolutions and decisions of the World Court in The Hague are notorious examples of institutional language uttered without the backing of executive authority—and they are widely ignored in the press and elsewhere, to no one's surprise.
2. The power of the hearer to hold the speaker to his or her words through the institution of legally binding contracts. A man may swear undying love to his wife to be, but no courts will hold him accountable for his oaths when they eventually separate. To get a court order, the couple need a prenuptial agreement.

In neither case are the whips or spears of the executive authority entirely out of sight.

These kinds of slippage or displacement between the symbolic action of language and events in the actual world (both of them consequences and manifestations of free will) come very close to defining the essence of language. In fact, my metaphor of language as a balloon of hot air anchored to the ground of reality by socially determined guarantees of sincerity and consequentiality is not that different from the familiar Saussurean model of the sign whose form (hot air) is anchored to its meaning (our conception of reality) by social conventions alone. Rather than its familiar arbitrariness, however, it is the *insincerity* and the *inconsequentiality* of language, the essence of which is summed up in my title, and in dozens of comparable proverbs, which is my present topic.

Without Cheapness, No Meaning

I've chosen a deliberately cynical characterization of this property for my title, but I could just as easily have emphasized its more positive aspects. Another apparently less pejorative but entirely synonymous term for "cheapness" is the *autonomy* or *displacement* of language, long recognized as one of its principle design features (cf. Hockett & Ascher 1964). It is this feature of language which emancipates human beings from what Loren Eiseley has famously called "the eternal present of the animal world" and makes possible the institutions of human culture.

This autonomy of talk is also implicitly captured in Erving Goffman's powerful metaphors of "frames" and "laminations" (Goffman 1974). Essentially, a frame is a code or set of principles for the interpretation of any ongoing activity (ibid.:10–11). It is *only* when the observer has been provided with interpretations that he or she can attempt to answer the question "What is going on here?" Relative to natural phenomena, cultural "guided doings" are framed; relative to cultural actions in general, talk is even more framed. Every additional frame "laminates" the ongoing activity further from the real world of fact (ibid.: chaps. 1, 2).

Some humdrum examples of frames in language are provided by the notion of shifters, signs whose interpretations are wholly or largely determined by the context in which they are uttered. Relative to semantically autonomous intersubjective words like "rosebush" or "pig," shifters or egocentric particulars like "I," "now," "here," and "ago" are framed by the speech act; that is, what they mean in the world depends entirely on who is saying them and when and where they are being said. Only a bit less apparently pragmatic are shifters like "exotic," "good," and "appropriate." Phonetic sounds are framed by emic slashes: the "meaning" of a given sound is provided by the sound pattern of the language in which it is uttered (cf. Sapir 1925, 1949). In that sense, they too are shifters.

The radically pragmatic perspective of authors like Mark Twain and J. L. Borges identifies every text and every strip of activity as a possible shifter. In *Tom Sawyer* the action of painting a fence with whitewash may be framed as either drudgery or the hottest game in town. (So, conversely, the narcissistic yuppie toiling at his rowing machine, if he were paid for his effort, would be pitied as a galley slave.) The text of *Don Quixote* has one set of meanings when uttered by the Spaniard Miguel Cervantes and a radically different set of meanings when uttered 300 years later by the Frenchman Pierre Menard in Borges's magnificent parable "Pierre Menard, Author of the Quixote":

> It is a revelation to compare Menard's *Don Quixote* with Cervantes'. The latter, for example, wrote (part one, chapter nine): ". . . truth, whose mother is history, rival of time, depository of deeds, witness of the past, exemplar and adviser to the present, and the future's counselor." Written in the seventeenth century, written by the "lay genius" Cervantes, this enumeration is a mere rhetorical praise of history. Menard, on the other hand, writes: ". . . truth, whose mother is history,

rival of time, depository of deeds, witness of the past, exemplar and adviser to the present, and the future's counselor." History, the *mother* of truth: the idea is astounding. Menard, a contemporary of William James, does not define history as an inquiry into reality, but as its origin. Historical truth, for him, is not what has happened; it is what we judge to have happened. The final phrases—*exemplar and adviser to the present, and the future's counselor*—are brazenly pragmatic. The contrast in style is also vivid. The archaic style of Menard—quite foreign, after all—suffers from a certain affectation. Not so that of his forerunner, who handles with ease the current Spanish of his time. (Borges 1962e:43)

Relative to instrumental behavior, all symbolic behavior or talk is framed or "one lamination further removed" from reality. Instrumental behavior is framed in turn relative to natural phenomena; and finally, natural phenomena that seem to obey physical laws are framed relative to the uncanny or supernatural phenomena. These last, according to Goffman (1974:28–30), are totally unframed: they are, then, the absolute real thing, "unmediated" ultimate reality. But what is this "ultimate" reality? Without frames, it is (to cite some familiar sources) "just one damn thing after another," "a vast garbage heap," "a blooming buzzing confusion," "a tale told by an idiot": immediate but inexplicable, vivid but incomprehensible.

It is only when a "strip" of activity is edited and framed (and an important part of the frame is the identification of when it has begun and ended: consider the infinite ambiguity of the strip of activity which is represented by the jagged line of stock quotations) and *represented* in a story that it becomes satisfyingly meaningful or can be said to have a moral. Robert Browning's Fra Lippo Lippi makes a closely related point about the ultimate framing function of art: "We first love things when first we see them painted." (For a lowbrow translation of this stunning psychological insight, I am indebted to John Bernstein for a ribald joke about the castaway who finds himself on a desert island with Sharon Stone and becomes restless after a few days of bliss because he *needs somebody to brag to*.)

There is no cynicism implied in the observation that we live, and that we need to live, in a forest of symbols. It is precisely our hunger for meaning that drives us to bifurcate all our experiences into signs, omens, and portents. But the essence of a sign is precisely this resulting duality: what it *is* (objectively or "etically") is different from what it *means* (in a language or "emically"). And in comparison to what it means, what it is is necessarily some kind of hot air, which is only arbitrarily anchored to what it means by social conventions.

Outline of This Book

Our point of departure will be an investigation of sarcasm and the ways in which speakers mark its expression. Sarcasm is a particularly transparent variety of "cheap talk" or hot air insofar as the speaker is overtly meaning (and saying) the opposite of what he or she ostensibly claims to be saying. The delimitation of sarcasm and its description are the subjects of the first part of the discussion (chapters 1–3).

But sarcasm is not the only variety of speech which is manifestly insincere: other genres of "schtick" which involve false fronts include simple politeness, hints, understatement, euphemisms, code, sententiousness, gobbledygook, posturing, bantering jocularity, affectation, and ritual or phatic language. All of these could be considered varieties of *un-plain speaking* and are more or less explicitly contrasted with plain speaking, which has a unique and privileged status in current American ideologies of both popular culture and academic discourse. Although there is an extensive tradition of study of politeness in language and some very insightful studies of ritual language have recently appeared, there have been no attempts to define the broad category of utterances to which sarcasm, ritual language, and polite speech belong. In outlining the kinship of these speech act types, I will be diverging from scholars like John Searle (1979) and Ellen Winner (1988), who have lumped them together with metaphor as examples of what *they* might call "un-plain speaking": a class of speech genres where the literal meaning of the words in a message (sentence meaning) is not the same as the speaker's intention in uttering it (utterance meaning). What is common to sententiousness, affectation, sarcasm, ritual language, and politeness, and what distinguishes them from metaphor, is the idea of the speaker as a divided self: more specifically the speaker's self-conscious alienation from the actual referential content of his or her message. In order to put my descriptions of these genres into some kind of perspective, however, I will also attempt to outline a description of a widespread attitude toward *plain speaking*, a mode of speech to which they are all apparently (but, in my view, quite mistakenly) opposed. What is common to all of these genres, *including self-conscious plain speaking*, is a marked degree of speaker's *detachment from* (which is the same thing as "awareness of") the social role which he or she is performing, as well as from the message which he or she is ostensibly delivering. In the second part of this book (chapters 4–7), I will focus on the ideas of alienation and the divided play-acting self as manifested in un-plain speaking genres and other formally unrelated linguistic behavior.

Finally, all self-consciously insincere language may be identified as a kind of formulaic stylization or ritualized version of plain speaking. A great deal is known about not only ritual but also the ritualization process and not only in language but also in other forms of both human and animal activity. I believe that the ritualization process (variously described and named in linguistics, not to mention other fields like art, sociology, ethology, anthropology, and law) not only is pervasive in the development of language but also may shed light on its origins as well. Not only is talk cheap; it is in the very process of "cheapening" that actions become talk. This is, at least, what I will argue in the third section (chapters 8–12). I will try to show that the transformation of ordinary language (primarily through repetition) into ritual alienated language is both formally and conceptually a very plausible model for the transformation of prelinguistic symptoms into the signs of human language. Both transformations are characterized by a large number of the same unidirectional changes. In enumerating and describing these changes with copious and more or less well-documented examples, I hope to offer some speculations concerning the genesis of the design feature of displacement in human language.

ONE

_____

Sarcasm and the Postmodern Sensibility

"Is the pundit you looking for, not so?"
The taxi driver said, "Nah. We come all the way from Port of Spain just for the
scenery." (Naipaul 1959:8)

Whatever our social or psychological purposes in being sarcastic, from a purely
linguistic or grammatical point of view, we are doing two things at once: we
are communicating an ostensible message to our listeners but at the same time
we are framing this message with a commentary or metamessage that says
something like "I don't mean this: in fact, I mean the exact opposite." This
metamessage makes sarcasm seem like a very abstract and quintessentially
"linguistic" activity, for when we engage in it, we are using language to talk
not about the world but about itself. Moreover, as there are many other devices
available for performing the act of denial or committing verbal aggression, it
seems like a needlessly roundabout way of performing this task.

Accordingly, we should not be surprised to find that sarcasm correlates with
some other kinds of "sophistication" or to find that it is far from universal even
among human beings. If language is what defines humanity, then irony and
sarcasm may conceivably define a "higher" or "more decadent" type of culture or personality or at least a geographically and temporally restricted use of
language to perform verbal aggression or other kinds of work. This idea has
occurred to a number of observers of contemporary American culture.

A recent article in _Spy_ magazine, for example, announces that the familiar
mimed "air quotes" sign of the second and third digits of both hands that says
"we're not serious" is "the quintessential _contemporary_ gesture" (emphasis

12

added) and attributes this to the influence of (somewhat mysteriously) television: "To get the joke, all you had to do was what you had always done best— *watch a lot of TV*" (Rudnick & Andersen 1989:40). Alienation and shallowness of affect are perceived as the exclusive moral preserve of the generation of Americans born between 1961 and 1981: "There's our 'attitude;' a coolness, a detachment. There's the way we dress—'mock' turtlenecks, way-too-big suits. And the way we speak: ironic, flip, uncommitted, a question mark at the end of every other sentence" (Nancy Smith, "25 and Pending," *Washington Post*, cited in Howe & Strauss 1993:181). In a perceptive undergraduate essay, Molly Test (1989) notes that irony on TV is so pervasive that its *absence*, as in the style of Dale Cooper, the lead character in *Twin Peaks*, sets off alarms:

> Dale Cooper . . . speaks in such a serious unaffected way that we cannot possibly take it seriously. The American audience is so used to television being light and totally affected that when a character doesn't crack a joke every five minutes, it commands attention. Cooper's rational honest form of talk is virtually nonexistent in real life as well and therefore absurd. He utters banalities with conviction (e.g., "You can't let personal feelings interfere with your work"; "mind, body, and spirit are up to the task") and describes, rather than expresses his emotions (e.g., "I have violated my professional code and now Audrey is paying the price").

In fact, in addition to the weird and surreal Dale Cooper, two currently accepted types embody the exotic virtues of speaking banalities with conviction in postmodern America: latter-day "fools in Christ" like the saintly Forrest Gump in Roger Zemeckis's popular film and innocent aliens who fall to earth like John Carpenter's extraterrestrial in *Starman*. If we need negative evidence for the ubiquity of irony today, the conception of the noble savages on whom we project its absence (morons and extraterrestrials) should provide some.

In his magisterial typology of games in human cultures, Roger Caillois (1967:164) suggests that we can interpret a culture from the kinds of games it plays the most, and there is no reason not to extend this insight to verbal games. F. Muecke (1969) suggests that irony is associated with a specific—Western?—worldview, which Susan Sontag, in a famous essay, called the camp sensibility. She restricted it to "affluent societies" and dated its origin in the West to the early eighteenth century (Sontag 1966a:280, 289). The essence of camp for Sontag is of "life in quotes."

Hardly an event or a relationship is possible which does not seem to the hip and sophisticated camper to be an implicit allusion to or, much worse, a trite repetition of some other event or relationship. Every response seems to be a quote of something already played out. The relevant postmodernist slogan (as Rudnick and Andersen 1989 very insightfully point out) is "it's been done." The hipster looks on life like the Grandmaster looks on chess, where dozens of opening combinations of moves are so familiar, so congealed by countless repetitions, that they have actually sprouted proper names (Ruy Lopez, Sicilian, etc.) and where many tournament games are quotes of some previously recorded game up to (in some cases) the twentieth move or beyond; and the deeper the players are steeped in chess lore, the more aware they are that what they are doing is very often not original.

The "postmodern" attitude that there is no new thing (including, notably, postmodernism itself) under the sun—and that this is somehow regrettable—is older than hip; it is older even than Ecclesiastes and has been held by all manners of people at various times. Indeed, a random assembly of some of the notable quotations to this effect (with a little help from Bartlett) might itself serve as a small object lesson on the ubiquity of recycling.

My first citation is attributed to Khakheperessenb, an Egyptian scribe of circa 2000 B.C.: "Would I had phrases that are not known, utterances that are strange, in new language that has not been used, free from repetition, not an utterance which has grown stale, which men of old have spoken" (cited in Lentricchia, 1980:318).

The Roman playwright Terence (190–159 B.C.) defends himself from charges of plagiarism in the prologue to *The Eunuch* (161 B.C.) (Duckworth 1961:255): "In fact, nothing is said that has not been said before." He is self-consciously cited by Robert Burton in *The Anatomy of Melancholy* ([1621] 1932:25): "We can say nothing but what hath been said . . . of that which I have is stolen from others."

Cicero (106–43 B.C.) in the *De divinatione* (45 B.C.) (Baiter & Keyser 1864:206) puts a twist on it: "There is nothing so ridiculous but some philosopher has already said it." These are words repeated almost verbatim albeit without attribution by Descartes in his *Discourse on Method* ([1637] 1912: 13–4): "No opinion, however absurd or incredible, can be imagined which has not been maintained by some one of the philosophers."

Jean de la Bruyère (1645–1696) in his *Des ouvrages de l'esprit* ([1688] 1951:65) acknowledges that originality is only possible in style, not content: "Everything has been said, and we come more than seven thousand years too late—seven thousand years since there have been men who have been thinking—to say anything which has not been said already."

Muecke (1969:125) cites Goethe's diaries: "The world is now so old, so many eminent men have lived and thought for thousands of years, that there is little new to be discovered or expressed." The literary critics speak of the poet's "horror of finding himself to be only a copy or a replica" (Bloom 1973:80) or assert that "when the pop song moans that there is no new way of saying that I am in love or that her eyes are full of stars, it touches one of the main nerves in Western literature. . . . Such was the acquisitive reach of Hellenic and Hebraic articulation that genuine additions and new finds have been rare" (Steiner 1975:23).

The most recent echoer of Khakheperessenb's eloquent despair in my informal collection is David Peters, a fast-food worker of the Bart Simpson generation: "So many things have already happened in the world that we can't possibly come up with anything else. So why even live?" (Howe & Strauss 1993:87). Curiously, Muecke (who calls this Ecclesiastical there-is-no-new-thing-under-the-sun attitude a "closed ideology") believes that irony flourishes only in times when the opposite attitude is predominant: "General irony, in its subjective aspect, is itself an 'open ideology' phenomenon" (ibid.:127).

Marx's trenchant observation that history repeats itself, the first time as tragedy, the second time as farce, may be closer to the mark. Indeed, Muecke himself is keenly aware of repetition and staleness of a model as among the indispensible preconditions for successful parody of that model.

One consequence of a jaded perception, I would stress, is that the hip ironic speaker is forever self-conscious and skeptical, particularly of his or her own originality and sincerity. If what I say has been very likely said before, then not only am I that most recognizably pitiful and contemptible of all kids on the playground, a *copycat*, but surely my sincerity in saying it is suspect. Like an actor on a stage, I am painfully conscious of merely repeating someone else's lines, playing a role. If I live in such a world, then possibly the only means I have available to express my superiority to the clichés which I find myself constantly spouting, to be cool, is to utter them as parody, that is, sarcastically.

A man cannot tell a woman "I love you madly" because "he knows that she knows (and that she knows that he knows) that these words have already been written by Barbara Cartland." So to stake a slim claim to some originality, he says instead, "As Barbara Cartland would put it, I love you madly." (I owe this example to Enright 1986:159, who, appropriately, is himself echoing Eco 1984:39.)

Brackman (1967:63) provides a wonderful example of the same preemptive strategy:

> At a large New York advertising agency, communication through hackneyed Madison Avenue-ese has become a source of embarrassment. Certain executives—usually the oldest and highest ranking—will use a chestnut unself-consciously; e.g., "Why don't we put it out on the back stoop and see if the cat licks it up?" Others employ such expressions only reluctantly, making it clear that they know a trite saying when they use one: "Why don't we put it out on the back stoop and see if the cat licks it up, as the cliché goes." Yet the phrase "as the cliché goes" has achieved such currency around the agency that a third echelon of junior executives has come to recognize *it* as a cliché. Still too lazy or unimaginative to break away into a fresh image, they simply incorporate this further self-consciousness: "Why don't we put it out on the back stoop, as the cliché goes, as the cliché goes."

It seems to me that this same "anxiety of influence," this same very Western terror of losing face through inadvertent sententiousness and uttering nothing but other people's shopworn clichés, is what motivates not only Bloom's "poet" and Brackman's adman but also the air quotes in one of Rudnick and Andersen's vivid examples from "The Irony Epidemic": "Bob tells his co-workers with a grin that he's got to get home to—raise hands, insert air quotes here—'the little woman' or to 'the wife and kids' as if his wife and daughter didn't really exist, as if he's still 'a wild and crazy guy.'" It's not that Bob thinks they don't exist. More probably, Bob, like Khakheperessenb or Brackman's Madison Avenue junior executives, is acutely aware that many of his phrases are necessarily prefabricated, and he does not want to be thought uncool. The ultimate in uncoolness is to be unaware of one's own lack of originality.

It is tempting to follow Sontag, Muecke, Brackman, or Rudnick and Andersen and speculate that sarcasm as an institution allows us to distinguish the sensibility of our own culture from others and look for other correlates (like TV and other mass media) which favor its presence. Neil Postman speaks of the "immunization and therefore indifference to reality itself that may be generated by [the mass media] . . . [as] life . . . becomes a stylized, edited media event, and it is not inconceivable that in the completeness of our immersion in media, we come to prefer media life to reality itself" (Postman 1987:428). And if sarcasm is motivated at all by anxiety of influence, then a host of observers have pointed out that our Anglo-American or "Western" cult of cool (basically a self-consciously phobic anxiety of influence) is not shared, apparently, by speakers of Japanese, Javanese, Maninka, Malagasy, Turkish, Arabic, or Greek, to name only a few (cf. the useful collection of articles in Coulmas 1981). I myself, in an earlier article (Haiman 1989a:165–6), speculated that sarcasm seems to be unknown among the Hua, a group of New Guinea Highlanders.

But sarcasm is not even specifically linguistic, nor is it specific to mass mediated culture; the metamessage that (in some sense) "this isn't for real" is one of the features which defines artworks, games, rituals, and drama wherever they occur, and these are surely not limited to TV cultures. The folklore of both theater and games reflects our understanding of the distinction between what it is now fashionable, following Tom Wolfe, to call the *reel* and *real* worlds and their mutual autonomy (cf. Caillois 1967; Huizinga 1955; Mead 1934; Piaget 1951; Szasz 1965). Whatever happens in the real world, "the show must go on"; and whatever happens in the reel world, "it's only a game." As Caillois puts it (1967:37): "Il y a un espace de jeu: . . . rien de ce qui se passe a l'extérieur de la frontière idéale n'entre en ligne de compte" (There is a playing field: . . . nothing that happens outside of it is of any account).

It could be argued that games, rituals, drama, and possibly art in general are all essentially linguistic manifestations, inasmuch as they are cultural institutions which would be inconceivable without human language, and are in fact parasitic growths or superstructure that could only be constructed on that foundation. In fact, students of human culture have at times suggested that just as subgroups of human beings are defined precisely by the games they play (Caillois), human beings as a whole are defined precisely by their penchant for playing games at all. The thesis of Johan Huizinga's classic *Homo Ludens*, then, is no different from the more familiar definition of human beings as animals with language. But even Huizinga's (universalizing) claim may be insufficiently general, because (unlike language) play is not even specifically a human invention.

Although the practice of sarcasm is no more universal than is any other cultural institution (and in fact varies from person to person, as we know), gamelike behaviors are by no means even restricted to human beings. Merlin Donald (1991) attributes play and games to a putatively prelinguistic *Homo erectus*, but even this speculation is overly conservative. As Gregory Bateson observed in a famous essay of 1956, the metamessage "this is play" is a crucial part of communication among puppies, otters, and other mammals, and their ability to make this known is what allows them to engage without injury in pretend fights. More recent research confirms that all warm-blooded animals exhibit play behavior of some kind (cf. Smith 1984). So, although there is undoubtedly cultural, as well as personal, variation in the penchant for sarcasm, I have given up on trying to assign different sarcasm quotients to languages and cultures.

What is the payoff that makes people engage in sarcasm? What are the specific metamessages which accompany ironic, sarcastic, playful, or nonserious utterances? How are these metamessages spelled out in natural languages? These are the questions I will deal with here. I believe that answering or even approaching them will bring us surprisingly close to the essence of language, even while it will show us deep parallels between language and other kinds of behavior.

The following chapters will treat irony as an ever-incipient (but never realized) grammatical category like the future tense or the subjunctive mood and will enumerate some of the specific cues or grammatical markers which broadcast the metamessage "I mean the opposite of what my words are saying" and similar messages.

TWO

Sarcasm and Its Neighbors

Sarcasm is not a totally isolated speech act. Among its conceptual neighbors are put-ons, irony, and outright lies. In somewhat pedantically distinguishing sarcasm from these, I will also demonstrate its kinship with parody and carica-ture, affectionate insults, and at least one other as-yet unnamed speech act type which I will call the guiltive modality.

2.1. The Put-On

It is possible to be ironic or sarcastic without any overt sign of the speaker's insincerity. The put-on, or deadpan act of sarcasm, still differs from a lie in that the speaker wants his or her actual meaning to be understood at least by some happy few members of the target audience from their knowledge of the world or from their knowledge of the speaker's character and opinions (cf. Brackman 1967). I will start with some examples of such put-ons, all culled from a political column by Noam Chomsky:

> The New "Soviet strategy" appears to be working among the *benighted* Europe-ans. (Chomsky 1989b:17)

> The Soviet Union supported indigenous elements resisting the forceful imposi-tion of U.S. designs, a *criminal endeavor*, as *any right-thinking intellectual* comprehends. (ibid.:20)

Businessmen might have to adjust to having workers on the boards of directors, among other *disasters*, if the Bolshevik virus is not exterminated. (ibid.:20)

We must not make the same mistake with Daniel Ortega, *poised for world conquest*. (ibid.:21)

Washington's rejection of the Soviet offer to cut aid "if Washington cuts its military assistance to its allies in the region" [is] *an utter absurdity*, as *outlandish* as a Soviet request that the US condition its military aid to Turkey on "democratic reforms." (ibid.:22)

Readers familiar with Chomsky's political views, as well as readers who subscribe to the outlet in which they are expressed (Z magazine), will have no difficulty in "hearing" Chomsky's venomous contempt in each of the phrases I have emphasized. But many people who are used to getting their ideology from network TV might take these remarks at face value. While the sarcastic intention of the writer is apparent to the in-group who shares his values, it is not formally marked in the examples above.

Another example is the following well-known passage from Gibbon's *Decline and Fall*, commenting on the startling absence of pagan corroboration for the miracles attested in the Gospels:

But how shall we excuse the *supine* inattention of the Pagan and philosophic world to those evidences which were presented by the hand of Omnipotence, not to their reason, but to their senses? During the age of Christ, of his apostles, and of their first disciples, the doctrine which they preached was confirmed by innumerable prodigies. The lame walked, the blind saw, the sick were healed, the dead were raised, demons were expelled, and the laws of Nature were frequently suspended *for the benefit of the Church*. But the sages of Greece and Rome turned aside from *the awful spectacle*, and, pursuing the ordinary occupations of life and study, appeared unconscious of any alterations in the moral or physical government of the world. (Gibbon n.d.:443)

Readers who are familiar with Gibbon's anti-Christian animus may "hear" the snigger in his voice in the emphasized phrases, but again, there is no overt mark of insincerity in this passage. The "sarcastive modality" is provided entirely by the reader's inference in put-ons of this sort, and of course, not all readers will get it.

In this discussion, I will focus on sarcastic messages where the metamessage *is* signaled by some overt cues, like mood markers. In such utterances, the positive message is visibly or audibly overlaid (or undermined) by the metamessage, which expresses the speaker's actual contempt, indifference, or hostility toward his or her target. One might say, in fact, that in sarcasm the ostensible message, like the meat or vegetables in a curry, is only the vehicle for the pragmatically essential metamessage. From a purely structural point of view, the message is like the lyrics while the metamessage is like the melody of a song. Pragmatically speaking, the "metamessage"—"I despise this message (and anyone who would utter it sincerely)"—is the main message that the speaker wishes to communicate. Sarcasm which includes the second (and optional) part of the metamessage is then clearly a form of verbal aggression directed either against one's interlocutor or against an absent speaker.

2.2. Sarcasm and Irony

There is an extremely close connection between sarcasm and irony, and literary theorists in particular often treat sarcasm as simply the crudest and least interesting form of irony (cf. Muecke 1969:20). I will take common usage as my point of departure, however, in establishing two important distinctions between the two.

First, situations may be ironic, but only people can be sarcastic. Second, people may be unintentionally ironic, but sarcasm requires intention. What is essential to sarcasm is that it is overt irony *intentionally used by the speaker as a form of verbal aggression*, and it may thus be contrasted with other aggressive speech acts, among them the put-on, direct insults, curses, vituperation, nagging, and condescension. The following contrast may help to make the familiar conceptual distinction clear. In the recent Jonathan Demme film *Married to the Mob*, the heroine, a mobster's widow, says to an FBI agent, "You're no different from the mob!" He responds: "Oh, there's a big difference, Mrs. De Marco. The mob is run by murdering, thieving, lying, cheating psychopaths. We work for the President of the United States of America." The irony of this statement was apparent to many members of the audience, who greeted it (on the night that I attended the film) with cynical guffaws. But the FBI agent *character* uttered it sincerely, with no sarcastic intention. The playwright sees both the message and the metamessage; so do the elect among the audience; the characters in the play itself, however, do not. That is, irony, unlike sarcasm, may be both unintentional and unconscious.

Compare the innocence of Demme's FBI agent with the late Abbie Hoffman's bitter assessment of the impact of the antiwar movement in the 1960s: "If it weren't for our efforts, we'd have a president today sending troops off to exotic countries like Lebanon and Grenada, and bombing cities like Tripoli" (*New York Times*, April 14, 1989, p. 17). Had Hoffman uttered those words in 1975, they would have been viewed by us in hindsight today as ironic: "The very things we *are* doing! If only he had known how wrong he was!" But since he uttered them shortly before his death in 1989, in full awareness of recent events in Lebanon, Grenada, and Tripoli, they constituted a sarcastic disparagement of (at least the effectiveness of) the Vietnam antiwar movement.

The stage metaphor, which allows us to distinguish between the playwright and the characters, is a useful one for approaching the second major difference between sarcasm and irony: irony (in the sense that Muecke proposes when he calls it an "open ideology" phenomenon) is relativistic, while sarcasm is absolute. The sarcast perceives only two versions of reality: that which obtains on the stage among the characters where he or she pretends to be and that which obtains for the playwright in real life, where the sarcast really stands. The sarcast's perspective is that of the know-it-all wise guy, who rolls his eyes while he mouths the lines of his "role," demonstrating that he appreciates their absurdity. The ironist, on the other hand, perceives that "all the world's a stage," and that what he or she honestly perceives as the absolute truth may be, from a loftier perspective, as limited and arbitrary as the stage he or she ridicules, or even, possibly, that the stage truth is closer to ultimate reality than what he or she thinks is "real life." As flies are to little boys, so we are to the gods, and so on ad infinitum (in both directions).

2.3. Sarcasm and Lying

Unlike the liar, the sarcast has no wish to deceive; sarcasm differs from falsehood in the presence of the honest metamessage. In Goffman's terms (1974: chaps. 3, 4), sarcasm is *keyed* and contrasts with *fabrications*. Among lies, however, sarcasm is especially close to self-referential paradoxical utterances like the Cretan's "this statement is false," the inflexible rule that "all rules have exceptions," double binds like "Be spontaneous!" or "Act natural!," or the hypocritical injunction to "never say never." One may legitimately inquire how a sarcastic "thanks a lot" differs from such well-known examples and why sarcastic expressions in general pose no paradoxical conundrums (for they do not). The difference between the two is perfectly clear on examination: the liar's single statement is both message and metamessage, while the sarcast is actually making not one statement but two clearly separated statements simultaneously: first, a message "X," and second, the commentary along the general lines that "X is bunk." One of my major concerns will be how this separate commentary is expressed in languages of the world. Nevertheless, the peculiarly self-referential (and self-conscious) nature of sarcasm is one of its most striking features, and one to which we shall return over and over again.

2.4. Sarcasm and Parody

Sarcasm is often a form of humor. If, following Stephen Leacock and many other brilliant theorist-practitioners, we identify humor as incongruity, the humor in sarcasm (as in irony) lies in the contrast between the speaker's flattering or sympathetic words (his or her ostensible message, the "lyrics" of his or her song) and his or her hostile intentions (conveyed in the often deniable but far more fundamental metamessage, or the "tune").

In its humor, sarcasm is, as it were, institutionalized in a number of perhaps culturally specific and closely related genres like mockery, mimicry, parody, and satire. To appreciate this fully, we might consider an example of a parody and remind ourselves how it works. The following parody of *The Decline and Fall of the Roman Empire* by Tom Weller (Weller 1987:55) is not a bad example of the genre:

> The Roman general exhorted, with persuasive eloquence, the empire's position;
> that neither the advantage and virtue of independent governance, or the amiability

of separate polities, to the divers tribes, or the expectation of favourable outcome, or beneficient resolution, of further trial at arms, could justify the maintenance, nor the removal of the civilising influence, and secure the protection of the empire, or the uncertainty of provoking further exertions of a powerful enemy, urge the wisdom, nor outweigh the benefits, of the former, could approve the risk, of continuing contention; the astonished chieftain asked to have the sentence repeated.

Clearly, Gibbon as a stylist is the target of this piece. Like all parodists, Weller ridicules the style of his target author through excessive imitation of some of its most characteristically recognizable features. In Gibbon's case, these are sonorous periods of indeterminate length (Weller claims that the *Decline and Fall*, far from being daunting and unreadable, consists in its entirety of only four sentences), balance, and overexploitation of the syntactic structure of right node raising to the point of unintelligibility. The ostensible message of this passage (the Roman general's speech to the barbarians, as conveyed by Gibbon) is fortunately unimportant, since it serves only as a vehicle for, and illustration of, the metamessage that "Gibbon's style is laughable."

2.5. Affectionate Insults

—I'll be seein' ya.
—Not if I see you first.

I also wish to exclude affectionate insults, such as the second line in the interchange above from the movie *Stand by Me*. Given the speaker's manner of delivery and the context, the hero's boilerplate insult to his best friend in this memorable scene is uttered (and understood) as virtually a declaration of love.

Similar in spirit are reclaimed epithets like "nigger," "fag," "dyke," and "bitch" used in a jocular fashion by members of stigmatized groups among themselves. What's going on here is very close in three ways to sarcasm: first, the speaker's actual feelings are the opposite of the ostensible meaning of the words used; second, the actual feelings "I don't mean this" or "I mock this" are signaled by overt cues. Third, intragroup use of terms like "fag" is clearly parodistic.

Yasue Kodama (1995) has drawn attention to the quasi-institutionalization of affectionate insults in Japanese, where they are known as *roakuka*, "pretending badness." It is a style affected by lovers and intimates who engage in it for presumably the same reasons as the young heroes of *Stand by Me*: to avoid the embarrassment of an overt avowal of affection.

She: So, do you miss me?
He: Not at all.

Or the somewhat more elaborate interchange:

He: Dou?
     "How (do I look in this outfit I am trying on)?"

She: Ara "Mago   ni mo ishai" tte   yoku itta   wa ne.
    Oh   stablehand on too clothes comp.well said top. focus
    "Oh, you know the saying, 'Even a stablehand looks good in good
    clothes.'"
He: Nakanii ga ii   kara,   suutu no yasa   ga hikaru n   da
    inside   sub. good because suit of goodness sub. shine nom. be
    yo. Wakatte   nai naa?
    focus understand not focus
    "The suit looks good because the person inside it looks good. You just
    don't get it, do you?"

All that seems to be missing is hostility directed against the interlocutor. However, not all sarcasm involves hostility toward one's actual interlocutor: the target may be the "conventional wisdom" or an absent parodied speaker, and this target may be the straight, sexist, or racist bigot in the case of jocular terms like "fag."

What clearly distinguishes affectionate insults from sarcasm, I propose, is that while the ostensible message in the former category is negative, the ostensible message in cases of sarcasm is invariably positive.

2.6. The Guiltive

In the following paragraphs, I will discuss a more elusive (though instantly recognizable) related modality which I'll call the *guiltive*, for which not even an adequate pretheoretical folk vocabulary exists. Like the put-on and other related acts of near-sarcasm, it differs minimally from the genuine article, though in a somewhat novel way.

Consider the following three examples from *Portnoy's Complaint*:

"Don't ask what kind of day I had with him yesterday." So I don't. "Alex," *sotto voce* still, "when he has a day like that you don't know what a difference a call from you would make." I nod. "And, Alex"—and I'm nodding away, you know—it doesn't cost anything, and it may even get me through—"Next week is his birthday. *That Mother's Day came and went without a card, plus my birthday, those things don't bother me."* (Roth 1969:39)

My father carries himself to the kitchen table, his head sunk low, as though he has just taken a hand grenade in his stomach. Which he has. Which I know. *"You can wear rags for all I care, you can dress like a peddler, you can shame and embarrass me all you want, curse me, Alexander, defy me, hit me, hate me."* (ibid.:70)

Yes, she *will* give me the food out of her mouth, that's a proven fact! And still I will not stay five full minutes by her bedside. "Run," says my mother, while Mrs. Re-ver-ed, who in no time at all has managed to make herself my enemy, and for the rest of my life, Mrs. Re-ver-ed says, "Soon Mother will be home, soon everything will be just like ordinary. . . . *Sure, run, run, they all run these days,"* says the kind and understanding lady—oh, they are all so kind and understanding, I want to strangle them!—*"walking they never heard of, God bless them."* (ibid.:75)

The sarcastive is recognized—and, crucially, is meant to be recognized—when the speaker's ostensible message is accompanied by a derived meta-message "I don't mean this." All it takes to be sarcastic is a single speaker who produces both the message and the denigrating commentary on it.

The guiltive, however, is something new: it is a cooperative venture, a linguistic pas de deux in that essentially the *same derived metamessage* is not produced by the speaker but is rather left to be supplied by the addressee, who is thereby made to feel like a worm.

As I will try to show, the sarcastive is overtly marked. Cues for the sarcastive metamessage (literally, "I don't mean this message") include "spitting it out with a sneer," nasalization, exaggerated duration, deadpan monotone, sing-song, caricatured courtesy, formality, and sympathy, such indices of *fakery* as mark rhetorical questions and commands (e.g., "Don't ask me what kind of day I had with him yesterday") and a small repertoire of the indices of *mimicry*, including most obviously the familiar (written, gestured, or pause-marked) quotation marks. Colloquial English includes as well a handful of segmental signs. All of these signs more or less iconically convey the framing metamessage "I don't mean this," *whence the inference* follows that "this message is bogus."

The guiltive is entirely different, in that, in order to properly trash her interlocutor, the guilter (typically but not always the stereotyped Jewish mother) has to sound perfectly sincere (and hence cannot be heard to broadcast the metamessage "I don't mean this," which must therefore be covert). This suggests a kinship between the guiltive and the *put-on* or between the guiltive and *polite* language, in which the speaker also suppresses his or her own emotions, is known to be suppressing them, and still manages to sound sincere.

Nevertheless, it is instantly obvious that the italic passages from *Portnoy's Complaint* above are in the guiltive modality rather than a put-on or polite. While the illocutionary force of a put-on is to fool at least some of the audience, and that of politeness is (presumably) to avoid aggression, the illocutionary force of guiltive utterances is clearly a kind of passive-aggressive one-upsmanship whose unambiguous purpose is to make the hearer do some work and then feel like an ingrate or a heel. How is this clear? How do the passages above do this, and how do they contrast with the same passages uttered with genuine politeness or with genuine sincerity, assuming that such a sincerity is even possible?

Some obvious suggestions that an advice columnist might provide for speakers wishing to achieve a nonguilting illocution include the following:

1. Don't exaggerate your selflessness. (If you want to be sincere, say: "*Of course* it bothered me that you forgot Mother's Day and my birthday." If you want to be polite, don't mention the incident at all.)
2. Don't exaggerate your pain. (If you want to be sincere, say: "It really hurts my feelings that you won't dress up for shul." If you want to be polite, don't show that you're upset at all.)
3. Don't exaggerate your forbearance. (Sincerity might impel you to say: "You wretched little beast, your poor mother is still at death's door, and you're

running off to play baseball!" Politeness, once again, would impel you to keep quiet.)

What's common to all of the ostensibly benign messages from Portnoy's elders is that the speaker's ludicrously *exaggerated* selflessness, hurt, and generosity; all express the explicit metamessage that "I who utter this am a long-suffering and absolute saint/martyr." This metamessage, then, is not so much a commentary on the message itself, as on the saintly nature of the person who can utter it sincerely. Implicit for Portnoy to elucidate are the derived meta-message "this message is therefore objectively bogus" and the accompanying inference that "you, Portnoy, are a heartless swine."

2.7. Conclusion: Definitions

I have briefly surveyed some acts of speech which are close enough to sarcasm that distinguishing them from the real thing provides us with a kind of definition. To sum up, sarcasm is characterized by the *intentional production* of an *overt and separate* metamessage "I don't mean this" in which the speaker expresses hostility or ridicule of another speaker, who presumably *does* "mean this" in uttering an *ostensibly positive* message. The "other speaker" may be the sarcast's present interlocutor, an absent third person, or a conventional attitude.

Two theories of sarcasm and irony are relatively well known in linguistics. The first is that sarcasm involves an act of *pretense* (cf. Grice 1975; Clark & Gerrig 1984): the sarcast pretends to an attitude which he or she does not feel and expects a privileged audience to recognize that he or she is indeed pretending. Like all pretense, then, and like all theater, sarcasm is a form of speech *play*. It belongs with other kinds of mimicry (cf. Caillois 1967) and is ultimately motivated by the same impulse that inspires people to play pretend games of any sort. In particular, Huizinga's remarks on games, cited by Caillois (ibid.:32–3), are very apposite: a game is a freely chosen fictive activity, and those who play it are conscious that things in real life (that is, outside the game) are different. It is easy to see how parody conforms with this account. The parodist pretends to be the author that he or she parodies.

The second (and much more restrictive) theory is that sarcasm involves *mention* rather than *use* of words (cf. Sperber & Wilson 1981; Ducrot 1984:192): the sarcast quotes or otherwise repeats other people's words (or possibly just the very words he or she used earlier) and, by repetition, draws attention to their peculiar inappropriateness. Again, it is possible to see how parody conforms with this account if the notion of quotation is made somewhat more general: one may quote not only another's actual words but also another's diction and syntax.

To be sure, there are many cases where sarcasm is achieved simply by derisory mention (that is, repetition or quotation) of inappropriate words. One of Sperber and Wilson's best examples (and a favorite among all students of irony) is Mark Antony's increasingly sarcastic repetition of the phrase "honorable men" in his rabble-rousing speech against the conspirators in *Julius*

Caesar. However, there are cases where only the pretense theory seems adequate. Among Clark and Gerrig's most telling examples is Swift's *Modest Proposal*, which surely cannot be considered even an "implicit echo" of another speaker's words. And even Antony in his use of "honorable" is surely pretending an attitude, which is more than simply repeating a sequence of sounds.

There is no real conflict between the ideas of pretense and quotation, which are intimately connected (both formally and semantically) in actual practice: the first simply subsumes the second. In its textbook sense, direct quotation, after all, is an act of mimicry above all and thus of self-conscious pretense. Both quotation and other kinds of overt pretense require the audience to understand that the speaker himself or herself is not committed to the words he or she utters and that these words originate from some other source. The metamessage in both cases is (loosely) paraphrasable as "this is not really me: I'm just playing a role, mouthing someone else's words."

I prefer the definition of sarcasm as pretense because this notion is more inclusive than that of mention. It will allow us to include examples of parody, which the mention theory can account for only if the notion of "mention" is relaxed to include "stylistic quotation"; it will allow us to relate sarcasm with verbal aggression, which the mention theory does not support; and it will readily accommodate clear examples of sarcasm, like the Abbie Hoffman remark, which the mention theory is utterly powerless to handle.

I wish to propose very seriously that the best metaphor in terms of which to understand sarcasm and irony is that of the stage or screen, with its frequently exploited contrast between (phony, pretend) "reel" playacting and (God's) "real" truth. One sarcastic perspective is essentially that of the actor on stage who steps out of character and shares asides with a privileged omniscient audience, inviting them to deride the other members of the play, who, unlike the sarcast, are seen to be playing a role in the limited world of the stage (this is the view developed by Ducrot, who distinguishes between the speaker as *locuteur* [character] and *énonciateur* [performer] [1984:211]). So Swift establishes a complicity with his readers in mocking the gruesome conventional wisdom of the (implicitly caricatured) English ruling class in Ireland, while he pretends to be one of them. So also Antony establishes a complicity with his audience in mocking the supposed "honor" of the caricatured self-righteous Brutus: Brutus may hypocritically play the role of an honorable man, but you and I know better. And so all parodists mock the phony, banal, or pretentious style of the targets whose viewpoints or mannerisms they pretend to adopt.

At the deepest level of analysis, which I will return to in the last chapter of this book, the difference between mention and pretense dissolves completely, in that both derive from the more fundamental notion of repetition (as do our ideas of style, rhythm, exaggeration, norms, standards, variation, order, and rules, to name only a few).

We generally take it for granted that the world of the theatrical stage is distinct from the real world, although a great deal of theater and of other (particularly modern) art plays with eliminating the distinction between the stage (or the artwork) and the real world.

I propose to call devices which demarcate art from life *stage separators* (what Goffman 1974 calls *framing cues*), and the effect of eliminating the distinction between them a *trompe l'oeil* effect. A put-on, then, is the verbal equivalent of a trompe l'oeil in painting. The metamessage "I mean the opposite of this" or "I mock this" is a stage separator.

This is the specific metamessage which distinguishes sarcasm from the expression of doubt, anger, distraction, sympathy, certitude, sorrow, or any other extraneous emotion with which a speaker may invest a given verbal text, such as the words "thank you." The fact that any of these melodies are possible is certainly evidence that words and melody are mutually independent. But our concern will be only with those cases where the melody is tightly bound with the words and constitutes an intentional commentary on the words (albeit a negative one).

For example, the phonetic expression of anger in probably all languages is unmistakable. It is characterized by Fonagy (1971b) in quantitative acoustic terms: fortition of consonants, particularly of stops and voiceless fricatives, signals aggression and anger, while lenition signals a more mellow mood (Fonagy provides measurements from French and Hungarian). Anyone who "spits out" words like "Thanks a lot!" is saying two things at once. On the one hand, he or she is going through the motions of expressing gratitude, but on the other, he or she is expressing a totally incompatible emotion. Fonagy also characterizes the articulatory properties and the acoustics of affection and spite in an earlier, pioneering study of 1962. Similarly, it may be possible to recognize a distracted tone of voice on the basis of purely acoustic properties: here again, the words may convey one message, but the tone in which they are spoken suggest that the speaker's thoughts are elsewhere. Strictly speaking, none of these "secondary" messages of rage, tenderness, and spite are really sarcasm, since the symptomatic message is delivered not as an intended commentary on the verbal message but quite independently. In spite of their extreme interest and their obvious kinship with sarcasm as examples of what Fonagy has called "double coding" in speech, I will therefore say no more about "manners of speaking" of this sort.

The overt and separate metamessage is the stage separator which alerts the listener or reader that what is said is in some way meant in jest or is pretended rather than sincerely felt.

In the following chapter, I will provide an informal survey of the ways in which this metamessage is expressed in different languages and in different media of expression. What makes this survey more interesting than a list of translations of "sarcasm" in ninety-nine languages is, first, that the attested expressions of this particular metamessage are few, highly motivated, and iconic. Second, as far as I am aware, there is no language in which any of these stage separators has achieved the institutionalization of grammatical stability; in other words, there is no language description in which these stage separators are either mentioned in the grammar (as the subjunctive or the interrogative are mentioned) or listed in the lexicon (as the word "sarcasm" itself is listed).

THREE

The Metamessage "I Don't Mean This"

"For a decade after the war, I was too much of a Nazi for any decent German to take coffee with me." He put the words "decent German" into roughly tongued inverted commas. (Deighton 1965:189)

Everyone who reads Deighton's novel *Funeral in Berlin* can supply the "roughly tongued inverted commas" which mark the speaker's *decent German* as sarcastic or fictional. We can also readily do the same with the examples given in figures 3.1 and 3.2. This chapter will deal with how the listener in English, and perhaps all languages, can both recognize and produce those inverted commas, not only in the spoken language but also in a variety of other media.

Most obviously, any verbal act may be performed, if the speaker wishes, "in a sarcastic tone of voice." The very triteness of this observation is important for two reasons. First, it underlines the fact that sarcasm is not one possible message among several but rather a commentary on any possible message. Second, it expresses the intuitive idea that sarcasm is primarily expressed by intonational or even paralinguistic means.

I propose that the "sarcastive" (if it were ever to become grammaticalized) could be called a mood like the traditional subjunctive, because it has the function of indicating a speaker's attitude toward the propositional content of his or her message (cf. Palmer 1986 for this definition of mood). It fails to qualify for the grammatical status of a mood only because it has not been grammaticalized. It is now time to survey some of the devices whereby this ever-incipient "wannabe" mood is expressed.

I will try to demonstrate that the formal expression of sarcasm is neither arbitrary nor particularly language specific. Irrespective of the medium, irre-

Calvin and Hobbes

by Bill Watterson

Figure 3.1. Calvin and Hobbes. (© Watterson; dist. by Universal Press Syndicate; reprinted with permission; all rights reserved.)

Dear Abby: I am a 29-year-old married man with a fine, bright, 8-year-old son. My wife and I have a wonderful marriage, and for the most part I have fantastic in-laws. The one negative aspect of my in-laws is the way they refer to certain ethnic groups. They are very close minded, prejudiced people who use offensive words to describe someone's race, color or religion.

I can live with it, but I don't want our son to hear talk like that from people he is suppose to respect.

Is there a tactful way to ask my in-laws to please refrain from making ethnic slurs around our child? Or should I let them say what they've said after they leave?

—Open for Suggestions

Abby says: Ask your *"fantastic"* in-laws to please keep their ethnic slurs to themselves in the presence of your son because you are trying to teach the boy to judge people by their character—not by their color or religion. Also ask your wife to join you in keeping her parents in line.

Figure 3.2. Dear Abby.

spective even of the code, *the sarcastic metamessage ("I don't mean this message" or "I'm not serious") is most frequently signaled by a very limited set of highly iconic gestures.*

3.1. Sneers and Laughter

The sarcast's face is wrinkled with disgust: the words of the message seem literally to taste bad in his or her mouth. (As Darwin [1873:254–62] pointed out in his study of the emotions in Man, the nearly universal facial gesture of disgust probably derives from the expression made by someone tasting or smelling something disgusting and—possibly—miming the gesture of expulsion.) This facial expression of distaste directly indicates the speaker's emphatic lack of commitment to the literal meaning of his or her words and is primarily a visual signal. But its phonological reflection is a heavy overlay of nasality, accompanied possibly by diphthongization and the lengthening of stressed vowels (cf. Fonagy 1971c:43–6). This visual pattern and the epiphenomenal auditory signals which accompany it allow the non-native speaker to detect sarcasm in languages which he or she may not understand at all. As someone who has the vaguest acquaintance with Italian, I can understand the sarcasm of Leporello's bitter comment on his master in my recording of Mozart's *Don Giovanni*:

> O, che *cārō* galantuomo.
> "Oh, what a dear gentleman."

I recognize exactly the same contemptuous inflection in the second speaker's voice in the following Mandarin dialog, of which I cannot understand a single word:

> — Ni   kan wo zhe jian   yifu   pianyi ma?
>   you see my this piece clothes cheap Q
>   "Do you think my clothes are a good buy?"
> — *Pianyi.*
>   "(Sure. Real) cheap."

Compare the nasality with which speakers of American English often express a sarcastic "thanks" or "sorry."

Why nasality? Darwin (1872) was the first to draw attention to the universality of the sneer as an instrumental gesture of disgust: following Darwin, Fonagy (1971c) suggests that when the speaker is expelling something nauseating, he or she wants to remove it not only from the mouth (where it can be tasted) but also from the nose (where it can be smelled): that is, the velum must be lowered to allow air to be expelled from the mouth and the nose simultaneously. This insight is incidentally preserved in the French idiom "rendre par les trous de nez" (literally, "to expel through the nostrils"), meaning "to utterly despise" (cf. Sartre 1947:15).

Alternatively, the sarcast may comment on the absurdity of the message by uttering it with a derisive snort. The more or less suppressed laughter with which the words are uttered is then the metamessage. We hear the same repressed snort in the most common (at least in North America) sarcastic expression in English:

Thanks (a whole bunch).

Apparently, it is also common in German, as attested by the readily elicited

Gratuliere.
"Congrats."

Die, die, die . . . "Freiheitskämpfer."
"The, the, the . . . 'freedom fighters.'"

Or compare in the contemptuous Italian:

Che uomo!
"What a man!"

The derisive snort may be partially grammaticalized (or at least, reducible to a conventional orthography) in various ways. Segmentally, it may be manifested as an extra-heavy expiration of air through the mouth. One of the sounds produced in this way, the aspiration of voiceless stops, is usually represented as [h] (whence *haha, hoho, heehee* and all of the other more or less onomatopoeic lexicalizations of laughter). For the corresponding expulsion of air through the nose which accompanies fricatives, I propose the related sign [H]. Both the [h] and [H] sounds, as the sublimated remnants of a laugh, in an ideal system of autosegmental transcription should probably be represented on the same level. Thus:

```
Nasal:  H             H
Oral:            h
        freiheitskämpfer

Nasal:  H
Oral:      h
        thanks

Nasal:
Oral:      h
        che uomo
```

3.2. Inverse Pitch Obtrusion

It may well be that the intonational pattern of inverse pitch obtrusion (in which the stressed syllable is uttered at a *lower* pitch than the surrounding material, and which I suspect is what Winner [1988:148] and others have in mind when they talk of a "contemptuous intonation") is also a partial grammaticalization of this same originally paralinguistic signal. Contrast sincere and sarcastic utterances of the phrase "her career":

Sincere:

Pitch:	High
Stress:	*

her   career

Sarcastic:

Pitch:	Low
Stress:	*

her   "career"

The latter occurs in the recorded interchange:

—I'm certainly not going to stand in the way of her career.
—Her "career"!

A comparable example with the same intonational pattern virtually guaranteed occurs in the dialog from Jane Austen's *Pride and Prejudice* ([1813] 1985:223):

—Who that knows what his misfortunes have been, can help feeling an interest in him?
—His misfortunes! [repeated Darcy contemptuously]. Yes, his misfortunes have been great indeed.

Jonsson (1995) has found pitch obtrusion to be frequent in German. The expression *Armes Ding!* "(You) poor thing!" for example, typically is uttered sincerely with a Low–High pitch contour, but sarcastically with High–Low.

In my materials, inverse pitch obtrusion tends to occur in English in two particularly favoring contexts: first, as suggested by the two examples I have provided above, in contemptuous echoes (which are also marked by exaggerated amplitude); second, when other signs of emphasis (prolongation, extra amplitude) are more likely to be taken at face value, as iconic signs of enthusiasm and sincerity. A construction which regularly favors inverse pitch obtrusion, then, is "don't you just LOVE it when. . . ."

The sarcastic metamessage can be conveyed more indirectly. A variety of inappropriate intonations can indirectly signal that the speaker's words do not reflect the speaker's feelings. We now turn to these examples of incongruity.

3.3. Intonational Misfits

In part, Saussure's notion of *linearity*—that we can say only one thing at a time—a notion to which sarcasm presents such a spectacular counterexample, was a totally predictable consequence of his failure to consider suprasegmental phenomena. Most often, sarcasm is overtly expressed by a discord between positive words and the negative tune of a spoken text, a discord which can easily be represented in any of a variety of formal notations.

Phonologically, sarcastic detachment (between the lexico-syntactic content of the "stage message" and the intonational content of the sarcastic "real-world metamessage") is often expressed by means of an emotively inappropriate intonation, a melody characterized as an "intonational misfit" (Cruttenden 1984:71). While a sincere or appropriate intonation reinforces the lexico-syntactic content of a message, a contraindicative, incongruous, or inappropriate one will undermine it, usually decisively. That intonation has the last word in conflicts of this sort (cf. de Groot 1949) only serves to confirm the widespread view that it is more fundamental than lexical or syntactic structure in conveying attitudinal meanings. Intuitively, it belongs among paralinguistic gestures like choking with rage, sneering, snorting with laughter, smirking, rolling the eyes, and pouting. Intonation is less nuanced than words but more genuine as an unaffected and spontaneous symptomatic expression of the speaker's real feelings. The following is an inventory of the most frequently encountered intonational misfits. Where I can, I will indicate how the same incongruity is signaled in other media besides the spoken language.

3.3.1. Exaggeration or Caricature

Aw, you poor thing!

Grenade gave me a deep bow of mock dignity and mock gratitude. (Deighton 1965:113–4)

Mr. Clotho did an impression of servile enthusiasm. "Yes, *suh!*" he exclaimed. "Yassuh." (Stone 1987:232)

As the second example makes clear, exaggeration as an index of sarcasm is by no means confined to intonation. Rather, it is characteristic of parody or mocking mimicry in general.

What is exaggerated in the intonation are the absolute amplitude, the absolute duration, and the variations in pitch which would be appropriate if the message were sincere (cf. Fonagy 1971c). Amplitude is typically exaggerated in contemptuous repetitions of the type exemplified in figures 3.1 and 3.2. The crucial role of duration is alluded to in the common orthographic representation of sarcastic "Excuuuuse me," as well as "Riiiight" in the interchange between the fat cat Garfield and his bathroom scales in figure 3.3.

A note on method: I and my students have elicited artificial examples of sarcasm from native speaker subjects in the laboratory by asking them to mime sincerity in hypothetical scenarios in which they would express gratitude, contrition, compassion, and other affects. Then they were asked to use *exactly the same words* they had recorded for sincere responses in another set of scenarios in which they would be expected to feel the opposite of these emotions. The questionnaire is included in the appendix at the end of the book.

Cheng (1989) and Xiao (1989) have both noted the prevalence of exaggerated duration in Mandarin:

Peifu   peifu.
admire admire
"I really admire you. Congratulations."

Figure 3.3. Garfield, by Jim Davis. (© Paws, Inc.; dist. by Universal Press
Syndicate; reprinted with permission; all rights reserved.)

    Peeeifu peeeifu.
    admire admire
"I 'admire' you. Congratulaaaations."

    Xiexie nide haoyi.
    thank your good-intention
"Thanks. I really appreciate it."

    Xieeexie nide haoyiii.
    thaaanks your good-inteeeention
"Thanks a whole bunch [sc. but I know the evil purpose behind your offer]."

    Ta shi qiondekelian.
    3sg. be poor-resultative-pitiable
"He is poor indeed [e.g., he can't even afford a book]."

    Ta shi qiondekeliaaan.
    3sg. be poor-resultative-piiiitiable
"[In a pig's eye] he's poor [sc. he's a millionaire]." (Cheng 1989)

    Ni zhen xing.
    you really capable

    Ni zhen xiiiing   a.
    you really caaaapable really (cf. Chen 1994)
"[Yeah right:] you're real capable." (Xiao 1989)

    Adachi (1996) and Jonsson (1995) have also demonstrated that in Japanese
and German *simple prolongation* is the most reliable and consistent indicator
of sarcasm, confirming Fonagy's results for Hungarian (cf. Fonagy 1971c). I
have subsequently found that prolongation is a fairly reliable index of sarcastic utterances in English, Russian, Greek, Tagalog, and other languages.
    A good case could be made that exaggeration is what marks not only camp
(Sontag 1966d:275) and not only parody but all *play*, and not only among
humans. For example, rough-and-tumble wrestling among many animals is
performed with "exaggerated movements, [which] together with the high
pounce that initiates the bout, seem[s] to inform the interactants of the bout's
'playful' nature" (Hole & Einon 1984:100). Nor is this exaggeration confined

to semantic communication. Exaggerated sweetness, for example, is perceived as fake in music as well as in speech. Although both "Täuschung" and "Frühlingstraum" (two well-known songs from Schubert's *Winterreise*) are in the same key, and both are by conventional standards sweet or melodious, audiences quite unfamiliar with both the German language and Schubert will spot the parodistic intent of what audiences of mine have called the "music box-like" melody of "Frühlingstraum," which contrasts with the poignant sincerity of the melody of "Täuschung" (see figure 3.4). The verbal text and the harsh continuation of "Frühlingstraum" make it unambiguously clear that parody is indeed what Schubert consciously intended, but the important thing to note is that these explicit later disambiguators do no more than clinch a contrast that is already explicit in the cited passage itself.

I am not claiming that the arch exaggeration of the former melody (or of any exaggeration) is totally absolute. In fact, it cannot be, *insofar as the very fact of exaggeration implies the existence of an original model whose features are to be exaggerated.* In other words, nothing is exaggerated the first time around. To be perceived as an exaggeration, a production must be recognized first as an imitation or repetition of something else, and an absolutely virginal audience (one totally ignorant of Western classical or popular music) would in fact probably fail to distinguish between the sweetness of "Täuschung" and the "sweetness" of "Frühlingstraum." My ideal audience for the taste test doesn't have to come from Vienna, but they can't come from Tibet, either.

I have a hunch, which I would dignify with another name if I were a musicologist, that the perception of fake sweetness in Frühlingstraum depends on our prior familiarity with the convention of grace notes, paradigmatically illustrated in the rhythmically and melodically very similar "Gavotte l'antique" by F. J. Gossec, familiar to every schoolchild veteran of Saturday morning cartoons, illustrated in figure 3.5, and the even more familiar passage from Ponchielli's "Dance of the Hours of the Day," familiar to everyone who has watched the hippo dance in Walt Disney's *Fantasia*, illustrated in figure 3.6. In other words, the perception of fakery depends directly on the perception of quotation in this case. It seems to me that the same is necessarily and self-evidently true of every other case of exaggeration.

3.3.2. Flattening

a) Wow.
b) Yippee skippee.
c) Great.
d) Ha ha.
e) My heart bleeds for you.

The words are excited, but the melody (as signaled by the full stop rather than the expected "!") is apathetic. Again, attestations in German, Japanese, Mandarin, Italian, Spanish, and Ukrainian suggest the near universality of this.

Täuschung

Etwas geschwind (Allegretto)

39.

Ein Licht tanzt freundlich vor mir her, ___ ich

Frühlingstraum

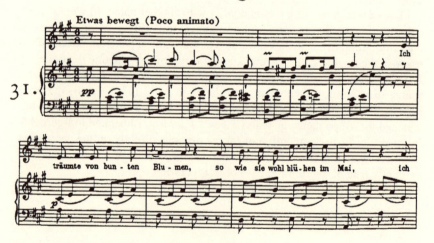

Etwas bewegt (Poco animato)

Ich

31.

träumte von bun - ten Blu - men, so wie sie wohl blü - hen im Mai, ich

Figure 3.4. "Täuschung" and "Frühlingstraum."

Figure 3.5. "Gavotte l'antique."

3.3.3. Singsong Melody

a) So sorree.
b) Boo hoo.
c) Thank you!

The singsong melody, whose core at least in English is a spondee on a descending third, is characteristic of calls. For extensive discussion of the (Low) High Mid melody of this "vocative chant," compare Ladd (1978a, b) and Liberman (1979). I agree with Ladd (1978a:248) that a function of this particular singsong melody is to signal "an element of predictability or stereotype in the message": note, for example, that it is the melody with which we utter "Ho hum" and "Bo-ring." (In fact, I think all chants signal clichés.) For this reason, the chant is often associated with expressions which the speaker feels to be banal.

Singsong as an index of insincerity has proved relatively difficult to find so far in other languages but is well attested in my present data from English, French, Italian, Turkish, Berber, Korean, and Israeli Hebrew. Adachi (1996:18, 33) has identified the stylized intonation extra-HLM in Japanese:

Figure 3.6. "Dance of the Hours of the Day." Note the grace-noted octaves—virtually a cliché of daintiness.

H   L   M
Maa joozu
wow be-good-at
"Wow! You're terrific!"

Uttered sincerely, it contrasts with the same expression uttered in a contemptuous singsong, shown in figure 3.7.

Fonagy and others (1983) note that saleswomen in France utter "Bonjour madame" on the same notes as the opening bar of the last movement of Beethoven's "Tempest" piano sonata. In my materials, I have a spectrogram of a speaker uttering an ironic "Te plains, ma pauvre" to roughly the same melody.

3.3.4. Falsetto

Falsetto is false. False what? I would say false delicacy and possibly false femininity. It is popular with sarcasts targeting women and gays. In each of the examples below, it is accompanied by heavy nasalization.

a)   Supermarket checkout clerk: Eating between meals? Tsk tsk.
     Lovable hero: *"Eating between meals, tsk tsk."* (from the
                                          movie *Stakeout*)
b)   *My nickname is Bambi and my favorite subject is science.* (Arsenio Hall,
     mimicking a hypothetical *Playboy* Playmate, June 17, 1989)
c)   You say some good things, we say some good things, and *we'll all do well
     together.* (Jimmy Swaggart, mimicking mainstream religious figures on a
     televised sermon, 1988; in the same sermon, he does a turn mimicking their
     effeminate "mincing" walk)

I have elicited this without exception in American English when I ask subjects to quote and mimic (with as much contempt as they can muster) a self-pitying monologue.

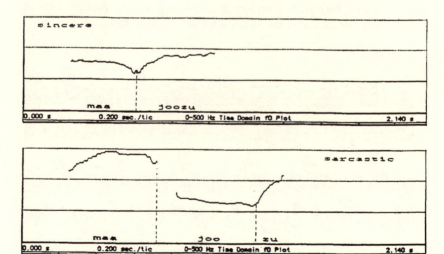

Figure 3.7. Stylized Intonation in Japanese.

3.3.5 "Heavy Sarcasm"

I use the phrase "heavy sarcasm" to denote a combination of heavy exaggerated stress and relatively monotonous intonation. It tends to occur most frequently in English with expressions which are uttered sarcastically so routinely that they have become enantiosemantic (like all of the examples below except the very last):

- a) BULLY for YOU!
- b) TELL me about it!
- c) THANKS a WHOLE LOT!
- d) Go ON!
- e) You're BREAking my HEART!
- f) BIG (FAT HAIRY) DEAL!
- g) That's really RICH.
- h) VEry FUNny.
- i) So SUE me.
- j) I could CARE LESS.
- k) ConGRAtulAtions!

There is a perfect acoustic parallel between these examples and one variety of ironic applause: a heavy monotonous, thoroughly controlled repetition of the clapping gesture. Attestation so far is confined to English (where it is extremely common), German, Mandarin, Hungarian, and Italian.

3.3.6. Separation by Heavy Pauses

Reagan's . . . freedom fighters . . . need new Gucci's.

Adachi (1996:11–5) finds that the framing pause is the only overt sign of sarcasm in utterances of the form "X" (pause) datte "'X' . . . says" in pairs like:

" Watashi wa ii mono shika   kawanai kara" (pause) datte.
I   top. good   things only not-buy because   says
"'I buy only high quality materials' (. . .) she says."

Jonsson (1995) finds that a framing pause is also accompanied by a strong initial glottal stop for all vowel-initial quotations in German:

Um diese . . . "Einheit" . . . zu bewirken
to   this   unity   to effect
"To effect this . . . 'unity'"

3.3.7. The Iconicity of These Metamessages

Undoubtedly, there are also cases where utterances exhibit a mixture of the melodic patterns idealized in these examples, nevertheless they can each exist as an adequate sign of insincerity by themselves. Although there are other means for conveying the required metamessage, let us focus for now on these relatively crude and more or less iconic devices.

It is widely recognized, even by scholars who deny iconicity in language, that expressive suprasegmentals (variations in pitch, amplitude, and length) are a special case. Sarcastic intonation in the examples I have listed here is virtually a charade of distaste and clearly iconic of alienation or detachment from the segmental text in each of the types given previously.

Iconicity which requires exegesis is not particularly successful, of course, but I do not think that the intonations listed here require a great deal of it. For the record, I will state the obvious: the *exaggeration* of a contextually inappropriate sign is what defines most kinds of mocking mimicry, including parody. It characterizes in particular a caricature in every medium. Exaggerated compassion is then an icon of other kinds of caricature. Why it should be the case that caricature is a sign of mockery is another question, with possibly more than a single answer.

In part, exaggeration, like mention in Sperber and Wilson's theory of irony, and like all mimicry, has the effect of drawing the audience's attention to some sign not just as a representamen but as an object in itself. What is exaggerated is of course most generally some feature which is perceived as a weakness rather than a strength. (The falsetto exaggerates what may be perceived as the essence of a child's voice, for example.)

In part, exaggerated *courtesy*, or hyperformality, is a kind of stylized behavior, and like all stylized behavior, it signals insincerity. It does this not only because whoever manifests it has control over his or her pretended emotions but also because stylization, like exaggeration, is impossible the first time around. It can only arise in imitation, and self-conscious imitation at that.

Flattening of affect, on the other hand, is clearly a symptomatic icon of exhaustion. The affectation of exhaustion is then a sign of boredom or indifference.

For the orthographic representation of frigid flatness, of course, the simple period or even zero instead of the expected exclamation mark can be deadly. There is no mistaking the mockery of "Wow." or of "Whoopee."

Singsong intonation—precisely because it is stylized—is an iconic index of the speaker's lack of spontaneous feeling or personal commitment to the too often repeated words of a stale, unfelt ritual, where the natural melody (originally lost, no doubt, because of flattening) is (as it were) artificially reconstituted. It is like painting a cement parking lot a "grasslike" shade of green. In the case of a sarcastic singsong chant, it is of course crucial that the hearer *not* be fooled into taking the cement for grass and that the hearer be able to distinguish the singsong tone from the genuine article.

A particularly rich example occurs toward the end of the film *Married to the Mob*. The philandering villain encounters his homicidally jealous wife, who points a gun at his crotch, smiles sweetly, and says:

Kiss it good-bye
  L   H M

This is no time (one might think) for clichés! The wife's threat is genuine and deadly. Why then is it apparently belied by the sweet smile, the playful diction, and the unserious intonation with which it is delivered? I believe that all of those signals which stress the woman's playfulness in this case serve to make the threat even more ominous. An enraged assailant may be mollified. But a playful one is deaf to counsels of pity, since she pretends not to be serious.

Finally, heavy sarcasm, the *slowing and heavy emphasis* characteristic of ironic applause and related expressions of "ridiculed enthusiasm," iconically conveys a rather complicated message: "I feel no enthusiasm or any other spontaneous emotion (hence, the slow, rhythmic, and, above all, controlled nature of my utterance), but—and this is crucial—don't delude yourself that I'm simply too tired to respond to you enthusiastically. I have plenty of energy to ridicule you with, and I am not tired, weak, or apathetic (hence, the exaggerated force with which I mark this)."

A sarcastic delivery presupposes and contrasts with a normal or emotively appropriate one. The conceptual distance between words and the speaker's true or intended meaning is then signaled not directly by the "distance" or "misfit" between the intonation and the segmental utterance but rather by the distance between the actual intonation and an unspoken intonational model which a sincere delivery would call for. The meaning of sarcastic intonation, like that of every other sign, consists in its contrast with other signs that are in a paradigmatic relationship with it.

3.4. Segmental Markers of the Sarcastive Modality

In my discussion up to this point, the incongruity between message and metamessage could be phrased as the misfit between words and music or between what you say and how you say it. There are also cases where the metamessage is expressed in signs of the same type as the signs of the message, so that the incongruity is between what you say and what you say elsewhere in the same linear string.

3.4.1. Hyperformality

He treated me with a civility that was too exaggerated not to convey an impression of sheer irony to even the most impartial observer. "Lo and behold, the heir apparent!" he would say, rising ceremoniously, whenever I came into the room, and waiting until I took my place before he sat down again, leaning forward as though waiting assiduously to hear what I had to say. Such behaviour was bound to confuse me as much as his always addressing me with "*Sie*" the polite form. (von Rezzori 1981:24–5)

The survey we have just completed of suprasegmental sarcastic devices has already touched on the issue of control. Three melodies (exaggeration, singsong, and heavy sarcasm) directly advertise that the speaker is in complete control of and hence distanced from his or her pretended emotions.

What is the connection between control and sarcasm? Control (politeness, etiquette) contrasts with spontaneity. If the latter is a symptom of sincerity, then *control signals artifice*. Surprisingly, then, one metamessage of politeness "this is not sincere" is almost identical with the metamessage of sarcasm. The speaker may signal *control* in two separate but deeply related ways: first, in the use of a "High" register (cf. Ferguson 1959); second, in the use of a code or the use of language itself.

3.4.1.1. FORMAL REGISTERS

Control can be manifested in all of the grammatical aspects of High register; phonological, lexical, and syntactic. For this reason, hyperformality is often used as a stage separator to indicate the speaker's lack of sincere commitment to the words he or she speaks.

3.4.1.1.1. SARCASTIC SEGMENTAL PHONOLOGY
"Try to remember," I said, "this is important."
"Oh, that's different," said the man. He rubbed his chin.
"If it's *important*, I'll have to remember."
He chewed each syllable carefully and presented the finished word on the tip of his tongue, anxious not to mutilate a vowel or drop an aitch. "I was getting it mixed up with the trivia of half a million people being fed into a gas chamber."
He looked up at me, frankly jeering. (Deighton 1965:161)

In a large number of classic studies, Labov has shown that the phonology of formal speech (manifested by self-conscious, language-conscious subjects uttering minimal pairs, reading word lists, reading aloud, and participating in formal interviews) contrasts with the phonology of informal speech (in which subjects speak unself-consciously with their peers) in fixed and predictable ways (cf. Labov 1966, 1972a, 1972b). Formal registers are marked by the relative absence of optional assimilation and neutralization processes and the retention of underlying syllable structure. Speakers work hard to enunciate clearly. Informal registers are marked by extensive assimilation, neutralization, and reduction. Speakers abandon themselves to the principle of least effort. This seems to be a universal, so much so that even nonspeakers of English can readily guess that [dId ju] is more formal than [ʒə], and so on.

Like exaggerated courtesy and compassion, the exaggerated clarity of pronunciation which characterizes High registers often signals mockery, as in the example from Deighton.

Jonsson (1995) notes the frequency of suspiciously clear diction as a marker of sarcasm in German: [a:məs diŋ] "You poor thing!" (with loss of post-vocalic /r/) contrasts with its sarcastic counterpart [a:ᴚməs diŋ].

3.4.1.1.2. ORTHOGRAPHIC HONORIFICS
Orthography in English can be used for the expression of respect. Typically, proper names are capitalized; even personal pronouns referring to God are capitalized; and personified virtues like Truth and Beauty sometimes qualify for the same respectful treatment. Consider now the orthographic sarcasm of the following passages from *Portnoy's Complaint*:

The impoverished districts that had been given him to canvass by The Most Benevolent Financial Institution in America. (Roth 1969:5)

Moreover, there had not been a Jewish manager in the entire history of Boston & Northeastern (Not Quite Our Class, Dear, as they used to say on the Mayflower). (ibid.:6)

No, no indeed—what we have before us, ladies and gentlemen, direct from a record-breaking engagement with his own family, is a Jewish boy just dying in his every cell to be *Good, Responsible, & Dutiful* to a family of his own. (ibid.:173).

Also:

None of this was reported in the *Free Press*, the "community of nations" being irrelevant when it fails to perceive the *Truth*. (Chomsky 1989b:18)

Right now, for example, they are busily administering the defense of El Salvador, a wretched little country that has suddenly become *Vital to Our National Security*. (Barry 1987:75)

With the ironic use of capitals, writers may attempt to suggest in their writing the same exaggerated courtesy and insolent respect that speakers can signal with mock High register or mock honorifics.

Of course, the use of capital honorifics suggests a pronunciation, which is why some writers indicate the sarcastic nature of a person's *speech* through this device alone:

But you're concerned, aren't you Mr. Rainey? I use the word concerned in sense of moral engagement. For example when you ask me a question like Do They Always Do Things That Way, I think I espy an uplifting reform-minded attitude. (Stone 1987:163)

3.4.1.1.3. FORMAL DICTION AND SYNTAX

—It's against orders, really, sir.
—Well, it's certainly very kind to do that for me. I'll certainly be most discreet in my conversation.
—There's no need to be sarcastic, sir. I'm only doing my job. (Deighton 1965:125)

The most famous example of exaggerated deference in the canonical literature comes in Mark 15:18–20: "'Hail, King of the Jews!' And they smote him on the head with a reed and did spit upon him, and bowing their knees, worshipped him."

The most grammaticalized lexical index of formality in most European languages is the use of a formal V pronoun for the addressee (Brown & Gilman 1960). This too is sometimes pressed into the service of sarcastic expression (Friedrich 1972).

In the same spirit, but using somewhat different materials for its expression, is the use of women's speech markers as an overt index of sarcasm in Japanese. In Japanese as in most European languages, there is an intimate connection between hyperformality and women's speech. Just as in English (Fisher 1958), it is men rather than women who tend to drop the final *g* in the -ing suffix, so too in Japanese, it is women's speech which signals hyperformality through the addition of certain segmental morphemes like the honorific prefix *o-*, the clausal nominalizer *koto*, and interjections like *maa* "wow." The sentence below, which is liberally festooned with such markers of feminine speech, is presumed to be sarcastic (Adachi 1996:15–6):

Maa o – joozu   desu koto.
wow hon. good-at cop. nom.
"Wow, you're good at it."

So, too, the sarcasm is patent in the incongruity between the hyperformal diction of "Meine Damen und Herren, höffentlich stört es Sie nicht, wenn ich hier . . ." and the exasperation of "schon zum fünfzehnten Mal um Ruhe bitte" (Jonsson 1995).

3.4.1.2. THE USE OF LANGUAGE

The difference between "Aaaa!!" and "That hurts" is sometimes labeled as the difference between an *expression* and a *description*; alternatively, it is described as the difference between a *symptom* and a *sign*. In either case, it is profound. The expressive symptom, an unmediated cry (or a sob or a laugh), is involuntary, and, to that extent, it is universal. It is so far beyond language that we can recognize and relate to screams of pain in other animals. The descriptive sign, on the other hand, is a *coded message*. It communicates information only to someone who recognizes the arbitrary code in which it is uttered. It is produced only by someone who is in sufficient control of his or her emotions to submit to the arbitrariness and the formality of a social convention.

In a word, to use a code, or to speak a language, is to exercise a degree of artifice or control in communicating. It may seem that this control is, if not minimal, at least universal. And if it is universal, the potential contrast *code/ no code* is not available, one might think, as a carrier of meaning. Nevertheless, the presence of even this much control may contrast with its absence and thus be used for insincerity (recall Voltaire's cynical dictum that "language was given to us in order to conceal our thoughts") or to signal sarcasm.

Sincere amusement is expressed by an uncoded laugh; denigration of pretended amusement may be signaled by its lexicalization, the language-specific "equivalent" "haha": "They gave him stationery with his own name printed beneath a picture of the Mayflower, their insignia (and by extension, his haha)" (Roth 1969:4–5).

Sincere pain may be expressed by an uncoded scream; ironic pain, by "ouch." Sincere grief may be expressed by a sob; grief is mocked by "boo hoo." Sincere enthusiasm may be expressed by clapping one's hands; ironic applause by substituting a lexicalization like *hakushu* "clapping" or its onomatopoeic representation *pachi pachi* in Japanese:

Umai umai umai hakushuuuu pachi pachi pachi!
good   clapping   <clap>
"Let's give (him) a real big hand!" (Adachi 1996:11)

Sincere commiseration may be signaled by clucking one's tongue; ironic parodies of this by saying [tisk tisk], a vocalization of the orthographic distortion of the click.

Slightly less sarcastic than lexicalized imitations are descriptions of the would-be stimulus, like "very funny," or of the speaker's response to it, such as "je rie," "je sanglote," or "my heart bleeds for you." By this stage, however, control has other functions besides that of signaling unwelcome insincerity.

"I am very angry" is a welcome sublimation (not an ironic denigration) of an inarticulate bellow of rage. So, too, the German "Beleidigung," which members of German dueling fraternities politely uttered to each other to initiate a sword fight (Austin 1975), is a ritualized abbreviation of a genuine insult and uttered with the intention of provoking a similar response—although not a "serious" one.

Again, there is an instructive parallel with play. A way of signaling insincerity in emotional responses is to substitute a label for the action. This is one of the ways in which animals signal that their bites are not for real: they substitute a pantomime for the thing itself (Hole & Einon 1984:100).

3.4.2. I Quote

Many different things can happen when a quoter cites a source. In one genre of quotation, which we may call performance, the quoter largely suppresses his or her own personality in order to speak with the voice of the source; examples are a priest intoning a ritual prayer, an actor playing a role, or a pianist playing a musical work. (We call the performer's attempt at empathy with the absent composer an interpretation.) In another, familiar as plagiarism, the quoter speaks with the voice of the source but wishes to convince the hearer that no other source than the quoter exists. In both performance and plagiarism, the effect is of speaking with a single voice.

Direct quotation of the sort that we are interested in here is different. Both the voices of the source and the quoter are heard. Quotation is the linguistic stage separator par excellence. In the same way that what happens on stage neither impinges on nor is affected by the outside world, so too what is quoted is not incorporated into the linguistic context in which it is uttered.

We may formalize the notion of incorporation in the following way. In a string $X A Y$, the element A is incorporated into the string $X \ldots Y$ if either the shape or the position of A is affected by X or Y, or the shape or position of either X or Y is affected by A. To say that quotation is a stage separator is to say that in a string X "A" Y, A is not incorporated in this sense. In phonology, incorporation is familiar as *sandhi*. In morphology and syntax, the various kinds of incorporation are not generally thought of under a single heading. Some instances of what we might call morphosyntactic sandhi include the following:

a) a verb agrees with a noun phrase with respect to certain features (more generally, all agreement);
b) a noun phrase occurs in a certain case when governed by a verb or a preposition (more generally, all government);
c) a noun phrase which is coreferential with another noun phrase is replaced by an anaphoric expression;

d) the presence of an affective phrase at the beginning of a sentence triggers subject-verb inversion;

e) a verb which occurs in construction with an object noun phrase must be a transitive verb;

f) a negative word in construction with an adjective may be replaced by an affix.

Quoted or mentioned material is exempt from agreement, government, or any other kind of modification by context. Moreover, it fails to induce agreement, government, or any other kind of modification in elements of the context. Consider only the following representative examples:

1. a) He goes "Aaargh."
    b) Who's "they"?
    c) I don't like the use of "I" here.
    d) What do you mean "we," white man?
    e) She said "Nothing" (*at all interesting).
    f) "Under no imaginable circumstances," { she said.
                                             { *did she say.

In (1a), the quoted material need not even be language (let alone English), and the quotative verb, as a number of researchers (Partee 1973; Munro 1982) have pointed out, does not have to be transitive. This indicates that the quote has not been (even minimally) incorporated into the matrix sentence as one of its arguments, that is, as the object of a verb of saying. It is interesting to observe, however, that such a minimal incorporation is at least possible with verbal quotation. The intransitive verb "go," as Heath (1984:559), among others, has pointed out, is obligatory only with nonverbal quotation or pantomime.

In (1b), the quoted material, apparently a plural noun, is either treated as a singular noun or does not cause subject-verb agreement. In (1c), the quoted material fails to appear in the accusative case or in the reflexive form, although apparently identical with the subject pronoun of the sentence where it seems to occur as an object. In (1d), as in (1a), the quoted material corresponds to no argument (subject, object, indirect object) of the matrix sentence, nor can it be identified as a separate vocative, like the apostrophic "white man." In (1e), the quoted negative morpheme fails to allow negative polarity items. Finally, in (1f), the sentence-initial negative quote fails to allow the normally obligatory inversion of the following subject and verb.

Like the activities which occur within the context of a game, so too the sounds which occur within the context of a quote are separated from the "outside world." In the stage metaphor, real people in the audience ideally cannot affect stage events: "the show must go on." On the other hand, real people cannot be affected by stage events: nobody really dies in *Rambo*, and, ideally, the spouse of the romantic lead does not sue for divorce on the grounds of adultery. This generalization as it stands is too strong (as are the ideals of the stage: real life can always slosh over the borders of the stage, and there are very famous cases where people have believed what was presented as fiction). However, it does represent a psychologically robust ideal and will serve as a suitable approximation of the truth.

Now the speaker may signal "I'm not serious" or "this is fake" by indicating that the words he or she utters are a quote. In the following sections, I wish to distinguish two kinds of quotation: contemptuous repetition of "fresh talk" (wherein the speaker mocks another speaker) and contemptuous repetition of banalities (wherein the speaker mocks the accepted wisdom of a stale cliché).

3.4.2.1. QUOTE

The word "quote" is of course a spoken rendition of the orthographic quote sign. Although in dictation "quote-unquote" is a discontinuous constituent with arbitrarily long strings within its scope, as a sarcastive "quote-unquote" is continuous and only the following word (or, at most, short phrase) is within its scope.

Your quote-unquote principles are nothing but snobbism.

The word "quote" is the only sarcastive morpheme which has lasted for any length of time in English. It is also the only one which has grammaticalized congeners that I have been able to find in other languages.

3.4.2.2. EVIDENTIALS

The *quotative* is an evidential category in a large number of the world's languages (cf. Chafe & Nichols 1986). In at least two of these, its meaning has been extended to convey irony as it does in English.

Thus, the following statement in Turkish "can convey not only hearsay, but doubting scorn when predicated of a well-known exercise hater" (Aksu-Koç & Slobin 1986:162; the authors also cite Kononov 1956:232, who notes that the evidential in Turkish conveys "an ironical attitude toward the carrying out of an action"):

Her   gün koş- uyor- muş.
every day run prog. evid. 3sg
"He reportedly runs every day."

And thus the Albanian admirative, which is "traditionally defined as the mood expressing surprise" but is "also used to express irony, doubt, and reportedness" (Friedman 1986:180):

E   na   i   dashka   bullgaret . . . ai e . . .e   pse keshtu u pritka
and to-us them loves(adm.) Bulgarians   he ha! and why thus   is-met
nje Bullgar?
a   Bulgarian
"And he 'likes' Bulgarians. Him? Hah! After all, is that how you treat a Bulgarian?"

Friedman (ibid.:183) perceptively notes that in this sentence, the speech event is *mocked* (rather than simply reported). In the written translation, the quotation marks seem to capture the admirative perfectly.

Lexical equivalents of the quotative morpheme in Rumanian are the sentential adverbs *parca* "seemingly" and *adica* "that is to say, in other words," as in

a) "Parca   noi am furat maşina?
    seemingly we have stolen car
    "I suppose that you're now going to say *we* stole the car?"
b) Adica, sa   fiu eu cel   care a   murit?
    i.e.   subj. am I dem=ms who has=3sg. died
    "I suppose you're going to say I'm the one that died?" (Mallinson 1986:6)

Note that Mallinson's felicitous English translation of the sarcastive as "I suppose you're going to say" is also a periphrastic quotative. For an example from colloquial English, consider figure 3.8.

Another possible congener is the Japanese postutterance *datte* "said" if it is separated from the preceding quotation by a slight—framing—pause (Adachi 1996:12), or even if it occurs as a freestanding commentary on a prior utterance. Adachi reports on the possibility of the following conversations:

A: Watashi wa ii mono shika kawanai kara.
     "I only buy good quality things." [exit A]
B: "——— datte. [disgustedly, to C]
     "(A) says."

Lexicalization of a quotative shades off into other imputations of an alien source for one's words. Consider the following French dialog:

— Tes parents savent que tu ne couches pas chez toi ce soir?
  "Do your parents know you're not sleeping at home tonight?"
— *Tu trouves que* j'aurais dû leur demander permission, hein?
  "You think I should have asked for their permission, eh?" (Gide 1966:35)

Nevertheless, natural as the extension from quoting to mocking mimicry may seem to us, it is by no means universal. Robert Oswalt (personal communication) emphasizes that neither the quotative evidential nor the actual direct quote followed by /nihcedu/ "say" can ever be used to signal irony, sarcasm, or doubt

Figure 3.8. Sally Forth, by Greg Howard. (Reprinted with special permission of King Features Syndicate.)

of the veracity of the source in Kashaya or in Southern, Central, or Northern Pomo. I would speculate that those languages in which the quotative cannot be sarcastic may be among those fabled languages and cultures immortalized by Douglas Q. Adams in *The Hitchhikers' Guide to the Galaxy* where, as in Betelgeuse, "they don't have sarcasm" (Adams 1979:15) at all.

3.4.2.3. IRONIC REPETITION OF FRESH TALK

a) What do you mean "we," white man?
b) Her "career"!
c) Reagan's precious "freedom fighters" need new Gucci's.
d) Checkout clerk: Eating between meals? Tsk tsk. (prissy)
   Customer: "Eating between meals?" (with caricatured prissiness)
e) I fear I wrong the "honorable men" whose daggers have stabbed Caesar. I do fear it.

In one of the first efforts I am aware of to distinguish between respectful and sarcastic quotation, Voloshinov (1973:123) suggests that "the stronger the feeling of hierarchical eminence in another utterance, the more sharply defined will its boundaries be and the less accessible will it be to penetration by retorting and commenting tendencies from outside." Compare Baxtin 1986:92–3: "the speaker's expression penetrates through [the quotation marks] and spreads to the other's speech, which is transmitted in ironic, indignant, sympathetic, or reverential tones. . . . The other's speech has a dual expression: its own . . . and the expression of the utterance that encloses the speech." Baxtin's insight that this dual representation occurs primarily in those cases where the other's speech is both openly introduced and clearly demarcated (i.e. in the case of direct quotation rather than in a variety of other closely related speech genres like indirect quotation, translation, plagiarism, or playacting) is very important.

The formal expression of the metamessage "I quote" is not entirely confined to iconic (and thus, perhaps, relatively primitive?) paralinguistic or intonational gestures. Most European languages (in fact, most languages I have investigated so far) have at least the adjectives "so-called" or "purported" which express the speaker's noncommittal to or disagreement with (or disparaging evaluation of) the following nominal label. A comparable segmental "sarcastive morpheme" for verbs, adjectives, or complete utterances is the frequent colloquial "quote-unquote," which is used to introduce material from which the speaker wishes to distance himself or herself. (The more grammaticalized evidential morpheme, which occurs in a large number of languages with the meaning "it is said," seems to introduce *indirect quotation* rather than direct quotation, as a number of diagnostics make clear.)

In making a meaningful utterance, Searle (1979:24) suggests, a speaker is actually performing several different speech acts: uttering actual words, forming propositions by naming a subject and linking it with a predicate, and investing this utterance with some illocutionary force so that the utterance is intended as a statement, an exclamation, a question, an order, a promise, and so on. Each of these acts may be imitated with sarcastic intent. In our discussion of quotation so far, we have focused almost entirely on quotation of the original speaker's actual words; in Searle's terminology, this would be quotation of the sentence. Literature is replete with examples.

"Young Sammy here is with us, aren't you, Sammy? *Young Sammy* was with them all right. *Young Sammy* was applying for the job of bugle boy in the proud little army that marched under the banner of $2,500 a week. (Schulberg [1941] 1971:126)

—Those friends of mine didn't know that.
—One of these days, Chico, you are going to face up to the fact that *those friends of yours* in what you persist in calling the War House know nothing about everything. (Deighton 1965:68)
—Try to remember. This is important.
—Oh, that's different. If it's *important*, I'll have to remember. I was getting it mixed up with the trivia of half a million people being fed into a gas chamber. (ibid.:161)

Or, as in the following case, the quotation is of a tiresome or hypocritical cliché:

I know what you are going to say . . . "Now you *understand for the first time.*" That's what they all say, and, believe me, it sounds silly. (ibid.:159)

Even sentence quotation may be quite subtle. In the course of normal conversation, it is common for speakers to avoid repetition of certain words and phrases: thus shifters change with speakers, and full noun phrases are replaced by anaphoric expressions. The metamessage "I don't mean this" may be communicated very sharply by the speaker when he or she simply *fails to translate* an original speaker's shifters, as in the interchange

—Do you think you all could pay for the cleaning up, then?
—No, "you all" certainly could not.

But it may also occur when the speaker simply fails to substitute an anaphor for a term previously introduced by himself, as in

Many people think asthma is psychosomatic, but *many people* are wrong.

Repetition rather than automatic translation of a referential expression may be sufficiently odd to call attention to the message and to the ignorance of the "many people" cited here.

But it is also possible to quote nothing but the illocutionary act itself. This is what occurs in one kind of rhetorical question: that exemplified by the response in exchanges such as

—Is she still mad at me?
—Do birds fly?

The semantic force of the response, I believe, is at least in part a denigration of the original questioner. The put-down is accomplished by quoting not the actual words or the propositional content of the original question but its illocutionary force alone. The implicit message "that is a stupid question" is conveyed by the frigid flatness with which the rhetorical question is asked and, of course, by the absurdity of the rhetorical question itself, whose answer is no more self-evident than the stupid original question which it "quotes."

The same thing occurs in exchanges like

—This will be easy.
—Oh yeah, sure. And I promise not to come in your mouth, and the check is in
    the mail. (from the movie *To Live and Die in L.A.*)

—I have a national reputation.
—And I'm the Queen of England.

What is quoted is neither the utterance nor the propositional content of the original speaker but his or her illocutionary intent, which is to make an empty promise or a vain boast.

Direct quotation, then, may be of the actual words, of the proposition, or of the illocutionary force of the utterance which is being mocked. Indirect quotation, while it seems to resemble direct quotation of all but the original speaker's words, differs crucially in that, unlike direct quotation, it does not attempt to draw the listener's attention to any aspect of the original message as an object in its own right. In each of the examples just cited, however, this is exactly what the sarcast tries to do.

Conventional orthography has always attempted to mark intonation with ancillary signs like exclamation and question marks. Not suprisingly, quotation marks are routinely used to mark a sarcastic attitude toward a text, even where no act of quotation has occurred. The last sentence of Hardy's *Tess of the d'Urbervilles*, for example, alludes ironically to "Justice" but quotes no one: "'Justice' was done, and the President of the Immortals . . . had finished his sport with Tess." The practice of using quotation marks for judgments and statements which are of alien origin and of dubious validity is widespread in journalism, letters to the editor, and political writing:

Do you have any idea how our troops feel when they see reports of "Americans" running around like idiots burning flags? (letter to an advice columnist from a Vietnam veteran)

Ask your "fantastic" in-laws to please keep their ethnic slurs to themselves. (Dear Abby's response to a parent worried about the ethnic bigotry of his in-laws)

The existence of this orthographic practice, misleadingly labeled "scare quotes," surely confirms the claim that pretense and quotation are intimately related; one may view the several functions of quotation marks as an example of motivated polysemy—the recurrent representation of related meanings through a single formal device. In this case, the related meanings are those of pretense and quotation.

It is, of course, no accident that both the adjective "so-called" and quotation marks allude transparently to the act of quotation. Quotation, as many authors have already noted, is a kind of mimicry or playacting (Voloshinov 1973:135; Wierzbicka 1974) and, therefore, a kind of pretense. To some extent, the quoter is putting himself or herself into the original speaker's role and playing a fictional part.

Finally, the ubiquity in North America of the mimed or "air quote," recently characterized as the "quintessential contemporary gesture" (Rudnick & Andersen 1989), is an obvious reflection of the orthographic sign of quotation.

3.4.2.4. QUOTATION OF CLICHÉS

A singsong intonation, as I have suggested, may be used to mark some expressions as wearisome clichés. In speaking with a chanted melody, the speaker is as much as saying "I've heard this song before." Another device which may mark a stretch of text as a fixed banality is to "chunk" it, that is, to utter it as though it were a single word. There are two ways to capture this pronunciation in orthography. The most direct is to simply run the words of a cliché together as a single word, as *The Nation* did in a recent editorial (August 12, 1996) lambasting Clinton and Congress for ending "welfareasweknowit." The second, a little more subtle, is to treat the words of a cliché like the letters of a spelled-out word. A number of authors, sensitive to the chunking process, artfully reproduce it in writing by the use of hyphens:

> Moreover, when she loses at mah-jongg, she takes it like a sport, *not-like-the-others-whose-names-she-could-mention-but-she-won't-not-even-Tilly-Hochman-it's-just-too-petty-to-even-talk-about-let's-just-forget-she-ever-brought-it-up.* (Roth 1969:12)

> But now these Democrats can find easy cover in the weak-kneed, *it's-just-not-politically-feasible* argument. (Corn 1989:239)

A purely lexical equivalent of the singsong intonation is the use of the artfully mangled cliché. The speaker parodies the cliché by quoting it in a totally ludicrous context or by changing it slightly to express a subversive sentiment, and the incongruity between the cliché and the novelty of the author's own ideas contributes to the humor of the combination:

> At Auschwitz, they managed things better. *They moved with the times.* With cyclon-B, they killed two and a half million. (Deighton 1965:135)

> But these *natural outward and visible signs of inward and spiritual disgrace* were not enough. (Crisp 1978:28, describing gayspeak voice mannerisms)

> When the discomfort and sometimes the downright degradation became too much for me, I moved on to *fresh pits and pendulums new.* (ibid.:83)

> *Never before in the history of sexuality was so much offered to so many by so few.* (ibid.:152)

> I became one of the *stately homos of England.* (ibid.:154)

> *Drink and the world drinks with you: eat and you eat alone.* (ibid.:156)

> Expensive as it is, I have been using them to jerk off into, to see if they will stand up *under simulated fucking conditions.* (Roth 1969:187)

> My, how time flies when you's doing all the talking. (Fierstein 1979:8)

> "I recovered, and I chose to face whatever there was. Because of the covenant."

"And so we have the benefit of your attentions," Mr. Clotho said reflectively. "My, my, doesn't *He worketh in devious ways?*" (Stone 1987:215)

3.4.3. Other Segmental Devices

There is no doubt that markers of quotation in both spoken and written language are the most heavily institutionalized overt segmental indices of sarcasm. I will list some others which are currently fashionable in North American English, with no confidence that they will still be put to such use by the time this study appears.

3.4.3.1. LIKE

The whole following utterance is in the scope of the marker "like." The hearer is warned that what is about to follow is what the speaker may be expected to believe but does not. (A predictable synonym is "as if.")

a)   Like I care. (=I don't care.)
b)   Like there's any difference. (=There's no difference.)
c)   Like I haven't heard that one before. (=I've heard that one before.)
d)   As if TV advertising weren't intrusive enough already. (=TV advertising is too intrusive already.)

A possible equivalent with invariably sarcastic meaning in Russian is *mozhno podumat*, literally, "it is possible to think":

Mozhno podumat' ja bespokojus'.
Like   I care

In French, *si tu crois* "if you think" has much the same function:

—"Etait-elle belle, au moins?"
   "Was she pretty, at least?"
— Si tu crois que je l'ai regardée!
   "Like I was looking at her!" (Gide 1966: 38)

And in German, *als ob* seems to do the same work (Jonsson 1995):

Als ob mich das was angeht!
as if me that what comes to
"AS if I cared."

3.4.3.2. ... NOT

The utterance deflater "... not" signals that the preceding utterance (often a compliment) was meant facetiously. Until it is uttered, the hearer may believe that the prior utterance was sincere.

a)   He's a snappy dresser ... not!
b)   Guess I'll hit the books in time for that quiz ... not!
c)   Real Life with Jane Pauley ... not.

   d)   Bush will kill that program . . . not.
   e)   That's a fabulous science fair project . . . not!
   f)   Bush/Quayle in 1992 . . . not! (bumper sticker)

According to conventional wisdom, this locution surfaced on *Saturday Night Live* around 1988. According to William Safire, however, the first known incident of this locution on *Saturday Night Live* occurred ten years before that, in 1978. And Larry Horn has identified an occurrence in a "Little Nemo" cartoon of 1910, although he notes that it is unlikely that the locution was original at the time it was used there (personal communication). A British English equivalent with a longer history is "I don't think," now almost entirely obsolete (Suzanne Kemmer, personal communication).

     Sarcastive ". . . not" is clearly an example of what Horn (1985) has called metalinguistic negation, and it differs from garden-variety epistemic or deontic negation only in its clause- or utterance-final position. It is interesting that the formal relationship between *de dicto* negation and the ordinary *de re* negation is parallel to the difference that Horn extensively discusses between "not" and the prefix *un-* in cases like

   a)   I'm not happy: in fact, I'm downright miserable.
   b)   I'm not "happy": I'm ecstatic.

The latter is what Horn calls metalinguistic. And it is the metalinguistic "not" which cannot appear as a derivational prefix:

   a)   I'm unhappy: in fact, I'm downright miserable.
   b)   *I'm unhappy: I'm ecstatic.

In each case, the "metalinguistic" negator contrasts with its garden variety *de re* opposite number in that it is *more separated* from the constituent or the utterance which it negates. I've argued that the simple temporal separation from its embedding context is one of the ways in which a speaker marks the peculiar otherwordly status of quoted or mentioned material: perhaps the external position of the negator in itself serves as a kind of iconically framing quotation mark.

     Jonsson (1995) notes that "a phenomenon of German 'Jugendsprache' is the mocking, clause-external [heehn] (where the 'eehn' is a long nasalized schwa). The sarcast may append this to the end of a proposition and thus ridicule it." He gives this example:

   Sieht ja super aus . . . heehn.
   "Looks real great . . . NOT."

3.4.3.3. . . . OR ANYTHING

The clause introducer "not that" is generally used to signal that the speaker's interest in what follows is minimal:

   a)   Not that I value my sanity so highly.
   b)   Not that I care about the money.

The motivation is clear. A reconstituted "full" paraphrase would be something like:

a) It's not that I value my sanity so highly. (What terrifies me are screams of my fellow lunatics, the curses of my keepers, and the clanging of the chains.) (with apologies to Pushkin)
b) It's not that I care about the money. (What I *do* care about is the principle of the thing.)

Like many other things, however, a meaning can be mocked through ostensible exaggeration or emphasis. (I have indicated that this is the essence of all caricature.) When strengthened by the tag "or anything," the belittling constituent "not that" is apparently strengthened: but in practice, the speaker's ostensible act of trivialization is *mocked*.

a) Not that I care about the money or anything. (=I care passionately about the money.)
b) Not that it's cold out or anything. (= It's real cold out.)
c) Not that you annoyed me or anything. (=You annoyed the hell out of me.)

If not for the fact that I have a teenager in the family, I wouldn't have heard this marker.

3.4.3.4. GIVE ME A BREAK

The speaker signals his or her impatience with a clearly absurd proposition attributed to the interlocutor by repeating what he or she imagines to be the gist of it, followed by an exasperated plea for mercy on his or her overworked credulity—"give me a break" (see figures 3.9 and 3.10).

3.4.3.5. INTERROGATIVE AND DUBITATIVE MOOD MARKERS

Brown (1979) describes lexicalized indices of irony in a Mayan language of Mexico. In ironic speech, the interrogative or dubitative markers, plus optional use of the possibilitative morpheme and the emphatic morpheme, convert spoken "P" into "not P," and vice versa.

Figure 3.9. Sally Forth, by Greg Howard. (Reprinted with special permission of King Features Syndicate.)

> **Because he's black?**
> Kevin Weston and Andrea Jones of YO! newspaper in
> San Francisco are absolutely correct (Commentary,
> June 27): O.J. Simpson's arrest as the prime suspect in
> the murder of his ex-wife and her friend is racism, pure
> and simple. It has nothing to do with the facts or the
> evidence gathered by police. They arrested and jailed
> O.J. because he is black. If Fran Tarkenton were facing
> charges of butchering two human beings, he would be
> free and walking the streets. Give me a break.

Figure 3.10. A letter to the editor.

Sentence Meaning	*Utterance Meaning*
It might not possibly be the case that they are there.	They're there.
Perhaps he didn't just possibly get drunk.	He got drunk.
Perhaps we don't possibly get tired from bending over to pick up coffee.	We get tired from bending over to pick up coffee.
Is it that the one who hears you is happy?	You make everybody miserable.

The usage instantly makes sense to a speaker of English, although we have not
come anywhere near as close to institutionalization of this stylistic device.
Compare our use of interrogation:

> Aren't you just a teeny bit ashamed of yourself? (=You ought to be ashamed of
> yourself.)
> You think I'm making it up? (=I'm not making it up.)

Or even our use of the dubitative markers "I suppose" and "maybe":

> And as if it wasn't clear enough what I was up to, I even tacked on "as recog-
> nized in principles expounded by the United Nations." *By the United Nations.*
> Now what could I possibly have said to make the whole thing any more inane?
> *Maybe* I was supposed to have told them "as recognized in principles expounded
> by the American Automobile Association." *Maybe* I should have given the whole
> speech in Pig Latin, and made funny faces while I was at it! *Maybe* I should have
> come out to make the statement in a clown's costume! (Roth 1972:29)

Jonsson (1995) points out the parallel use of *vielleicht* "perhaps" (clipped to
[flaixt]) in German:

> Du bist mir v'leicht ein guter Freund.
> "Some friend you are."

3.4.3.6. MANNER OF SPEAKING VERBS

> He said science was going to discover the basic secret of life someday, the
> bartender put in. He scratched his head and frowned. "Didn't I read in the paper
> the other day where they'd finally found out what it was?"
> "I missed that," I *murmured.* (Vonnegut 1970:26)

The self-righteous narrator of *Cat's Cradle* is certainly making it clear to his enlightened reader, if not to his dim-witted interlocutor, that he means more than he is saying simply by drawing attention to his manner of speaking. At this point, the indices of sarcasm and the differences between the put-on, the aside, and the sarcastive speech act become a matter of personal style.

3.4.3.7. REPETITION

A general grammatical point that can be illustrated by this literary example, however, is that almost any mark which draws attention to the actual words spoken (as opposed to their intrinsic content) may signal that the words are to be taken with a grain of salt. And it may be that the most prevalent of these (and one that is closely akin to both quotation and exaggeration) is the mere act of repetition itself. The most plausible interpretation of repetition is an iconic one: if you say something once, you may mean it, but if you say it two or three times, you *really* mean it. Thus, reduplication, as often noted, typically has the iconic function of signaling plurality or intensification.

It is therefore remarkable that *repetition of signs of assent*, like "sure," "right," "of course," or "yeah," signals not heartiness but irony. "Yeah, right" in American English has by now achieved a quasi-institutional status as a sarcastive marker because it is a kind of repetitive. Nor is this limited to colloquial American English. The same is noted by native language consultants for Turkish, Russian, Hungarian, Berber, and Oromo renditions of expressions like "excuse me" or "of course." To be sarcastic, the repeated words have to be pronounced in a weary deadpan way, of course, but for some reason, repetition (as in "yeah, yeah") helps to achieve this.

Perhaps singsong is one means of marking an oft-repeated cliché. But another may be the mimicry of the act of repetition itself. I suggest that a possible reason for the sarcastic flavor of repeated "yeah, yeah" is that speakers who repeat such expressions are themselves *mimicking the process* whereby these words, like any others, have lost their original meanings through repetition by other speakers. It is notable that sarcastic repetitions are uttered on a series of downstepped tones, mimicking a fading of intensity over time.

In language after language, saying something once is unexceptionable but repeating it (which serves to draw attention to it) has the ambiguous function of emphasizing it but also encouraging skepticism.

3.4.3.8. SYNTACTICIZATION: A FINE ROMANCE THIS IS

The closest approach to a pure syntacticization of the sarcastive is the word order exemplified in expressions like the one above. If the "sincere" utterance has the form

X copula a [positive adjective] Y
1 2   3

then the transformation of this structure into 3 1 2 seems to mark sarcasm fairly reliably at least in English:

A fine friend you turned out to be!
Some party this is!

3.5. Conclusion: The Nongrammaticalization of Affect

A major question is: if the sarcastive is a candidate for being expressed by a grammatical mood like the subjunctive, why have virtually none of the all-but-transparent devices for signaling lack of speaker's commitment achieved the status of the subjunctive, the interrogative, or the evidential in any human language? (The only ones that come close are "quote-unquote" and stylized intonation, both of which have other, more central functions.) An alternative way of posing this question is: Why are the indices of sarcasm so widely shared and so iconic? Indisputably, there are steps toward the grammaticalization of sarcasm which may be language-specific: for example, Adachi (1996:21–5) reports that utterance-final glottal stop is an almost totally opaque and arbitrary sign of sarcasm in Japanese. Nevertheless, there is considerably more overlap between English, Berber, and Japanese ways of sounding sarcastic than between English, Berber, and Japanese ways of naming cats and dogs.

I suspect that institutionalization has not happened because the indices of sarcasm, like those of anger and other personal emotions, belong to the same communicative realm: they are not really representative signs of thought but presentative symptoms of affect (For an early and explicit recognition of the contrast, cf. Fonagy 1956.) Raising one's voice is probably a symptom of anger in whatever language one chooses to speak; nevertheless, no language has grammaticalized increased amplitude as a sign of anger. Why? Maybe because it's too universal, too natural, and too self-evident. Signs don't get codified (i.e., they are not recognized as signs) until they're at least a little bit arbitrary. Codification is arbitrariness, and *affect tends not to get coded* (cf. Lotz 1950; Sebeok 1962; and Fonagy 1971a for statements of this position, and also Chen 1994 for some extremely interesting counterexamples drawn mainly from Mandarin). It remains rather as the "last word" (cf. de Groot 1949) in communication. Having said this, I must note that logically alternatives are possible. One could imagine a mythical (and, I think, probably inhuman) language in which it is affect which is coded, and cognitive information is expressed in the tone of one's voice. In English, we say lexically and grammatically things like the affectionate insult from *Stand by Me*:

Referential insult, in words: "Not if I see you first."
("Last word," in tone of voice: "I love you.")

In the languages of a mythical universe like Borges's "Tlön" (and it would take a Borges to develop this notion), it's the other way around. They say grammatical things like "I love you." But the last word, as evidenced by their "manner of speaking," is "I'll need three dozen of these by four o'clock Thursday," or whatever else we express in English and human languages with grammatical devices and the lexicon.

But there may be another purely human reason for the fact that expressions of affect like sarcasm in particular resist syntacticization more than other ex-pressions of affect. One can, after all, say "I love you" in words. But one can-not rely on conventional coding techniques to say "I don't mean this."

And maybe the reason is simply that *we can't handle the complexity such institutionalization would make possible.* It is an essential defining property of a sign (and, incidentally, of a language) that it can be used insincerely. We have at our disposal a number of metalinguistic devices for signaling insincerity of the first order: "I don't mean this." Imagine now that we had a perfectly grammaticalized indicator of sarcasm, like the grammatical subjunctive mood, analogous to the orthographic device of quotation marks. There would then be nothing to stop us from embedding messages to an arbitrary depth in over-arching metamessages, as there is nothing to stop us from putting quotes within quotes within quotes ad infinitum.

But perhaps as humans at the present stage of our evolution we are limited by a purely performancelike constraint (similar to the constraint on syntactic center-embedding) which inhibits us from signaling insincerity of the second or higher orders. *"I don't mean 'I don't mean ("I don't mean) this" ' " (ortho-graphically " ' " this " ' "), which we could utter once the symptomatic "I don't mean this" was harnessed as a sign, is simply not readily interpretable by the average person, even in postmodern America.

The reason it is not interpretable may be that while we can appreciate the difference between sincerity and a bluff, and even between a bluff and a double bluff, our minds aren't yet rigged up to appreciate the difference between, say, a triple and a quadruple bluff. The virtual impossibility of higher order subtlety when there are only two possible choices is vividly caricatured in a wonderful passage from William Goldman's *Princess Bride*: the Man in Black proposes a battle of wits to the evil Sicilian hunchback Vizzini. One of the goblets of wine he offers the villain is poisoned, and the other is not. Can Vizzini figure out which one he should take?

> The Sicilian smiled and stared at the wine goblets. "Now a great fool," he began, "would place the wine in his own goblet, because he would know that only another great fool would reach first for what he was given. I am clearly not a great fool, so I will clearly not reach for your wine."
> "That's your final choice?"
> "No. Because you knew I was not a great fool, so you knew that I would never fall for such a trick. You would count on it. So I will clearly not reach for mine either."
> "Keep going," said the man in black.
> "I intend to." The Sicilian reflected for a moment. "We have now decided that the poisoned cup is most likely in front of you. But the poison is powder made from iocane, and iocane comes only from Australia, and Australia, as everyone knows, is peopled with criminals and criminals are not used to having people trust them, as I don't trust you, which means I clearly cannot choose the wine in front of you." (Goldman 1974:139–40)

And so the sly Sicilian goes on for another two pages. As Goldman makes clear, human beings just lose track as rarefaction grows and increasing subtlety becomes (to mortal minds, including the reader's) indistinguishable from aimless dithering.

And, possibly, our patience with it declines. There is a case to be made that bluffing and sarcasm are currently passé for some of the same reasons, and that we may be currently in the throes of a revival of the good, the true, and the beautiful. Whether this revival has any chance of success, or whether it is even logically consistent, is a question which I will return to in chapter 7, when we discuss the cult of plain speaking.

FOUR

Alienation and the Divided Self

Like every actor, the sarcast has a divided self, existing both as the performer and the persona—the character portrayed. Unlike Laurence Olivier, however, who succeeds in submerging himself as a performer and appearing as a virtually unrecognizable person in each new role that he plays, and also unlike typecast performers like Clint Eastwood who hardly seem to be acting (that is, playing roles) at all, the sarcast is a *disdainful* playactor who advertises his or her insincerity by self-consciously keeping the performer and the persona alive, distinct, and opposed. The ostensible message delivered in character expresses the role, but the metamessage—an aside directed to the other members of the play—expresses the performer's sincere alienation from the role which, for whatever reason, he or she elects to play.

Sarcasm is not the only speech genre that enforces such a distinction, which is reminiscent of the useful distinction made by Searle (1979) between the literal and the intended meaning of an utterance. I will call all speech genres in which the (speaker's) utterance meaning differs from the (words') sentence meaning "un-plain speaking." Un-plain speaking is, of course, opposed (or seems to be opposed) to the prose-like-a-windowpane ideal of blunt, sincere, plain speaking, which has an extensive and familiar folklore of its own. In particular, however, I will be concerned with those varieties of un-plain speaking which express the performer's *alienation* from the content of his or her role.

The notion of self-alienation (as opposed to alienation from the social order) is a very simple one, as a cursory view of some of the most pertinent social and psychological literature on the topic should confirm. It consists in this: People may, in various ways, repress their private spontaneous genuine selves and play instead a public role (Mead 1934:210) or, more accurately, a number of public roles (James 1890:294). When they do, we can say they are alienated from themselves.

Mead's idea of such a divided self and the literal self-consciousness with which one half regards the other is a very ancient one in Western culture. The image of Narcissus; the Socratic injunction to "know thyself"; the Stoic conception of heroism as "playing one's part"; the Christian tension between the willing spirit and the weak flesh; Polonius advising Hamlet "to thine own self be true"; Goethe's Faust complaining of "two souls residing in his breast"; Will Rogers telling you to "be yourself"; Sigmund Freud's recognition of the id, the ego, and the superego—like the notions of sincerity, hypocrisy, politeness, affectation, and image, these metaphors, adages, and similes are all based on the assumption of a divided or multiple self and have been part of the Western tradition for a long time.

The divided self is lexically cognized in many other non-Western languages also. In Chewong, a language of Malaysia, a familiar body-and-soul distinction is made between one's *bi loy* "true person" and *ruway* "life force" on the one hand and one's *bajo ruway* "the cloak of the life force" or body on the other (Howell 1981:138). (Compare our own metaphor of the trivial container and the genuine contents, expressed in images as diverse as "the naked truth," the proverbs "you can't tell a book by its cover" or "beauty is only skin deep," or the Biblical image of the body as the "temple of the soul.")

Meyer Fortes (1959, cited in Rosaldo 1984) notes that a number of "African peoples" distinguish between "the person," who plays a social role, and the "individual," who enjoys a uniquely personal destiny.

Japanese exploits the metaphor of a mask in distinguishing between *tatemae* "the outward presentation of a socialized self" or *omote* "one's face, front, or public self" and *honne* "one's hidden inclinations or proclivities" or *ura* "one's private inner self" and recognizes *enryo* "reserve" as an institutionalized and ceremonialized form of denial of the latter two (Johnson 1985:123, citing Doi 1973; cf. Doi 1986).

Javanese also has a notion *sungkan* "respect," more properly "an attitude of constraint, a repression of one's own impulses and desires" (H. Geertz 1959:233), which closely corresponds to Japanese *enryo*.

But the very possibility of this kind of alienation from oneself, however ancient and widespread it may be and however self-evident to ourselves, is perhaps not a priori a universal of human conceptualization nor of social behavior. For example, Rosaldo (1984:142), in arguing for the relativity of self and feelings, claims flatly that the contrast we take so much for granted between the inner and public self does not exist: "Ilongots [a Philippine people] do not conceptualize an autonomous inner life in opposition to life-in-the-world," and that "most of the time, there is no gap between the inner heart and what one does or says" (ibid.:146). Duranti (1985:48) makes a similar claim about Samoans. For a very similar impression of a Papuan group, the Gahuku-Gama (now Alekano), see Read (1959).

On the basis of everything I have said here, I would have to say that either playacting of any sort (from theater and hypocrisy all the way down to simple concealment) is unknown among the Ilongot, the Samoans, and the Alekano, or the claims and judgments of their ethnographers are mistaken. If alienation and a divided self are culture-specific, as these students of "sincere" and "nonsophisticated" cultures suggest, then sarcasm may also be. The same suggestion that alienation may be culture-specific is ventured by Western cultural historians closer to home, beginning with Durkheim and Tönnies, who associate alienation with the modern Gesellschaft. In particular, Morris (1972) and Lyons (1978) venture the view that the tradition of a divided self, although an ancient one, may have been only intermittent in Western civilization, disappearing with the fall of the Roman Empire and reemerging in the Renaissance.

The sociologist David Riesman saw the—to us very familiar—separation between the inner heart and the outer action occurring only in some places, even in "Western culture." In presumably prestate (Gemeinschaft) communities, he speculated, "the traditional directed character hardly thinks of himself as an individual. . . . He is not separated psychologically from himself" (Riesman 1950:17).

This impression is echoed by Colin Morris in his study of the discovery of the individual in Western Europe, an event which occurred, he ventures, around 1200 A.D. (Morris 1972:121):

> Primitive societies are usually conformist societies not in the sense that a single code of behaviour is forced upon their dissenting members, but in the more fundamental sense that their members are not aware of alternative patterns of conduct. The individual is instructed in the wisdom of the fathers and expected to allow his mind to be shaped by the common mind of the tribe. There are few options open to him.

Matters are different with Riesman's inner-directed character (a later type who appeared with the "Protestant ethic" of Max Weber and who is isolated before his God) and the other-directed character (who trades on his public image) (Riesman 1950:17). Like the literary and cultural critics Colin Morris (1972), Lionel Trilling (1972), John O. Lyons (1978), Norbert Elias (1978), Philippe LeJeune (1980), and Yi-Fu Tuan (1982), Riesman saw in such culture-specific institutions as separate bedrooms, table manners, and clothing and such culture-specific activities as portrait painting and diary-keeping (and the much later public autobiographical account) "evidence of separation between the behaving and the scrutinizing self" (1950:44), between protagonist and narrator.

The psychiatrist Ronald Laing separated an inner "true self" and an outer "false self," which "arises in compliance with the wishes and expectations of the other" (1965:105). A man's social façade, like the ritual language he employs, "becomes stereotyped . . . caricature . . . characterized by a compulsive excessiveness . . . and hypercompliance which turns his behaviour into a bitter 'satire' on the persons he hates and fears" (ibid.:109).

But unlike Durkheim, Mead, Elias, Riesman, and other sociologically inclined theorists, Laing saw this suppression of the inner self not as a cultural consequence of some "civilizing process" but as the truly pathological behavior of the schizophrenic individual. Either way, however, the sociologist and the psychiatrist are in agreement on one thing: although "the capacity for sham is universally human" (Henry 1973:99) (and perhaps largely unique to human beings), the hypertrophied division of the self with which we are so familiar is much less so. In proposing the cultural specificity of self-consciousness and its attendant vices, and in their implicit glorification of the sincere medieval peasant or Ilongot tribesman, Riesman, Read, and Rosaldo are following in the footsteps of Jean-Jacques Rousseau, Karl Marx, Emile Durkheim, and Ferdinand Tönnies.

It was Tönnies who proposed the labels "Gemeinschaft" and "Gesellschaft" for local and large-scale societies. We have already considered one difference between the two in our discussion of the guarantors of sincerity and consequentiality: in a Gemeinschaft, personal bias is bleached out of an utterance by the use of proverbs, rituals, and oracular utterances (DuBois 1986, 1993), while in a Gesellschaft, the appearance of oracular impartiality is created by officialdom and bureaucracies. In a Gemeinschaft, consequentiality is guaranteed by the ultimate sanctions of ostracism and ridicule; in a Gesellschaft, by the police. The world of the Amish community, immortalized in the barn-raising scene from the movie *Witness*, is a Gemeinschaft. Anonymity (and therefore also the possibility of glamor), rootlessness (and therefore also the good of social mobility), and alienation (and therefore also the freedom to choose other ways to be) are all impossible in such a small world. And *so, perhaps, is any kind of playacting*.

The world of the lone atom jostling other atoms in a void, represented in Kafka's *Trial* or *The Castle*, in Charlie Chaplin's *Modern Times*, and in scores of bitter-loner movies (Westerns, cop and private eye movies, and dark future fantasies including the science fiction classic *Blade Runner*), is a Gesellschaft. This is a world which is haunted by an escapist nostalgia for the eternal verities of nature and the Gemeinschaft but one which offers to those who are willing to try faking it the possibilities of glamor, freedom, and "being someone." This is the world which on the one hand offers some scope to the "self-made man," the wise-guy "rebel," the competitive individual, the playactor. It is at the same time a world whose citizens (like the female office workers in Dolly Parton's *Nine to Five*) know that "there's a better life / And you think about it, don't you?" and for whom the pursuit of personal happiness is synonymous with dropping out of the rat race—"il faut cultiver son jardin"—because the public domain offers no prospect of true happiness (cf. Bellah et al. 1985 and the review in Ehrenreich 1991). The two major prospects for personal fulfillment in the Gesellschaft (faking it and dropping out) are equally predicated on the existence of a divided self.

If we survey the possible payoffs of sarcasm—the avoidance of the stigma of nonoriginality; the scope for putting down one's interlocutor; deniability, self-camouflage, or the avoidance of commitment; and the opportunity for asserting one's superiority over social conventions while nonetheless adhering to them (in the immortal words of the hero of Tennessee Williams's *Glass Menagerie*: "I'll rise—but I won't shine," that is, claiming for oneself the "diplomatic immunity" of internal emigration)—then it seems plausible that sarcasm is far more likely to feature in the discourse of the prisoners of the Gesellschaft.

Some commentators have viewed the hypertrophied development of the divided self as a product of one or another of the specific features of the Gesellschaft: movable type, the Protestant Reformation, capitalism, or such consequences of the Industrial Revolution as mass production and the mass media. Daniel Boorstin in *The Image*, Christopher Lasch in *The Culture of Narcissism*, Stewart Ewen in *All Consuming Images*, and Mark Crispin Miller in *Boxed In* view the individual's creation of an (essentially "glamorous") public image as a central obsession, in fact "the highest form of creativity" in our (late twentieth-century Western) advertisement-driven culture of narcissism. Charles Derber in *The Pursuit of Attention* and Philip Slater in *The Pursuit of Loneliness* see the spirit of capitalism underlying our unquestioned ideology of personal isolation and competitiveness. According to them, it is this spirit, itself a consequence perhaps of the Protestant ethic, which fosters this culture of narcissism, wherein individuals alienated from both nature and each other compete for the commodities of insulation or privacy for their inner selves on the one hand and attention for their personas on the other.

Capitalism (alone?) is blamed for creating an isolated "me," estranged from both his or her fellows and his or her true "I." Klapp (1969:11–3) provides a checklist of symptoms: self-dislike, touchiness, self-concern, a feeling of being a stranger in society and of unrealized potentiality, a wish to be someone else, an excessive consciousness of role playing, an excessive other-directedness and adaptability, and despair. (The countervailing, perhaps nostalgic yearning for community, often phrased as "getting out of oneself" or "losing one's ego in order to find a higher non-personal identity" [Klapp 1969:35], is for Klapp the essence of orgiastic raptures as apparently diverse as barn raisings, the Superbowl, Nuremberg rallies, rock concerts, psychedelic drugs, and ecstatic religion. In passionate, mindless uniformity as in every other kind of community lies one kind of liberation from the solitary confinement of one's sweating self.)

More conservative observers like Colin Morris think they can trace the beginnings of the ideal of individualism to a much earlier period, in the twelfth century, and correlate it with the generally popular ideal of self-knowledge (Morris 1972:66), the rediscovery of the personal portrait as an image of an individual rather than as an image representative of office or rank (88), the rebirth of satire (122), and the institution of the individual pilgrimage (122).

We come finally to students of the postmodern sensibility like Walter Truett Anderson who claim that "stepping out" of our frames with self-referential metamessages ("this is play"; "this is a copy"; "this is fake"; "I quote"; "I repeat") is precisely what defines citizens of the late twentieth century (Anderson 1990:255). We may not know for sure whether the Middle Ages were an age of faith, but observers 1,000 years from now will surely know that ours was an age of image and irony precisely because of a wealth of documents like *Reality Isn't What It Used to Be* and "The Irony Epidemic."

Reading these cultural gurus and historians, our first reaction to their claim that irony may be culture-specific has to be somewhat skeptical. There is something a little suspicious about projecting our yearning for the abolition of presumably human traits like self-consciousness onto ethnographic black holes like "The Dark Ages" or stereotypes like "the noble savage." They serve as convenient repositories for our own fantasies because we know comparatively little about them. Even if the difference between the Ilongot and Manhattanites is merely one of focus and emphasis, there is something a bit too pat about the all too familiar dichotomies (simple tribesman, jaded decadent cosmopolitan) being used once again in ways they have been used ever since Horace and Tacitus. But perhaps it may be possible to buttress some of these speculations with some relatively hard linguistic data.

The distinction between a (fake) behaving and a (genuine) scrutinizing self is linguistically expressed not only in sarcasm but also in phenomena as disparate as the strategies for identifying *coreference* between the behaving and the scrutinizing self. This will be the subject of chapter 5. Having surveyed sarcasm as one example of the genre, we will turn our attention in chapter 6 to other varieties of un-plain speaking. After completing a survey of these, in chapter 7 I describe the language with which they implicitly contrast: the possibly mythical plain speech of the almost certainly mythical noble savage or equally mythical strong, silent, non-quiche-eating "real (Marlboro) man."

FIVE

Reflexives as Grammatical Signs of the Divided Self

At least since the appearance of Paul Postal's article (1971) on reflexivization and the method of "universal grammar," modern grammarians have treated the reflexive as a universal structure or, if not a universal structure, at least a universal concept. That is, there exists in every language something like a set of pronouns whose function is to indicate that the entity they refer to (typically some object) is *the same as* the entity (typically a subject) referred to by another expression. The structure is motivated by the fact that people do various things not only to others but also to themselves.

From our perspective, nothing could be a more innocently plausible universal. For openers, there is surely nothing more universal than *self-awareness*: hearing your own voice when you speak, being aware of the posture and position of your body, seeing a great deal of this body, touching it, smelling it, and so on. So universal is this concept that some scholars—I believe mistakenly—have even toyed with the idea that self-awareness and consciousness itself are the same thing: "Perhaps consciousness arises when the brain's simulation of the world becomes so complete it must include a model of itself. . . . Another word for this might be self-awareness" (Dawkins 1978:63). For a more conventional separation of consciousness and self-consciousness, see Donald (1991).

From *sensing* your self, it is surely only a short step to manipulating it— grooming it, moving it, pinching it, and so on—and, finally, to having attitudes toward it. And for all of these the reflexive is the natural syntactic structure in English. It remains for universal grammar only to inquire how this structure is translated into every other human language. Or so it seems.

My position here will be different. I will argue first that the so-called middle voice—which makes the verb a predicate with only a single argument—is truly a universal, but that *the self*, both as a common noun and as a separate reflexive pronoun, is very far from being a humdrum morpheme in the universal inventory of human language concepts. Further, I would like to venture the speculation that its presence may be one grammatical symptom of a quite culture-specific mind/body dualism or even a divided or alienated self. Specifically, I would like to show how syntactic developments in the history of English offer some (fragile) support for the speculations of cultural historians like Lyons, Morris, and Riesman.

5.1. No Representation of the Self

What would it be like to be linguistically absolutely unself-conscious, a state of "grace" which we so typically project onto animals (cf. Savage-Rumbaugh 1986:25, cited in Masson & McCarthy 1995:xxi) and one that is the object of so many religious practices? Grammatically, the state is one where there is no pronoun "I." I will begin with a brief description of this state of *nonrepresentation of the observer*.

The observer who is lost in the rapt contemplation of the scene is like Thomas Edison, who on one legendary occasion was allegedly unable to remember his own name. Such an observer may signal total absorption in the external world by failing to include himself or herself in the linguistic model of this world which he or she provides for the hearer—what Langacker calls "the objective scene" (1985:122).

This nonrepresentation of the self is not the same thing as "scientific objectivity," a narrative ideal typified by the injunction to avoid the first person in scientific or bureaucratic language. In fact, false "objectivity" is often humbug and properly attacked by relativists for its implied claim to divine omniscience. But another reason for avoiding "I," which is generally overlooked, is that the observer, like the mystic, the medium, or Thomas Edison, may be so absorbed in what he or she is doing or observing as to have lost track of his or her identity entirely. Total participation is the very antithesis of total objectivity. Like the latter, however, it may also result in the nonrepresentation of the speaker/subject. Formally parallel to objective protocols like "the rain in Spain falls mainly on the plain" in this respect are sentences like

1. a) There's snow all around—.
    b) Ed is sitting just across the table—.
    c) It's behind the mug—.
    d) It's to the left—.

A large number of relational words like "left," "across," and "behind" involve reference to a fixed point, which may be culturally determined or defined relative to some person whose viewpoint is particular to himself or herself. For example, in a phrase like "behind the bookshelf," it is clear for most speakers

of English that the location is between the bookshelf and the wall, irrespective
of the speaker's viewpoint. This is a cultural fact shared by all people who agree
that bookshelves are usually placed against walls, with their fronts accessible.
But the sentences of (1) are different. Here the point of reference (also known
as the "ground" or Langacker's "landmark") is the speaker. The blanks correspond to various phrases referring to the speaker, as indicated in the near-
translations of (1):

2. a) There's snow all around me.
    b) Ed is sitting just across the table from me.
    c) It's behind the mug from me.
    d) It's to my left.

The subjectivity of these sentences is beyond question. Yet the speaker of the
nearly synonymous sentences of (1) suppresses reference to the "landmark,"
and certainly not to foster the appearance of omniscience.

Langacker suggests that these sentences signal total *participation*, not alienation, on the speaker's part. The perfect participant, like Meister Eckhart's mystic, *looks outward and is visually unaware of himself or herself*. Nonrepresentation
of the speaker in (1) is thus an icon of the total participant's lack of self-awareness.
The speaker of (1), far from being divided from himself or herself, is not even
divided from the world he or she watches. Duranti (1985:48) suggests that such
nonrepresentation of the speaker/subject is common in Samoan.

From here on, alienation increases. I would maintain that the increasing reality of the divided self is demonstrated by any or all of the following behaviors:

a) self-address
b) self-reference
c) shame, stage fright, and other self-conscious emotions
d) affectation and image cultivation in general
e) distinct representations of the self by reflexive pronouns

The last of these is my particular focus here, but all of them are closely related.
They may even tend to occur together, so that languages lacking one are likely
to be lacking the others.

A first approach to locating any of these phenomena in a language is to verify
the existence of a monolexemic equivalent for any of the terms above. Failing
to find a label (and we should not be surprised to fail), we should look for the
thing itself. With the exception of the last category, the search is necessarily
ethnographic rather than linguistic; compendious grammars will be of little use
in telling us whether people talk to themselves or use sarcasm and affectation
in talking to others.

5.2. Self-Address

In self-address, the speaker *talks to himself or herself*. (For extended examples
of the second person in self-address, see McInerney 1984.) For shorter examples, consider any case where an athlete berates himself or herself or gives

himself or herself a pep talk, in effect assuming the distinct roles of "coach" and "athlete" (or teacher and pupil, director and actor, parent and child).

3. a) Come on, Jeremy, play it properly. (said by a frustrated tennis player, having muffed a volley)
    b) Oh, Alice! (said by a drum majorette, having dropped a baton, in Roth 1969:59)
    c) Wile E., you genius! (said by Coyote in the familiar Saturday morning cartoon series)
    d) You will have to learn everything all over again. (narrator, closing sentence of McInerney 1984:182)
    e) Fame proclaims you in your writing forever, Eadwine, you who are to be seen here in the painting. (inscription on a portrait of the scribe in the *Canterbury Psalter* of 1150 A.D., cited in Morris 1972:85)

Clearly, any language with a pronoun "you" has the *structure* to allow its speakers to address themselves. But do all cultures allow their speakers to avail themselves of this structure? Are there any languages or cultures in which such self-talk or any kind of talking to oneself is unknown except as a sign of insanity? (Myron Bromley has reported [personal communication] the apparent absence of such auto-apostrophization among the Dani of Irian Jaya. But—with all respect to Bromley as a consummate ethnographer—how could he tell for sure? How could anyone?)

5.3. Self-Reference

I want to consider here two related phenomena: that of the divided speaker and, much more familiar to English speakers, that of the divided hearer.

The divided *speaker* talks about himself or herself in the third person. This is affected by public figures (most recently Robert Dole) who refer to themselves by name; by writers who refer to themselves as "the author"; by announcers who waggishly refer to themselves as "yours truly"; by obsequious letter writers of Addisonian English who refer to themselves as "your humble and obedient servant"; and, of course, by parents who adopt their child's perspective in referring to themselves as "Mom" and "Dad."

4. a) The Fonz does not dance. (*Happy Days*)
    b) From now on, Calvin the Bold will begin referring to himself in the third person. (*Calvin and Hobbes*)
    c) As long as there is one Filipino who is poor, Imelda's work will not be over. (Imelda Marcos, *New York Times*, November 5, 1991)
    d) Come to Mommy.
    e) Susan Sontag decides that if someone as smart as Susan Sontag is amused by pop culture dreck, it must be OK. (Bruce Handy, *Spy*, April 1988, reprinted in *Utne Reader*, July/August 1989:65)
    f) The man is tortured—Jerry Lee thinks Jerry Lee is too wicked to be saved. (*People*, July 10, 1989:52)

This identification of the speaker with an institutional role is taken furthest in languages like Persian, Vietnamese, and Cambodian, where the constant first-person pronoun is still identical with the common nouns denoting "servant" (Vietnamese *tôi*) or "slave" (Persian *banda* < *bandaka* "slave," Cambodian *kñom*); and in languages like Japanese, where there is arguably no first-person pronoun at all, only a set of kinship and status terms analogous to "Mommy," from which the speaker selects the one that is empathetic to the viewpoint of his or her present interlocutor (T. Suzuki 1986).

It is the divided speaker's "me" or social self which is on the "discourse stage": his or her real "I" or personal self (if he or she even has one) is never mentioned at all.

I would like to claim that a related phenomenon is that of the divided *hearer*: that is, the familiar formal register conceit of referring to the respected "V" addressee (cf. Brown & Gilman 1960) as if he or she were absent in languages like Hungarian, German, Spanish, or Italian. Here it is the addressee whose social self is identified with a third-person "onstage" role, while his or her private self is exempt from participation (as in "your excellency") or even from mention (as in "his excellency"). Note that if we define the discourse stage as the one that is created by the speech act, the effect of these devices, if taken together, is to remove both the speaker and the hearer from it. In languages like Vietnamese and Cambodian, *only* a third-person "V" form comparable to "Sir" or the interlocutor's name is possible for any addressee—the "true" private "T" addressee as an onstage individual, target of the speaker's words, strictly speaking does not exist at all.

The motivation for this kind of self-alienation is the same as the etiquette which underlies all euphemisms: the "true" speaker and hearer, both absent from the stage, never interact and thus ideally never bother or offend each other. Only their social projections, insubstantial holograms, meet (as excellency and slave) in the arena of discourse.

5.4. Stage Fright

I am borrowing here from Clifford Geertz, whose account of Balinese *lek* (ostensibly, "shame," provocatively retranslated as "stage fright") appears in his *Local Knowledge* (1983). Geertz provides suggestive evidence (though not as much as we might like) that in Bali the individual counts for very little and that his or her social role is what determines entirely who he or she is. What the Balinese call *lek*, Geertz argues, is the fear of not being able to perform one's role. Clearly, if Geertz (who follows Bateson and Margaret Mead) is correct in his impression of "the never-changing pageant of Balinese culture," where "only the dramatis personae, strictly speaking, exist" (not the actors who play these roles), then alienation (in the sense of a self divided between a private "I" and a public "me") is attested in the "theatrical culture of Bali," as possibly nowhere else on earth.

Stage fright is only one of the emotions that are self-conscious or otherwise implicitly reflexive. Others are the emotions related to self-esteem (cf. James 1890, who cites Hume's *Treatise of Human Nature*, I, 4:6)—shame, modesty, guilt, contrition (variations on the theme of feeling bad about oneself); pride, vanity, conceit, arrogance (similar variations on the theme of feeling good about oneself)—and the behaviors of camouflage or concealment—sham, pretense, playfulness, and hypocrisy (all variations on disguising oneself) and stoicism (controlling or denying oneself). Explicitly reflexive are a legion of emotions like self-doubt and self-hatred. In a slightly different category are feelings of selfishness itself (best defined as "wanting things only for oneself"). These seem related to the consciousness of oneself as an individual apart from the group.

Equivalents of these are notoriously hard to come by in many local languages (see Shweder & Levine 1984).

5.5. Mind-Body Splits: Reflexive Pronouns

Self-representation, even by a shifter like "me," represents a kind of introspective self-awareness: the speaker sees himself or herself as an actor (indeed, as others see him or her) on a stage shared with others. He or she is still an actor on the world stage but also a critic. Similar (in some ways) to the contrast between (1) and (2) is the familiar one between the sentences below:

5. a) I expect —   to win.
    b) I expect myself to win.

In classical versions of generative grammar, these two sentences were assigned the same deep structures, and the choice of Equi-Noun Phrase Deletion or Raising was open for certain verbs. I have suggested (Haiman 1985) that in a number of languages a similar contrast between reduced and full reflexives signals different degrees of self-alienation:

6. a) I got —   up.
    b) I got myself up.

As suggested by its syntactic structure, (6a) is an intransitive sentence with one participant. But (6b), with its two (coreferential) participants, suggests a subject mind–object body dualism. Since this is also precisely what is suggested in (5b), it seems advisable to account for the consistent difference in meaning by a single theory.

My central claim in this chapter is that *the representation of reflexivity by a separate (nonclitic) reflexive pronoun in sentences like (5b) and (6b) originally signaled the recognition of not one but two participants and thus implied some kind of detachment from the self.* No less than the ringing Socratic injunction to "know thyself," ordinary sentences like the following and the hundreds of English nominalizations like self-abuse, self-assertion, self-confidence, self-consciousness, self-esteem, self-awareness, self-centredness, self-loathing, self-pity, and self-regard still continue to reflect a degree of self-alienation which—unlike unmarked reflexivization—is probably far from universal.

7. a) I (don't) like myself.
   b) He restrained himself with difficulty.
   c) Don't be so hard on yourself.
   d) Stop patting yourself on the back!
   e) Be yourself.

The evidence for this comes not only from the large number of languages which have no reflexive pronoun at all (for a recent survey, see Levinson 1991) but also from the behavior of familiar languages like English, which do have such a pronoun but also allow reflexivization to be expressed by an intransitive middle voice, as in "I washed."[1]

All languages have means (simple intransitive verbs, the middle voice as a verbal inflection, clitic object pronouns) to indicate that some action is performed on oneself; relatively few of them have separate reflexive pronouns, and even the Indo-European languages seem to have come by them only recently. The middle voice and the reflexive are semantically distinct in that *the separate reflexive pronoun indicates a separate entity.*

The simplest typological evidence in favor of this hypothesis is the fact that the oft-noted homophony between impersonal passives and impersonal reflexives (functionally motivated by valence reduction) *involves only one-participant reflexives*. In languages which have both *verb + bound morpheme* and *verb # separate word* reflexives, only the former can be used as impersonal passives (cf. Haiman 1985:144).

Second is the evidence from minimal contrast pairs in languages which have coexisting extruded reflexives (what I call reflexives) and incorporated reflexives (what I call middles). The incorporated reflexive is used with what I have called "introverted" verbs—verbs denoting an action typically performed on oneself. The extruded reflexive is used with "extroverted" verbs—those which denote an action typically performed on others. In Haiman (1985), I presented data from Hungarian, Turkish, and Russian, relatively familiar languages which make this distinction. But there are many others.

In Thai (Haas & Subhanka 1945), the reflexive pronouns *'eng* and *tua* are used for extroverted verbs. Introverted verbs like *ko·n nùad* "shave beard," *lúg* "get up," *khŷn* "rise," *tɛ·ngtua* "dress (body)," *'a·bná·m* "bathe," *lâ·ng nâ·* "wash (face)," *si· fan* "brush teeth," and *wi· phom* "comb hair" are syntactically intransitive and become extroverted (transitivize) by means of an auxiliary verb *haj* "give," which has acquired the status of a benefactive preposition.

In Alamblak, a Papuan language, there is an extruded reflexive word *tu-*:

8. "Na tukia hïti - më -   a.
   I   self see   rec.past 1sg.
   "I saw myself."

But this is not required for introverted verbs like "bathe" (Bruce 1984:233):

9. Nafuk- a.
   I bathe 1sg.
   "I bathed."

In Amele, another Papuan language, the extruded reflexive is the same as the emphatic, consisting of the NP followed by the word *dodoc* "self" (Roberts 1987:122). With introverted verbs, the reflexive is unnecessary:

10.   as-ec   "wipe one's ass"
      cus-ec "wash"
      qal-ec "turn around"
      taq-ec "dress"

For the facts in Hua, another Papuan language, see Haiman (1982, 1989).

In consequence, I think we must reject the plausible but morphologically unsubstantiated claim (voiced by Faltz 1977, among others) that *all* instances of bound middle or reflexive morphology originate as grammaticalizations of some historically prior reflexive pronoun. It is far more likely that it is the nominal reflexive which is the later development and that it derives from the grammaticalization of some ordinary common noun like the one meaning "the same one" (as in English "selfsame"), or "body" (as in Middle English [Mustanoja 1960:148], Vietnamese, Cambodian, Kwa, or Ibibio), or some body part (in Bantu languages, as in modern Hebrew, the reflexive pronoun is derived from the noun "bone"; in Hungarian, it is derived from the noun "seed" or "kernel"; in Palestinian Arabic, it is derived from the noun meaning "soul"). The latter etymologies betray some recognition of a divided self in the mind/body split. But the most extraordinary etymological confirmation of this divided self comes from Thai: the language has an emphatic reflexive pronoun *'eng* with no other meaning than "self," but there is another, *tua*, whose original meaning is "body, part (in a play)." This is the form that is used with expressions like *triam tua* "prepare onself."

The fact that the reflexive pronoun is so often identical with the emphatic appositional pronoun (as in English) still reflects the idea that sameness of reference—in at least some contexts—is marked, noteworthy, or *surprising* (cf. Faltz 1977).

In the spirit of the morphology of those languages whose reflexive is still formally identical with the emphatic pronoun, I contend that reflexivization originated as a marked structure rather than a universal one. Note that in actual written and spoken language (as opposed to the standard textbook examples, most of them significantly involving artifacts like mirrors), the use of the reflexive in English is still often indicative of a divided self:

11.   a)   Judge removes *himself* from birth control case.
      b)   You don't have to call *yourself* a feminist to see and understand the realities of the status of women in this country.
      c)   If only my parents could allow *themselves* to see what I saw.
      d)   Pull *yourself* together.
      e)   However, the main reason you should attend graduation is for *yourself*.
      f)   No significant major thinker designates *himself* or *herself* as a philosopher of religion.
      g)   I don't know how they live with *themselves*. (Lauren Bacall, cited in *People*, March 6, 1989)

5.5.1. Developments in English

Old English had no reflexive pronoun to indicate coreference. The oblique form of the personal pronoun was adequate (Sweet & Davis 1953:23; Mitchell 1987:112; Ogura 1989:7):

12. a) þa ætiewde se   coccel *hine*.
         then showed the tare   him[self]
         "Then the tares appeared." (Matthew 13:26)
     b) Gaþ to þæm ciependum and bycgaþ *eow*   ele.
         go to the sellers   and buy   you[rselves] oil
         "Go to them that sell and buy oil for yourselves" (Matthew 25:9)

The "reflexive" nominal was reserved for emphasis:

13. God foresceawaþ, min sunu, *him self* þa offrunge.
     God provides   my son   himself   the offering. (Abraham and Isaac,
     in Sweet & Davis 1953:66)

Or it was used for unexpected cases of identity:

14. ic swerige þurh *me selfne*
     I swear   by   my own self. (ibid.:67)

This usage continued into the fifteenth century (Mustanoja 1960:153), alongside the development of the reflexive to signal unremarkable coreference, and we find in Chaucer's *Canterbury Tales* some cases of apparent free variation between oblique and reflexive pronouns:

15. a) The nyght was short and faste by the day
         That nedes cost he moot *hymselven* hyde. ("Knight's Tale":1477)
     b) In that grove he wolde *hym* hyde al day. (ibid.:1481)
     c) He took *hymself* a greet profit thereby. ("Friar's Tale":1344)
     d) Yet nolde I, for the oxen in my plogh
         Take upon *me* more than ynogh. ("Miller's Tale":3160)

Chaucer nevertheless had a strong tendency to use the distinctive reflexive where self-alienation is indicated:

16. a) What should he studie and make *hymselven* wood. ("Prolog":184)
         "Why should he try to make himself crazy?"
     b) He thoghte wel that every man
         Wol helpe *hymself* in love if that he kan.
         And eek delivere *hymself* out of prisoun. ("Knight's Tale":1767–9)
     c) Dianyre, that caused hym to sette *hymself* afyre. ("Wife of Bath's
         Tale":726)

This contrasts with the use of the oblique nonreflexive pronoun to signal unremarkable coreference, typically with what I have elsewhere called "introverted" verbs:

17. a) And he hadde been somtyme in chyvachie . . .
         And born *hym wel*. ("Prolog":87)

b)   He hadde geten *hym* yet no benefice. (ibid.:291)
c)   And right anon he chaunged his array,
     And cladde *hym* as a povre laborer. ("Knight's Tale":1409)

Indeed, traces of this stage are still visible in the English of the Renaissance. In the prose and verse of Shakespeare and his contemporaries, the nonreflexive form of the pronoun was still in common use for cases of *expected* coreference, as in:

18.   a)   He turned *him* right and round about. ("The Demon Lover," in Grave
           n.d.:28–30)
      b)   But from his spreading arms she cast *her*;
      c)   With that he stripped *him* to the iv'ry skin;
      d)   She overcome with shame and sallow fear
           Like chaste Diana when Actaeon spied her
           Being suddenly betrayed, dived down to hide *her*. (Marlowe, "Hero and
           Leander," ca. 1598)
      e)   There he unarms *him*. (Shakespeare, *Troilus and Cressida*:1:2:260)
      f)   And there she takes upon *her* to spy a white hair on his chin.
           (ibid.:1:2:132)

The reflexive was reserved for cases of unexpected coreference, as in:

19.   Lord of *himself*, though not of lands. (Wotton, "The Character of a Happy
      Life" ca. 1651)

5.5.2. *A Case of Semantic Reversal*

Stephen Levinson's (1991) conjectured diachronic progress in the development of the reflexive includes the following stages:

a)   The oblique pronoun alone functions as the reflexive (Old English).
b)   Another pronoun (the emphatic) is pressed into service as a reflexive, and for
     a while the regular pronoun and the emphatic both function as reflexives[2]
     (Middle and Renaissance English).
c)   The regular pronoun gradually ceases to function as the reflexive. This last
     change is almost completed in Modern English, although we should
     recognize familiar examples like "He always kept a gun on him." Where
     coreference is expected, the unmarked pronoun is used.

To these, I would add a final problematic stage, which modern English now has reached:

d)   The regular pronoun can *once again* function as a reflexive but by now only
     to indicate the most extreme self-alienation. Once the reflexive has become
     established as the normal marker of coreference, as in Modern English, the
     ultimate pronominal strategy for indicating a divided self is to use some
     nonreflexive nominal expression where coreference would call for the
     reflexive. I will call this the strategy of distinct representations. A paradig-
     matic instance of this strategy might be "*I'm* out for *number one*," but
     distinct representations include the ordinary oblique pronoun.

The set of reflexive pronouns with which we are familiar in English and similar languages signals a kind of "syntactic coreference," albeit one which is often

unexpected. If using the word —*self* in a defined set of syntactic contexts signals "sameness of reference," failure to use it no less clearly marks "distinct reference."

Thus the contrast between (20a), with the expected reflexive pronoun, on the one hand, and (20b):

20. a)   I'm in charge of myself.
     b)   I'm in charge of ME.

In (20b) the subject/speaker "I" is treating the object "me" as an entirely separate entity (this is not too surprising in the present example, which occurs in copy for a body-building advertisement). Other examples include:

21. a)   Wade Boggs plays for Wade Boggs. (*People*, March 6, 1989)
     b)   I like me. My best friend is me. (title of a children's book)
     c)   Apparently you don't listen to you either. (*Dilbert* cartoon)
     d)   Margo, I think we should talk about us. (*New Yorker* cartoon)
     e)   It hit me when I realized that I wouldn't take myself out or go to bed with me.(Dustin Hoffman, cited in *People*, March 6, 1990)
     f)   I have a hard enough time separating my garbage from *me*. (*Shoe* cartoon)
     g)   I had a little meeting with myself tonight and I talked *me* into it. (*Family Ties*, January 23, 1990)
     h)   Harvey Gantt made government work—for Harvey Gantt. (Jesse Helms ad campaign 1990)

It is notable that sentences like this often occur when the lexically, but not syntactically, coreferential object is implicitly contrasted with other people. The functional basis for this is that one cannot contrast things that are too different from each other; contrast is only possible between entities which are both formally and conceptually on a par. In this case, "being on a par" means the *elimination of subject privilege* or being *equally alienated from the subject*. (Compare Mead's notion of the "social self": the self seen *as others see it*.)

The failure of reflexive pronouns (himself, myself, etc.) to occur in syntactic contexts where they should be expected is usually a sign that the individual is divided into a self and a counterpart—and not necessarily in some other imagined world (cf. Lakoff 1970, for the famous "I dreamed I was Brigitte Bardot, and I kissed me").

The motive for this expression of self-alienation may be quite transparent, as in the *Family Ties* example: the speaker represents himself as two distinct people. No less transparent is the Wade Boggs example: the subject is both a person and an institution. Or the motive may be indirect, as in the *Shoe* cartoon, and involve the avoidance of "subject privilege": the subject is no different from any other actor with respect to the object.

5.6. Conclusions

Having spent the major portion of this chapter arguing that linguistic structures reflect some kind of social or psychological reality, I seem to have ended

Talk Is Cheap

by systematically demolishing this view in 5.5.2. In Old English, I have argued, the use of oblique pronouns to signal coreference may have been a sign of Eden, an index of Life before Alienation. In Modern English, the use of *these same pronouns* seems to signal very clearly extreme alienation between subject and object. In the face of examples of such extreme semantic indeterminacy, surely it is misguided to suggest that linguistic structures provide any basis for inferences about the nonlinguistic world. Rather linguistic structures, like texts, are infinitely ambiguous shifters, and extra-linguistic context is the only thing that determines their interpretation. The story of the reflexive pronoun in English is then a pedantic redo of Borges's fable of Pierre Menard, author of the *Quixote*.

A partial answer to such deconstructive skepticism, in this case, is Saussure's dictum that the meaning of signs lies mainly in their otherness: that is to say, yes, context is very important in the interpretation of a sign, but the most important context in this case is the paradigm in which the sign occurs. The meaning of the reflexive pronouns, like the *valeur* of signs in general, is partially determined by their (paradigmatic) linguistic context. Oblique pronouns mean one thing when they stand alone in a paradigm (as they did in Old English or do in languages like Samoan or Hmong) and something else when they contrast with reflexive pronouns.

But it is not the whole answer; reflexive and oblique pronouns with coreferential meaning coexisted in Middle English no less than in modern English. But in the meantime, their meanings seem to have gotten reversed, as summarized in table 5.1. What has happened in the interim, of course, is the grammaticalization of the reflexive pronouns; frequent repetition has dulled their meaning and, from indicating remarkable coreference in earlier stages of the language, they now indicate routine coreference. Syntagmatic context also can affect the meaning of a sign; in particular, the more often it is repeated, the less it comes to mean.

If we continue to bear in mind the undisputed and tremendously important fact that repetition causes meaning to erode (we will return to this in chapters 8–11) we can still venture respectable hypotheses about the ways in which languages reflect aspects of the external world. In particular, we can relate observations and speculations of cultural historians concerning isolation, estrangement, and alienation to humble facts of syntax and morphology.

Table 5.1. Meanings of Oblique and Reflexive Pronouns

Pronouns	Old English	Middle/Renaissance English	Modern English
Oblique	Indifferent to coreference	Nonalienated coreference	Alienated coreference
Reflexive	—	Alienated coreference	Nonalienated coreference

NOTES

1. Stephen Toulmin reports (1977:298–9) that J. L. Austin used to indulge in the Whorfian speculation that Cartesian mind–body dualism resulted from the absence of a middle voice in modern European languages. I contend that in languages like modern French, German, Italian, and Spanish the contrast between a true reflexive and the middle voice has become neutralized insofar as the reflexive morpheme is a clitic and is used indiscriminately for both true reflexives and middles, impersonal passives, inchoatives, and the like. The contrast between "I washed" and "I washed myself," with which this chapter mainly deals, simply does not materialize here.

2. Cognate with English and German "self" *selbst* is Dutch *-zelf*, which is not found on all reflexives. With introverted verbs, it is possible to use either *zich* or *zichzelf*:

Jan wast *zich(zelf)*.
John washes himself.

With extroverted verbs, the emphatic *zelf* is obligatory:

Jan schiet op *zichzelf*.
John shoots himself.
(*Jan schiet op zich.)

The contrast between Dutch *zich* and *zichzelf* neatly parallels that between Modern English *him* and *himself*. Like medieval English, Dutch is a language where the contrast is not between "extruded" and "incorporated" reflexives but between what Kemmer (1993) has characterized as "heavy" and "light" reflexive forms or what we could simply call "marked" and "unmarked" forms.

SIX

Un-Plain Speaking

Switching gears now to a very different set of structures, we will find that different manners of speaking also allow one to express the difference between a behaving and a scrutinizing self. It's intuitively plausible that a oneness of personality is expressed in sincere language, whereas a two-ness is expressed not only in sarcasm but in every other manner of speaking which advertises the speaker to be in some way and to some extent a role player of some kind. In this chapter I will enumerate with a few examples some other genres of what I have decided to label un-plain speaking. Most of these are familiar, even if they have not been extensively described by linguists, and my survey will do little more than acknowledge their existence and suggest their kinship.

In an odd, rather paradoxical way, irony and sarcasm are advertisements of *the speaker's sincerity*. If the divided self is seen as consisting of a private personal core and a social front or image, then sarcasm is meant to provide a revelation of the core: "Yes, I am playing a role, but look! my inner nature rebels against it" is a possible paraphrase of the metamessage "I don't mean this." The other genres of un-plain speaking are all advertisements of the front; it is not I who speak but my mask, The Culture, or The Deity.

Like irony and sarcasm, these genres of un-plain speaking are apparently ambiguous. Some, like hypocrisy, seem to be examples of pretense, while others, like clichés, seem to be paragons of mention or quotation.

6.1. Code and Euphemisms

> We know now that "committee," "task force," and "commission" are really code words for stall, confuse, and delay. (Clinton Collins, Jr., *Minneapolis Star & Tribune*, July 9, 1993)

> First there was a long silence, after which party chairman Paul Kirk announced a meditative retreat in search of "new ideas," which optimists interpreted as a code for "white male voters." (Ehrenreich 1991:77)

> In 1984, "supply-side economics" was code for "redistributing the wealth upward to those who already have more than they know what to do with." (ibid.:79)

> "Maturity," in the fifties, "had been a code word, even in the professional literature, for marriage and settling down." (ibid.:129)

> In campaign rhetoric, "consensus-driven" is a code phrase for "spineless"; "get government off people's backs," for "eliminate welfare"; "saving our cities," for "breaks for the rich." (David McKee, "Glossary of Enscripted Campaign Messages," *Twin Cities Reader*, November 2–8, 1994:13)

> "What we want in this country is equal opportunity for everyone, not affirmative action for a few." The author of this statement is David Duke, and everybody knows he doesn't mean it. . . . What he's really saying is: "Those niggers and kikes and faggots have come far enough; it's time to stop them before they take our jobs, cheat our children out of a place in college, and try to move in next door." (Fish 1994:89)

> Cats are less loyal than dogs, but more independent. (This is code. It means: "Cats are smarter than dogs, but they hate people.") (Barry 1987:24)

All of the phrases above are introduced as examples of *code*. How does "code" (in this vernacular sense, not—for the moment—to be confused with "code" as in "Morse code") differ from euphemism? Let's look at some examples of the latter.

> By sometime in early 1987, every last member of the electorate had figured out that the president was not all there, out to lunch, or—as we have learned to put it delicately—*cognitively impaired*. (Ehrenreich 1991:83)

> "Non-performing assets" is banker talk (as Nicholas von Hoffman calls it in his book *Capitalist Fools*) for *bum loans*; "landscaping" is a euphemism for *raking and mowing*. (ibid.:210)

> In Cuban political discourse today "this special period" is the euphemism for the economic agony caused by the Helms-Burton law passed earlier this year to tighten the 36-year embargo of Cuba. (*Eugene Register-Guard*, July 27, 1996:12A)

> "Rope in the ring," "obelisk in the Colosseum," "leek in the garden," "key in the lock," "bolt in the door," "pestel in the mortar," "nightingale in the nest," "tree in the ditch," "syringe in the flapvalve," like "sword in the scabbard," were desperately arch euphemisms in Renaissance pornography for *penis in vagina*. (Aretino 1971 apud J. O. Lyons 1978:182)

Recently, politically correct speech has also become a rich source of easily lampoonable euphemism, parodied by phrases such as "vertically challenged" for "short," and so forth.

Both code and euphemism substitute something with vaguely flowery or high-flown—or simply vague—associations for something whose actual denotation is vulgar, unpleasant, pejorative, insulting, or embarrassing. A recent definition of euphemism (Allan & Burridge 1991:11) is equally applicable to both: euphemism, they write (and it is notable that their book includes no reference to code at all), is an "alternative to a dispreferred expression in order to avoid possible loss of face: either one's own face or, through giving offense, that of the audience, or some third party." Both are essentially strategies of core concealment or linguistic camouflage.

Nevertheless, I hope that the examples I have cited clearly demonstrate that there is a tangible, if not always systematic, difference between euphemism and code. Part of the difference between them is that, unlike euphemism, code is both intended and perceived as pretense, as fundamentally dishonest; it is euphemism uttered in the service of hypocrisy, inasmuch as it gives us the means for sanctimoniously expressing or endorsing socially unacceptable opinions which we might otherwise be ashamed to state openly or even admit to ourselves. Speaking in code, as Fish expresses in the subtitle of the chapter from which his example is taken, is a socially accepted way of pretending to be better than you are or turning bigotry and ignorance into moral principles (Fish 1994:89). Euphemisms in general merely provide us the socially sanctioned means for talking antiseptically about socially tabooed or unpleasant subjects. The honorific camouflage is worn by the referent in cases of euphemism rather than by the speaker, as it is in cases of code.

Using this provisional definition, we can easily identify as "code" the otherwise unidentified use of "alternative" lampooned by Doug Henwood in the following passage from the October 21, 1994, issue of the *Left Business Observer*:

> These toilers, ranging from a homeless can collector in . . . Minneapolis to scrap dealers in Accra, aren't really desperate marginalized people doing the best they can, but the self-reliant plucky heroes of an emerging "alternative" economy.
> (Oh, that magic word "alternative," a tipoff that convention is disguising itself in false hipness.)

Both code and euphemisms allow people to remain alienated from unpleasant reality by substituting words with pleasant or perhaps no associations for words which directly denote nastiness of some kind. Unlike hints, however, they impose no interpretive burden on the hearer. As Fish (1994) suggests, they are so transparent they can almost be taken *literally*.

The provisional and tentative nature of this distinction (a distinction which recalls the one proposed between mention and pretense in our discussion of sarcasm), however, becomes clear when we examine relatively new expressions whose usage is still not entirely fixed. For example, it seems to me that the populist phrase "real people" (as in the familiar advertising slogan "Beef:

real food for real people") is coming to designate not only nonphony, unglamorous, *sincere* people from Gemeinschaftlike places like Des Moines and "The South" but also *working class stiffs in general*. Is it then euphemism or code?

> Campaigning in Omaha, Nebraska, the other day, President Bush ecstatically told a room full of people, "How nice it is to be out where the real people are— outside of Washington, DC!" (Russell Baker, *New York Times*, October 27, 1990)

When George Bush uttered this phrase (for the literal absurdity of which Baker gleefully lambasted him), was he being hypocritical in using it? Clearly, he, like Michael Dukakis driving around in a tank four years earlier, was trying to establish a common bond with his audience by implying that he too was a "real person." But, presumably, what he was primarily trying to claim was that he was not a phony, not that he was a member of the proletariat. (Not that the latter was beyond him: *this* claim he made by publicizing his love of country and western music and his hatred of broccoli.)

I am conscious of a similar hesitation in categorizing the word "lifestyles":

> The term, introduced as a useful shorthand for a variety of domestic living arrangements, achieved longevity because, as it incorporated consumer behavior into its range of reference, it obviated direct allusion to class. (Among American sociologists phrases such as "lifestyle enclaves" are now preferred alternatives to class-based terminology). (DeMott 1990:35–6)

I first heard a Cambridge neighborhood organizer caustically dismiss "lifestyles" as a euphemism for "class" in the spring of 1969. But DeMott's passage is still a striking and welcome insight in 1990, because I'm not sure most of us are really aware that we are using the phrase in that way. And if we're not, then can we really say that we're being hypocritical or even using a euphemism?

6.2. Scire Licet: Hints, Understatement, and Veiled Speech

In perhaps the most famous and widely quoted example of indirect speech in recent English literature, King Henry "soliloquizes," "Will no one rid me of this troublesome priest?" and his guards (who are, as he well knows, in earshot) get the hint to assassinate Thomas á Becket. Hinting is also the very widespread language of gentility, spoken stereotypically in the American South.

When a Yankee neighbor of mine drove down to Texas to meet his southern wife's family for the first time, she warned him that the question "Do you want potatoes, Paul?" is southern for "Pass the potatoes." In other words, Paul, manners! To say "No thank you" would be unthinkably rude, sort of like responding with "Yes" to the question "Have you got the time?"

The novels *A Pale View of Hills* and *Artist of the Floating World* by Kazuo Ishiguro have copious examples of characters using even more elaborately veiled speech, confirming the impression that hints, repression, and indirection are a valued cultural norm in Japanese. In fact, *A Pale View of Hills* is a

kind of tour de force of authorial veiled speech inasmuch as the shocking identity of the narrator is almost entirely concealed except for a single slip at the
very end, which is easy for a casual reader to miss. Ishiguro's *Remains of the
Day* is an even more extreme example of veiled speech as dramatic irony in
that the deeper meaning of the narrator's words is hidden from the narrator
himself almost to the same extent as in *Oedipus Rex*. The reader, who appreciates the tragedy of the butler Stevens's lifelong repression, is in a position to
weep, as Stevens himself is not, at the irony of his final resolve to cultivate a
"bantering" style to entertain his new American master. If by "banter" we mean
(jocular) insincerity, the butler has been engaging in something very like it for
all of his professional life. The point of the novel is that it has cut him off from
every sustaining human relationship. But Stevens's is an innocent or unself-
conscious banter, much as George Bush's use of "real people" is innocent. It
is his failure to realize that he has been using veiled speech all of his life which
makes his resolution to begin to do so in the closing lines of the book so
poignant.

Hints differ from euphemism in much the same way that the guiltive differs
from the sarcastive modality. In the interpretation of both guiltive statements
and hints, the hearer has to do some translation work. The speaker's or author's
intended meaning in each is *deniable*; it is not communicated directly but left
for the hearer to infer, with the speaker then being free to disclaim all personal
responsibility for his or her intended interpretation (and the hearer free to claim
credit for having made the requisite inferences).

Aoki and Okamoto (1988:64–5) note the prevalence of a relatively blunt
institutionalized hinting in polite Japanese in overtly fragmentary constructions
of the form

Sentence + Conjunction ———

where the hearer is invited to fill in the missing parts of the sentence:

Nee   chotto nodo kawaiteru n   da   kedo ———
excuse me little   I'm   thirsty   nom. cop. so
(sc. Can you give me something to drink?)

Anoo sumimasen kodomo ga   nete imasu, kara ———
uuh, excuse me child   nom. asleep   so
(sc. Please be quiet.)

The overt message is silence; the metamessage is "you said it, not I."

6.3. Gobbledygook

In a way, gobbledygook is the exact opposite of veiled language or hints, insofar as the speaker's intention may be to bury his or her intended meaning so
deep in circumlocution and bafflegab that no hearer can make any sense of it
at all. There is probably very little language that was originally constructed
with this intention, and if we consider academese, bureaucratese, and legalese,

all rich traditional sources of gobbledygook, it may be clear, at least to the
charitably minded, that the original intention of such language was to avoid all
possible misunderstanding and misinterpretation through a tremendous preci-
sion of wording. Nevertheless, when we are confronted with examples such as
this passage from Hegel, it is hard not to share Karl Popper's feeling that this
is "bombastic and mystifying cant" (1966:28), whose pseudoprofundity was
designed to mask total emptiness at the core:

> Sound is the change in the specific condition of the material parts, and in the
> negation of this condition;—merely an *abstract* or an ideal *ideality*, as it were, of
> that specification. But this change, accordingly, is itself immediately the negation
> of the material specific subsistence; which is, therefore, *real ideality* of specific
> gravity and cohesion, i.e.—*heat*. The heating up of sounding bodies, just as of
> beaten or rubbed ones, is the appearance of heat, originating conceptually
> together with sound.

People in the academy or government will have their own favorite examples
of such pretentious gibberish, but everyone in these niches will also concede
that it is so widespread there that we need explanations that are perhaps less
sharply contemptuous than Popper's or than George Orwell's scathing and
memorable indictment of academese in his "Politics and the English Language."
    Here, for example, is a representative passage from a sober workmanlike
grammatical description of Cape York Creole, an Australian-English-based
trade language spoken in North Queensland:

> There is a second set of aspect markers that appear not at the beginning, but at the
> end of a sentence. These aspect words are:
>
> | | |
> |---|---|
> | pinis | (Completive) |
> | gen | (Repetitive) |
> | trai | (Attemptive) |
> | nau | (Inceptive) |
> | wanwan | (Sequentive) |
> | yet | (Continuative) (Rigsby & Crowley 1979:193) |

There is, of course, more than a touch of well-intentioned linguistic political
correctness in translating the homely and perspicuous English words "finish,"
"again," and "try" with seven-dollar words like "completive," "repetitive," and
"attemptive." The authors are attempting to counter bigotry and racism by any
means necessary, and using pseudoscientific terminology in the description of
Cape York Creole is one way of preemptively asserting something that can never
be stressed too much: that *there are no "primitive languages."* It is particularly important and laudable to make this assertion in defense of a language
which seems to be a barbaric form of English (and thus in defense of its speakers, who have been subjected to unspeakable savagery). But opaque and pseudoscientific terminology of exactly this sort is part of the stock in trade of all
grammarians and grammatical descriptions. "Completive" as gobbledygook is
no worse than "subjunctive" or "nominative" from the lay person's point of
view in giving an appearance of rigor and profundity to often vague and un-
examined ideas.

One may disagree with Popper about Hegel's cynicism (he believed that Hegel's pretentious language was a front to disguise an absence of ideas at the core) but still ask what there is about the academy or the bureaucracy which allows such a style to flourish unpunished there. In fact, as all purveyors of gobbledygook are well aware, a fair bit of prestige is involved in slinging around this kind of language, since by its very uselessness it broadcasts the meta-message "Look! I've gone to school." I will return to the question of prestige later on.

6.4. Politeness in Language

Speakers may be alienated from the social roles they play in uttering socially prescribed speech—that is, linguistic etiquette may function precisely to alienate them from what they think of as "their true, spontaneous selves." "Javanese is ... full of small talk and polite conversation draws on a large store of stereo-typical remarks. To use them is not thought stultifying, as some Westerners find, but rather gracious, comfortable, indicative of the desire to make every encounter smooth and effortless for all concerned" (Keeler 1984:xvii apud Wolfowitz 1991:58).

Polite speech in general is virtually a linguistic icon of the R. D. Laing meta-phor of the divided self. In this model, the self is represented as two concentric circles consisting of a private core and an inflated image (Laing 1965:81). It is a structural universal that "greater politeness implies greater length" of the message (Haiman 1985:151–5; Aoki & Okamoto 1988:9). The "core message" is "wrapped" in so much packaging that it is hidden. In extreme cases of politeness, as in extreme cases of gobbledygook, the ostensible message at the inner core may actually vanish, as Laing pointed out (Laing 1965:85), and the packaging is left as all the message there is; for example, in Japanese, the expression *maa* is a classic example of a mitigating hedge: *maa X* "sort of X," or "I wouldn't go so far as to say 'X'":

> Maa   majimena hoo   desu ne.
> sort of hard   working cop. focus
> "I couldn't say he is really hardworking, but I could say he is more or less on the hardworking side." (ibid.:228)

Consider now the unexceptionable (and surprisingly easily translatable) interchange:

> Speaker A: Doo desu ka?
>   how cop. Q
>   "How are things?"
> Speaker B: Maa maa desu.
>   sort of   cop.
>   "Oh, you know how it is." (Aoki & Okamoto 1988:229)

Speaker B's response is pure metamessage.

6.5. Ritual Language

In a culture which prizes individualism as much as ours does, speakers uttering clichés and formulaic expressions may wish to be considered alienated (or
simply estranged) from the words and forms of an unfelt tradition. (Typically
they may betray their estrangement by a variety of recognizably "inappropriate intonations," such as singsong; or they may signal their awareness of their
lack of originality by artfully mangling and thus parodying those clichés.)

But the same indices of alienation occur as well in languages where conformity and blandness are highly cherished values. For example, in Javanese, "respectful style" is characterized by a very similar singsong or crooning intonation:

> This intonation is characterized by the elongation of phrase-final syllables,
> typically with an overall downward intonation and a slight upward lift at the end.
> The example most often used by native speakers in educating a foreigner is the
> polite form "please" used as an invitation:
>
> 3   1 1 2
> mongg o - o - o
>
> Respectful speech seems to be made up of brief but sometimes drawn-out
> phrases, exhibiting a consistent intonation pattern
>
> 3 1   2
> —, mba–ah
> "—, grandfather." (Wolfowitz 1991:39)

As DuBois has shown in his valuable essay on ritual language, the speaker
of formulaic utterances conceals or submerges his or her true core self in order
to "speak the culture," and the style in which he or she does this is characterized by the same features in many (possibly all) languages: fluency, formality,
stylization (DuBois 1986). I would like to subsume under the heading of "speaking the culture" not only ritual liturgical language of the sort that DuBois, Chafe
(1981), and Wheelock (1982) have described but also more generally what goes
by the name of sententiousness.

In each of the following literary examples, a character is speaking sententiously. We can get a handle on what this means by looking at the examples
(from French, Russian, American English) carefully.

> —As-tu bien travaillé?
> —Pas mal. Mais pas si bien que j'aurais pu.
> —*Les bons travailleurs ont toujours le sentiment qu'ils pourraient travailler
> davantage, dit Edouard sentencieusement.* (Gide 1966:99)

> Vse my pozdravljali ego, govorili s vazhnymy litsami raznyje poshlosti, vrode
> togo-de, chto *brak jest' shag ser'eznyj.* (Chekhov 1963:175) ("We congratulated
> him, spoke various banalities to him with important faces, along the lines of
> *marriage is a serious step.*")

> Furst raised his eyebrows. "I thought he was the competition." Hellman had his
> own used-car lot next to his showroom. "Charlie," Buddy said sententiously, "*I
> never try to succeed by knocking someone else.*" (Berger 1975:119)

To practice sententiousness is not so much to utter clichés as if they were your own as to cloak oneself in the wisdom of the proverbs of the culture. Being sententious, at least in our culture, is risky: you risk getting laughed at as a copycat if you are caught unself-consciously "uttering banalities with conviction," and the fear of running this risk is one of the principal reasons why people resort to sarcasm. For example, like many other would-be hipsters, I am afflicted in sophisticated company by Bloom's "anxiety of influence": the fear of uttering derivative opinions, of being a sententious copycat. When a sophisticated colleague once sneered at my characterization of "Nazis who played the cello at night and exterminated Jews by day," I was mortified at having been caught uttering what was by then a commonplace platitude.

The obsessive quotation of caricatured figures from pop culture, all of which are comical to begin with, may be a result of our fear of sounding sententious. But why engage in sententiousness in the first place? What motivates the speakers in the quoted examples above to express themselves in copybook maxims and run the risks they do?

Copybook maxims are a variety of cliché, but speakers who use these cliches sententiously are using them in order to sound *impersonally* pious or wise. Whatever their reasons for wishing to sound this way, this also incurs well-known risks: the risk of being thought to be personally smug, conceited, or self-righteous. It may be that to avoid such charges, speakers avoid personal responsibility for their words by appealing to "conventional wisdom." They do not claim wisdom for themselves but are speaking the wisdom of the community.

In their grammatical sketch of Maninka, Charles Bird and Timothy Shopen (1979) describe an oral culture in which sententiousness is carried to extremes as a norm of verbal behavior. The widespread use of proverbs is motivated by the desire to avoid direct confrontation: "The person who utters [the proverb] is not considered responsible for its meaning, only for the context in which it is used" (ibid.:94). Their example:

Teenager: But dad, why can't I have the car tonight?
Father: Ah, my son, the words of the elders are like the droppings of the
                  hyena. Grey at first, they become clear with time.

Aoki and Okamoto (1988:249) urge the use of stock phrases in Japanese for exactly the same purpose; "the implication is that these are not the speaker's own words":

Speaker A: Uwasa made tatte iru no?
                    "You mean everyone's talking about it?"
Speaker B: Shiranu wa tu hu bakari naritte naa.
                    "They say 'only the husband doesn't know.'"

In her discussion of ritual insults among the Wolof of the West African Sahel, Irvine makes similar claims about the distancing function of proverbial expressions (1993:109). If what is said is recognizably part of a ritual, then it does not count as fully serious, and the speaker can deny personal responsibility for it. Exactly the same nonseriousness is attributed to African American practitioners of the stylized rhymed insults known as The Dozens by William Labov (1972a:335, 352) and other researchers.

In his imagined world of medieval Islam (a world, incidentally, in which the concept of "theater" turns out to be incomprehensible), Borges (1962a) has his characters speaking in sententious dicta from the Koran to "vindicate the traditional" and to avoid embarrassing commitments of the sort outlined by Bird and Shopen, Aoki and Okamoto, and Irvine:

> Farach observed that the learned Ibn Qutaiba describes an excellent variety of the perpetual rose, which is found in the gardens of Hindustan and whose petals, of a blood red, exhibit characters which read: "There is no god but the God, Mohamed is the Apostle of God." He added that surely Abulcasim would know of these roses. Abulcasim looked at him with alarm. If he answered yes, all would judge him, justifiably, as the readiest and most gratuitous of impostors; if he answered no, he would be judged an infidel. He elected to muse that *the Lord possesses the key to all hidden things and there is not a green or withered thing on earth which is not recorded in his book.* These words belong to one of the first chapters of the Koran: they were received with a reverent murmur. (Borges 1962a:150)

Sententiousness is again a kind of camouflage; the metamessage may almost be paraphrased as "there's nobody here but us chickens." In particular, there's no "me" among the chickens, no "proximate speaker" (DuBois 1986), no "locuteur" (Ducrot 1984), only the wisdom of the ancestors.

6.6. Affectation

By affectation, I mean not only phony mannerisms but also the reification through playacting (and, hence, the creation) of any stable image of a social self. The essence of reification is this: structures and objects that were originally instrumental means toward the satisfaction of some ad hoc goals are routinized and simultaneously emancipated from this instrumental function to become "ends in themselves." Doing so, they "take on a life of their own" (Merton 1968:133–4; Israel 1971:58).

A bureaucracy is reified when its purpose is not to do the tasks for which it was created but to expand. Commodities are reified when they no longer have use value (like shoes, and ships, and sealing wax) but some kind of symbolic value, which may be merely exchange value (like credit) or ostensive (like gold, a platinum credit card, or a Ferrari). News is reified when the empirical reporting of events when they happen to occur (punctuated by periods of silence when there is nothing doing) is replaced by a daily newspaper or the nightly 6 o'clock news for which pseudo-events must be staged on a regular basis (Boorstin 1962). Scientific theories are originally constructed to "save the phenomena." They become reified (and this happens very early) when the phenomena which the theory purports to explain are relabeled or rejected to "save the theory."

The movie *The Bridge over the River Kwai* is a parable of reification: a captured British officer maintains the morale of his men in a Japanese labor camp by inspiring them to build a bridge for the Japanese not as slaves but as crafts-men taking their orders not from the commandant but from him. They do a far better job than their jailers could have ever dreamed. By the end of the movie, the bridge project has been so effective in maintaining the morale of the POWs that the Japanese commandant is on the verge of suicide and the British pris-oners are triumphant. The British officer has by now invested so much blood, sweat, and tears into the project that he regards the bridge as the meaning of his life, and he has completely forgotten that the purpose for which the bridge was built was to help the Japanese war effort. At the climax of the movie, he murders the Allied sappers who have come to blow it up and rescue him and his men from their now-forgotten captivity.

How do analogs of reification look in the world of human personality? Reification occurs, I contend, when "you give a dog a bad name," or more generally when a single motivated act becomes the basis for a decontextualized habit and a reputation. For example, the pragmatic sycophancy whereby one gains a special favor may become reified as tact. A character becomes a *type*; an individual becomes a role-player in a defined social world (cf. Berger & Luckmann 1966:72–4; Geertz 1983).

The self-conscious knowledge that one is playing a role and the accompa-nying feelings of disdain for the role or stage fright at possibly muffing it are so much a given for us (particularly, it seems, in the years of adolescence) that it is difficult to imagine that there may be a typology of cultures in this regard. When Douglas Q. Adams asserted that "they don't have sarcasm on Betelgeuse" in *The Hitchhiker's Guide to the Galaxy* (1979:15), he was writing inspired science fiction. Michelle Rosaldo (1984:142), however, came close to saying the same thing when she said in effect that "the Ilongot don't practise hypoc-risy," but she was engaged in hard-core anthropology. At the other end of the affectation spectrum, in the opinion of Clifford Geertz, are the people of Bali. Geertz (1983:62) claims that social life in Bali is "a pageant" in which the socially defined dramatis personae are the only reality, the individuals who play these prescribed roles leading a relatively shadowy existence.

In the same way, it may well be that there is a typology of subcultures. In North America, atavistic Gemeinschafts like the Amish (as portrayed in the film *Witness*) may not have sarcasm, but in the academy and on MTV the bulk of mainstream Americans surely do.

When a college student with an aggressively anarchic and hip persona said to me, an aggressively casual slob much given in my lectures to the use of four-letter words, in a casual conversation, "I know there was something else I wanted to ask you—DEAR DEAR, what was it?", he was indulging in a (very mild) affectation, insofar as he was speaking with a mock gentility. His "target," the role he was affecting, was that of a *Victorian churchlady*, or a schoolmarm.

When a male high school student walks up to a puddle, lifts his hands, and says with a mock shudder and a prissy falsetto "NASTY!," he is indulging in a more marked affectation, insofar as he is mimicking an (instantly recogniz-able) *caricatured homosexual*.

When my daughter comes into the kitchen for a snack, announcing that "I am one hungry little muchacha," she too is indulging in some kind of affectation common to junior high school language students, though at the moment it's not clear what she is mimicking (Spanish speakers? classroom behavior?).

Many forms of alienation (rote language, quotation, parody, sarcasm) indicate mockery of a present target. The metamessage is in every case a commentary on a current text. Affectation can be a conscious mocking, albeit possibly affectionate, imitation of an implied but absent target. (It is clear that I do not wish to consider respectful imitation or sarcastic quotation here.) The everyday conversation of many people is replete with nonce affectations, and we will assume it serves a useful purpose. Discovering this purpose, however, is a real challenge.

My student's guying of an imagined or stereotyped Victorian old maid would seem to have some satirical point if his interlocutor or the person they were discussing were a Victorian schoolmarm. My high school friend's affectation of effeminacy would have been motivated if we had been talking about, say, our German teacher. In any event, we were not. My daughter's use of "muchacha" would have been motivated if she had been making a point about (rather than a mere playful or phatic allusion to) junior high Spanish.

These cases, and others of a similar nature, seem to illustrate purely ritualized decontextualized and pointless jocularity or "just kidding." Unlike sarcasm, affectation lacks even a satirical point, unless what is being satirized is the (speaker's or interlocutor's?) habit of mimicry itself.

Affectations which harden into habits (and which are therefore totally humorless) are often called mannerisms. So, if my student develops the verbal habits of a schoolmarm, if my high school friend develops the habits of a queen, if my daughter peppers her conversation with unnecessary Spanish words to the point where she no longer expects or elicits a smirk, or if I lard my conversation with Latin tags and quotes from Shakespeare then we are engaging in mannerisms.

Now the thing about mannerisms is that they are hardly ever appreciated. We firmly believe that nobody likes a phony. If the speaker's goal is to be accepted, mannerisms should never get off the ground. Nevertheless, it's a rare teenager who isn't completely engulfed by affectations, a rare academic who doesn't show off his or her book learning, and a rare adult in America who has no mannerisms. Where do they come from? I would say that the actual materials from which everyday affectations are constructed come largely from our entertainment and (to a much more limited extent) our education. In writing this book, I may ostensibly "demonstrate" the antiquity of our revulsion toward affectation by self-consciously citing Horace (here goes: "Persicos odi, puer, apparatus"), thereby actually uttering the metamessage "Look! I studied Latin in high school." In the same way, I may do a Fred Flintstone imitation of "WilmAAAA!!!" to "call my wife," thereby actually demonstrating that I have WATCHED *The Flintstones* and (crucially) that I am NOT like Fred at all.

Characters in real life may not be caricatures of Joe Sixpack, effete pseudo-intellectual snobs, psychotherapists, schoolmarms, jocks, cheerleaders, housewives, southern rebs, Frenchmen, tough cops, Mae West, teacher's pets, and so forth. But characters in children's cartoons and (to an only slightly lesser degree) in sitcoms and commercials are such caricatures. They are parodies, sometimes parodies of parodies (e.g., the Jetsons are a parody of the Flintstones, the Flintstones are a parody of the characters in the *Honeymooners*, and the *Honeymooners* characters are a parody of a blue-collar couple). They are as stylized or as phony as characters in a Kabuki play.

Formal indices of affectation are hard to describe but instantly recognizable. Compare, for example, the stylized, *caricatured* voices of characters like Darth Vader or Bugs Bunny with those of the animated animals in equally fantasized films like *Watership Down* or *Babe*, whose parts were read by actors with normal speaking voices.

Many of us spend a lot of time playacting these roles. Why? Many of us don't. Who? The obvious answer to the first question, "to be funny," is suggested by the fact that laughter is often indeed the desired response to a vocal affectation. Yet most such affectation is far from witty or original. Some other possible reasons for engaging in it may include the desire to

1. avoid self-revelation; to be serious is to expose one's core self to ridicule for being a *naive geek* or overly sweaty or for having nothing interesting to say;
2. mock the stereotype portrayed; this is very plausible if the stereotype is viewed as fair game on account of being pretentious or absurd, like the stock blue-collar, beer-swilling boor, Viennese psychiatrist, or Jewish mother; it is also plausible if the sterotype is *unfair* game, like the redneck hick or other lowbrow type, whom it is not OK to disparage openly without incurring charges of elitism;
3. identify oneself as a member of the tribe by creating a phatic bond with others who not only get the allusion but also engage in similar behavior;
4. lampoon not the stereotype but the dominant culture which propagates it (this is analogous to affectionate insults: the hypercoristic use, within the stigmatized group, of terms of opprobrium like "nigger," "dyke," and "kike");
5. establish that the speaker is just pretending and not like that himself or herself.

To illustrate very briefly, I would like to survey three kinds of affectation which seem to me to be somewhat gender-related: acting great (showing off or grandstanding), banter, and gayspeak. All of these, I believe, are far more typical of males than of females.

6.6.1. Acting Great

The essence of grandstanding may seem to be summed up in the phrases like "showing off" or "acting great": the pretended image one projects is of someone more heroic and portentous than the playacting individual, so we clearly have a divided speaker. But grandstanding also implies a *divided hearer*; the pretense is that one is addressing a multitude. One is not so much "speaking" as making a speech, not so much writing as "publishing" one's words. Hence the hollow portentousness of the heroic dialogues in films like *Lawrence of Arabia* and novels like Hemingway's *For Whom the Bell Tolls*:

> "And you," Pablo said. "If you are wounded in such a thing as this bridge, you would be willing to be left behind?"
>
> "Listen," Robert Jordan said, and, leaning forward, he dipped himself another cup of the wine. "Listen to me clearly. If ever I should have any little favors to ask of any man, I will ask him at the time."
>
> "Good," said the gypsy approvingly. "In this way speak the good ones." (Hemingway 1940:25)

Hence too the billowy portentousness of supervillains in popular culture from Fu Manchu to Dr. No to Darth ("It-is-your-Destiny") Vader. (This perhaps explains some of the delicious relief so many of us feel in listening to the dialogue of Quentin Tarrantino's mobsters and hitmen in films like *Pulp Fiction*. Finally someone has actually converted Hannah Arendt's phrase about the *banality* of evil into art.)

A recent *Doonesbury* strip features Roland Hedley, star TV reporter, in interviewee mode (see figure 6.1). Note the tell-tale false modesty of Hedley's "little something called the First Amendment," which neatly echoes the false modesty of Robert Jordan's "little favors." The Trudeau piece is particularly insightful because it clearly marks Hedley's posturing as a self-consciously chosen framed activity. He's acting great, grandstanding, showing off ("code-telling") for the microphone and the public in the first frame and being real ("truth-telling") when speaking just to the interviewer in the last (cf. Nash 1980). Nash defines "code-telling" as "the intentional, selective presentation of information about a norm governed set of activities, with the design to impress upon the receiver the validity of a particular identity" (ibid.:94). Posturing of this sort is more likely to be used by men, possibly because it is much more difficult to validate "particular identities" such as that of "hero," "wise guru," "superfiend," or "ace journalist" than it does to be a mother (a role which requires no validation whatsoever).

Doonesbury BY GARRY TRUDEAU

Figure 6.1. Doonesbury, by Garry Trudeau. (© G. B. Trudeau; reprinted with permission of Universal Press Syndicate; all rights reserved.)

Neither, for that matter, should the role of a humble father:

> And I find no argument for the existence of God . . . in the fact that the most re-
> ve-red man in all of Newark came to sit for "a whole half hour" beside my
> mother's bed. . . . To him, uttering beautiful banalities to people scared out of
> their wits—that is to him what playing baseball is to me! He loves it! . . . This is
> a man who somewhere along the line got the idea that the basic unit of meaning
> in the English language is the syllable. So no word he pronounces has less than
> three of them, not even the word *God*. You should hear the song and dance he
> makes out of *Israel*. For him, it's as long as refrigerator! . . . Coming to the
> hospital to be brilliant about Life (syllable by syllable) to people who are shaking
> in their pajamas about death is his business, just as it is my father's business to
> sell life insurance! It is what they each do to earn a living, and if you want to be
> pious about somebody, feel pious about my father, God damn it, and bow down
> to him the way you bow down to that big fat comical son of a bitch, because my
> father *really* works his balls off and doesn't happen to think he is God's special
> assistant into the bargain. And doesn't speak in those fucking *syllables*. "I-a
> wan-tt to-a wel-come-a you-ew tooo thee sy-na-gawg-a." Oh God, oh Guh-ah-
> duh, if you're up there shining down your countenance, why not spare us from
> here on out the enunciation of the rabbis! (Roth 1969:80–2)

6.6.2. Banter

Jocularity is so much a given in popular discourse that we sometimes have to
signal its *absence* with the special metamessage "I am sincere" (cf. Goffman
1974:502; Haiman 1990:204). So pervasive is the jocular style that we become
aware of it only in its absence, an absence that is explicitly noted in the version
of the standard lightbulb joke that targets feminists:

> —How many feminists does it take to change a lightbulb?
> —That's not funny.

Probably one of the reasons for the backlash against feminism (of which this
joke is one expression) is that feminists, perhaps even more than most women,
refuse to play the jocularity game.

Probably many of us know people (more likely, men) whose conversational
style approximates that of the pathetic character in the xerox room on *Saturday
Night Live*, whose *entire* verbal stock in trade consists of meaningless jocular
greetings: "It's the Stevemeister, come to make some copies." A minor variation
on this character is the man (and it is invariably a man) whose conversational
repertoire consists of nothing but other people's jokes. A respected colleague,
whom I have known for over ten years, a man of deep erudition, wide interests,
and remarkable talents, has conversations which almost invariably take the form:

Speaker A:	Hi, have you heard the latest O.,J. Simpson joke?
Speaker B:	What?
Speaker A:	[Tells joke.]
Speaker B:	Har.
Speaker A:	Thank you.
Speaker B:	See ya!

A common interpretation of Speaker A's behavior is that it disguises the speaker's shyness or sense that he lacks anything to say. But it seems to me that there is another possible motivation. The metamessage which accompanies all banter is something like "I don't really stand by this; confronted by opposition, I will cut and run." In this sense, banter is a kind of self-protective and preemptive self-abasement, comparable to the submissive posture of dogs and wolves in the presence of the alpha male ("You thought I was *serious?* Ha ha!").

6.6.3. *Gayspeak*

The same motive of preemptive self-abasement to forestall outside attacks may even play a role in the creation of the variety of un-plain speaking which stands most visibly opposed to the plain speaking of laconic supermen like Clint Eastwood: the hyperstylized camp affectations of what is meant to be recognized as gayspeak (cf. Hayes 1976; Gaudio 1991). In the conventional wisdom (cf. Goffman 1974:194; R. Lakoff 1990:204), gayspeak is caricatured effeminacy in language and therefore *must* originate as a self-conscious imitation of a marked model, whether it originates in adulthood or considerably earlier. But the motives are unclear; in fact, one of the most striking findings in recent research into the phenomenon is that although gayspeak is instantly recognizable with a fair degree of accuracy by untutored observers (Gaudio 1991), the majority of its speakers (certainly not all gay men by any reckoning) profess to be unaware that there is any such thing, let alone that they engage in it (cf. Matthews 1995).

There is as yet no reliable sociolinguistic study of the phonetics of gayspeak. It is yet again a prime example of an area where, in Gaudio's words, "the proper work of linguists is barely being done at all" (1991:30). Failing such documentation, we will be forced to base our remarks exclusively on literary sources, in this case screenplays written by gay men: Mart Crowley's *The Boys in the Band* and Harvey Fierstein's *Torch Song Trilogy*.

In the Crowley play, only one of the gay characters, Emory, engages in gayspeak. The falsetto tone, the stylized intonation, and the breathy langor of his voice are in keeping with his diction, which is one of stylized effeminacy. "Who do you have to fuck to get a drink around here?," he asks, flouncing about "provocatively," and then waits for (and receives) the laughter which is his due as the official buffoon of the gathering (Crowley 1968:28). His walk and gestures are also egregiously effeminate. He camps relentlessly and is treated with affectionate contempt ("you're such a fag!" [ibid.:32]) by his friends, all of whom are straight-acting gays. It is hard not to think of his behavior as a version of *banter*, ritualized and nonserious self-diminution.

The lead character in the Fierstein play is a female impersonator, but his voice is a gravelly and rumbling bass. Phonetically, it would be difficult to imagine any vocal style more removed from the version of gayspeak exemplified by Emory. What advertises the cross-dresser as gay is another kind of nonseriousness. More than hip speech in general, gayspeak is marked by the continual use of artfully mangled quotations, proverbs, and clichés: "I've been beautiful. And God knows I've been young. *But never the twain have met*" (Fierstein 1979:7). Or "Face it. *A thing of beauty is a joy till sunrise*" (ibid.) This is also the rhetorical signature of Quentin Crisp, whose autobiography (Crisp 1978) teems with parodic utterances like "*the intimations of immorality* had come and gone some time back" (14), and "I became one of *the stately homos of England*" (169). It also occurs frequently in the writing of William Burroughs: "Well when that record starts around for the billionth light year *and never the tape shall change* us non-junkies take drastic action" (1968:17) and "Paregoric Babies of the World Unite. We have nothing to lose but our pushers" (ibid.:18).

Needless to say, it is not only gay speakers who utter clichés tongue-in-cheek. What is the payoff in such cases? Like all advertisements of nonseriousness, it seems to me that in signaling self-contempt they exempt the speaker from the opprobrium of others. Philip Roth's Portnoy flaunts and mocks his obsessive masturbation: "To be sure that these Trojans really hold up under pressure, I have been down in my cellar all week filling them with quart after quart of water—expensive as it is, I have been using them to jerk off into, to see if they will stand up under *Simulated Fucking Conditions*" (Roth 1969:187). Sneering at himself makes it easier to confess. If you, the listener, are disgusted with Portnoy's confession, so is Portnoy. You can't look down on him any more than he looks down on "himself."

Using proverbs also exempts the speaker from commitment, as we have seen. Like sententiousness, the cynical use of clichés is a kind of camouflage but one in which the speaker announces: "I am here, but I am only joking or play-acting. Nothing that I say is of any importance whatever." Much of the dialogue of Beckett's *Waiting for Godot* (1952), for example, is of this sort:

Pozzo:	Si vous me demandiez de me rasseoir. (Maybe you could ask me to sit down.)
Estragon:	Ça vous aiderait? (Would that help?)
Pozzo:	Il me semble. (I think so.)
Estragon:	Allons-y. *Rasseyez-vous, monsieur, je vous en prie.* (Here goes: Please do sit down, sir, I beg you.)
Pozzo:	*Non, non, ce n'est pas la peine.* [A voix basse.] Insistez un peu. (No, no, it's not worth it. [Muttered.] Insist a bit.)
Estragon:	*Mais voyons, ne restez pas debout comme ça, vous allez attraper froid.* (Come on, don't just stand there like that, you'll get cold.)
Pozzo:	*Vous croyez?* (You think so?)
Estragon:	Mais c'est absolument certain. (Why it's absolutely certain.) (Beckett 1952:50)

Matters are different with the naive speaker who is not haunted by the anxiety of influence and utters banalities not sententiously but honestly, as if they were his or her own ideas. Depending on our own sophistication and compassion, we can wholeheartedly agree with the well-intentioned pro-Zionist who passionately says the Israelis "*made the desert bloom*," or we can wince, or we can sneer. But there is all the difference in the world between a self-conscious and a sincere quotation of a fixed saying. And it is not a difference between pretense and quotation but between innocence (the absence of both) and sophistication (their presence).

It is interesting to observe that all but one of the features enumerated here as characteristics of gayspeak (falsetto, singsong, prolongation, and the mangling of clichés) are features which also identify sarcasm in general. The intimate relationship between the two styles is alluded to by Sontag in her famous essay on camp but still not explained.

Is gayspeak an affectation? Is it a register? Or is there, perhaps, no significant difference between the two? At some level, I would argue that there is not; both register and affectation are self-conscious presentations of oneself, presentations that are tailored for the recipient. Nevertheless, register seems much more automatized and conventionalized. Although gayspeak originates perhaps as an affectation or pretense with satirical intent, it has become emancipated from this motivation to a considerable degree and is adopted with as little self-consciousness by many speakers as a formal or casual register of one's native language.

6.7. Polite Self-abasement

An extreme form of politeness which is somewhat disprized in English is ritual self-abasement. It consists in being "nicer" than one's interlocutor, turning aside compliments and at the same time complimenting the interlocutor in a kind of verbal potlatch. We project this obsequiousness onto Frenchmen in the "After you Alphonse" routine and project it onto egregiously self-humbling Asians in parodies like the Kai Lung stories of Ernest Bramah. We recognize faint echoes of the type in characters like the sycophantic Mr. Collins in *Pride and Prejudice*.

Aoki and Okamoto (1988:100, 191–207) provide examples of this strategy of out-nicing in Japanese, and point out that it is an endlessly repeatable routine (ibid.:192). To respond to a compliment with a simple "thank you" or other acknowledgment, as we might, is "indicative of lack of manners, absence of proper upbringing, despicable family background, and other manifestations of low life" in Japanese (ibid.). There is no mistaking the authors' chuckles over this to-us-oh-so-alien behavior. But it seems to me that if banter and possibly gayspeak are also motivated by the same strategy of preemptive self-abasement, then these Alphonse routines are not so alien to modern Americans as they may at first appear.

6.8. Response Cries

We all crave good attention ("being seen") and dread bad attention ("being seen through" or "exposed" to ostracism or ridicule). The contrast between the two kinds of attention suggests the contrast between the core and the image and the unfortunately widespread feeling that the core is not only vulnerable but somehow discreditable. When our image suffers, we experience a momentary exposure of unflattering nakedness and make efforts to cover it up.

Erving Goffman's classic article on self-talk (1983) points out that "spontaneous expressions" of our "naked selves" like "Oops!" or "Shit!" are in fact acts of pretense and no less recipient-tailored performances than any other kind of affectation. But whereas grandstanding is acting as though the single interlocutor were an audience, "self-talk" is acting as though the actual audience of one's discomfiture were not present at all. Goffman points out snidely but absolutely correctly that such behavior is engaged in only after the speaker has surreptitiously checked to see whether there is an audience present and then it is recipient tailored to be uttered in the appropriate register. When one trips in a day care center, one says "Oopsadaisy!"; in a factory, one says "Shit!"

The purpose of self-talk, as of every other variety of un-plain speaking, is, of course, to save face. If you trip, your image has suffered. In saying "Oops!" or some version thereof, you are advertising that your core is still at the controls and unaffected.

6.9. Summary

We have been considering in this chapter a variety of speech genres which signal the existence of a divided or alienated self. R.D. Laing's metaphor of the concentric circles, in fact, can be used to describe not only the division between the core and outer speaker but also the parallel division between the core and outer text which the speaker utters: message and metamessage. And in the same way that a possible and possibly pathological development of the divided speaker is an atrophying of the inner core, so that nothing is left but a grinning mask, another a possible development of the text is an atrophying of the message, so that nothing is left but the purely formal etiquette of the metahusk.

We have seen it asserted that in extreme cases of gobbledygook (Hegel on sound), politeness (Japanese hedges with nothing to hedge), and banter (the Stevemeister in the Xerox room on *Saturday Night Live* with nothing to say), the metamessage is the only message there is. Nor are examples of pure self-referential ritual confined to the linguistic. Dave Barry points out that Science fair projects (metamessage: "Look! I've done a science project" [1994:2]) and holiday gifts (metamessage: "Look! I've bought you a gift!" [1987:281]) are comparable purely ritual constructions.

The existence of both duplicitous and hollow versions of un-plain speaking implies, of course, a benchmark of sincerity or plain speaking; the recognized duplicity of sarcasm, politeness, sententiousness, affectation, or hypocrisy implies the more fundamental existence of an undivided self who tells it like it is. (In fact, it may seem that the existence of such a genre is so self-evident as not to require any kind of separate external indication.) The ideology of such plain speaking is given sober expression in the famous conversational maxims of Grice (1975). According to Grice, conversation in general is governed by injunctions to tell the truth, to be relevant, to say no more than is required, and to avoid obscurity. As Wheelock (1982) rightly emphasizes, these maxims clearly do not apply to ritual language, and as Aoki and Okamoto (1988:3–9) point out, they do not apply to polite language. In fact, their point could be as easily made for any of the un-plain genres I have sketchily surveyed here. The Gricean maxims apply, presumably, to the version of conversation with which all of the varieties of phoniness considered here contrast.

For Grice, the central goals of conversation are "giving and receiving information" and "influencing and being influenced by others" (Grice 1975:47). It is instructive that the nonlinguistic analogs for conversation which he provides in order to illustrate his points are purely instrumental activities like fixing a car and baking a cake (ibid.).

For Goffman (who follows Malinowski's famous 1923 account of phatic communion), the central goals of conversation (1974:chap. 13) are not to give information at all but to get strokes and save face:

> What the individual spends most of his spoken moments doing is providing evidence for the fairness or unfairness of his current situation and other grounds for sympathy, approval, exoneration, understanding, or amusement. And what his listeners are primarily obliged to do is to show some kind of audience appreciation. (ibid.:503)

One may side with the philosopher or the sociologist in asserting the primacy of the referential or phatic functions of language here. But in any case, the enormous influence of Grice's article attests to the feeling that plain speaking is still widely perceived, at least in the community of linguists, as the default mode of communication: "There are of course, all sorts of *other* maxims (aesthetic, social, or moral in character) that are *also* normally observed" (Grice 1975:47, emphasis added). But the bedrock of conversation is plain referential speaking. In that sense, the stylized extravagances and affectations cataloged in this chapter are still viewed (to the extent that they are considered at all) as departures from some kind of norm. To an examination of this norm we now turn.

SEVEN

The Thing in Itself

A traditional metaphor which goes back in our tradition to Aristotle holds that style is a kind of afterthought or nonessential wrapping around a core of honest content. Many of us have a puritanical suspicion of the *insincerity* of "pure style" (cf. Sontag 1966b: 16), a skepticism which is reflected in the folk etymologizing that we engage in when contrasting pairs of words like the following:

form	formalism
style	stylization
affect	affectation
religion	religiosity
art	artifice, artiness
method	methodology
legal	legalistic

The words in the second column consist of a root (the word in the first column) plus some derivational suffix. In one case (methodology), the seven-dollar word is absolutely synonymous with the root, and the suffix adds absolutely nothing but pomp. In each of the others, the seven-dollar word has an additional pejorative meaning, one that is contributed by the suffix alone. Each of these words would require an essay considerably longer than a dictionary definition to elucidate, but the common pejorative meaning seems to me to be "fraudulent *fake*." For example, affectation is the display of fake emotions; to be legalistic is to engage in pointless and mean-spirited adherence to the outward conventions of the law; religiosity is the expression of the outward conventions of religion without any true religious feeling; the other examples are comparable.

The language in these cases is an icon of a widespread attitude toward style as ostentatious and useless dandyism—away with the wrapping and the fakery! (I share this attitude, incidentally, being violently allergic to the word "methodology.")

In this chapter, I want to explore three expressions of this bluff and puritanical attitude: the "cult of plain speaking" in America today; efforts to provide an unframed object language in various branches of linguistics; and the drive to get behind the formal façade and interpret works of art.

7.1. (The Cult of) Plain Speaking

> God must have loved poor people, or He wouldn't have made so many of them. (Abraham Lincoln)

> Let your yea be yea, and your nay be nay. (Jimmy Cliff)

A recurrent specter—that of wimpdom—is haunting the yuppie men of the United States today. (Since this is my group, I will use the first person in alluding to them from now on.) Not only do we fear that we are the spiritual clones of Caspar Milquetoast, Dagwood Bumstead, Walter Mitty, or Woody Allen and yearn to be real men, but we also believe in the moral superiority of the oppressed (cf. Russell 1950) and of poor people in general. We think of "real" (folksy, unsophisticated) *people* as more spontaneous and more natural (as Flaubert put it, "dans le vrai") and above all we think of "real" *men* as more virile than members of the etiolated and decadent "croissant crowd" that we belong to.

> Camp Sharparoon was a camp for youths from inner-city New York, who were popularly known at the time as "disadvantaged," which meant they knew a LOT more about sex than I did. I was in charge of a group of 12- and 13-year-old boys, and when they'd get to talking about sex, I, the counsellor, the Voice of Maturity, the Father Figure for these Troubled Children, would listen intently, occasionally contributing helpful words of guidance, such as: "Really?" And: "Gosh!" There were times when I would have given my left arm to be a disadvantaged youth. (Barry 1988:281–2)

Two strands can be distinguished in this cult of the commoner: a somewhat affected egalitarian reverence for the unaffected wisdom of "real people" in general and a much more heartfelt, frankly sexual envy of strong, silent "real men" in particular (cf. Feirstein 1982). Sometimes one of these strands or another clearly predominates, and the two notions can, of course, be mutually contradictory. (Nietzsche's "blond beast," although a real man, is a natural aristocrat.) However, they are also so deeply intertwined that trying to keep them separate is sometimes impossible.

The cult extends to a kind of adulation of the unaffected vigor of the one-syllable words in which "real people" express themselves, and this cult of plain speaking (CPS) will be my subject here. I hope, first, to demonstrate that the ideology, although not ubiquitous, is nevertheless not restricted to the white-collar elite of the United States today. And then I would like to present some of the reasons why I believe that it is a cultural construct and, like all such constructs, fundamentally artificial.

7.1.1. The Spread of the Cult

That the worship of "real men" is at least a reality is easily demonstrated by reference to the stereotyped figure of the action hero and its exploitation in recent American films from *The Godfather* to *The Last Action Hero*. Or we could point to the phenomenal (and deserved) success of Bruce Feirstein's witty ethnography of the white-collar male psyche, *Real Men Don't Eat Quiche*, or countless articles in magazines like *Esquire* with titles like "How to Be a Man" which obsess over this preoccupation or recruitment propaganda for the armed forces ("We're looking for a few good men") which exploit it. A particularly subtle manifestation of this cult is the widespread sense among white males that the term "man" is an altogether too grandiloquent and pretentious term for ourselves and the resulting general use of the more humble label "guy" (cf. Barry 1995:1).

The familiar populist worship of "ordinary people," on the other hand, is currently exemplified in the glamorization of doggedly unglamorous "real people" as represented not only by Jeff McNelly's cartoon idealizations of "Pluggers" but also by a spate of contemporary advertising campaigns for beef and beer, virtually incomprehensible in themselves, which can be understood as an extremely sophisticated reaction against the glitz of the star system, with its extreme glorification of impossibly affectless, sophisticated, hip, and glamorous models or the proverbial rich and famous icons of the reel world. *The Waltons*, *Little House on the Prairie*, Garrison Keillor's "Lake Wobegon," Jeff McNelly's *Pluggers*, and country and western music in general may be celebrating the same folksiness, sincerity, and authenticity whose artist laureate a generation ago was Norman Rockwell.

In the United States today, the populist component of the CPS attitude may derive in part from a very strong local tradition of anti-intellectualism in American life in general. This is ably described and analyzed in Richard Hofstadter's book of the same title (1963), as well as in Dwight MacDonald's critique of *Kulturbolshevismus* or "anti-intellectualism for intellectuals" ([1941] 1958). In recent years, the attitude has been exploited in the United States, with differing degrees of success, by midwestern and southern political figures from Harry Truman to George Wallace to Ross Perot, and even effete eastern millionaires like George Bush have attempted to cash in on it (with miserable results, as numerous lampoons by Garry Trudeau in *Doonesbury* made clear [see figure 7.1]).

The essence of the old idea that there is a necessary antithesis between honesty and civility is encapsulated in a memorable interchange in Goethe's *Faust* II (6770–1):

Doonesbury
BY GARRY TRUDEAU

Figure 7.1. Doonesbury, by Garry Trudeau. (© G. B. Trudeau; reprinted with permission of Universal Press Syndicate; all rights reserved.)

Mephistopheles:	Du weisst ja nicht, mein Freund, wie grob du bist. (You don't know, my friend, how rude you are.)
Bacchalaureus:	Im deutschen luegt man, wenn man hoefflich ist. (In German, politeness is lying.)

Although, as this interchange suggests, populism is generally associated with egalitarian and progressive sentiments, it is just as easily appropriated by the right and is quite compatible with the most thuggish *Blut und Boden* know-nothingism. Indeed, in a recent article in *The Nation* (February 17, 1992), Christopher Hitchens was right to draw attention to the "near-perfect symmetry" between Jesse Helms's attacks on the National Endowment for the Arts and Josef Goebbels's attacks on the "incomprehensible and elitist"—and hence, "degenerate"—expressionist art of the 1930s.

More generally, both strands of our current populism may derive from a Western European tradition that is associated with Romantics like William Wordsworth, William Blake, Johann Wolfgang von Goethe, Johann Gottfried von Herder, and Jean-Jacques Rousseau and the latter's familiar staple of "the noble savage." We encounter this figure (at once a "real person" and a "real man") again and again in canonical Western literature. Often he is explicitly contrasted with narrators like Gustave Flaubert, Franz Kafka, and Thomas Mann, the nerds who regularly present and describe him to us. Isaac Babel, the great twentieth-century Soviet writer, speaks as an inheritor of this tradition in his description of the virile brigand Benya Krik, "the king" of Odessa gangsters:

> Forget for a while that you have spectacles on your nose, and autumn in your heart. Leave off raising a ruckus at your writing desk, and being timid in public. Imagine for a moment that you raise a ruckus out in public, and you're timid on paper. You're a tiger, a lion, a cat. You can spend a night with a Russian woman, and leave her satisfied. (Babel 1965: 166)

But our idealization of the language of the salt of the earth and a concomitant revulsion for linguistic artifice and sophistication (as in the passage from *Faust*) is much older than Goethe, Rousseau, or even Shakespeare, whose Marc Antony ("a plain blunt man that love my friend") has given lessons in sophisti-

cated demagoguery to English speakers for nearly 400 years. In fact, it easily goes back within our Graeco-Roman-Judeo-Christian tradition at least
to the Sermon on the Mount (Matthew 5, 6), the idealization of the "good
shepherds" of Virgil (L. Marx 1964:19), the "Germans" of Tacitus (Russell
1950:58), and a comcomitant detestation of Persian effeteness in Horace and
continues to the present, where it is represented not only in high but also in
popular culture.

In high Anglo-American culture, notable apostles of the cult of plain speaking include Walt Whitman and George Orwell. The first inveighed against all
"style" in the introduction to his *Leaves of Grass*: "I will not have in my writing any elegance or effect or originality to hang in the way between me and
the rest, like curtains. I will have nothing in the way, not the richest curtains.
What I tell, I tell precisely for what it is" (cited in Sontag 1966b:16).

In the same tradition is George Orwell, who not only strove to achieve for
himself a kind of "prose like a windowpane" (1953d:316) but also excoriated
every variety of bombast, cant, and gobbledygook in his famous essay on "Politics and the English Language." The most memorable passage in this master-
piece of invective is Orwell's comparison of the eloquent power and simplicity of plain speech with its translation into officialese:

> Here is a well-known verse from *Ecclesiastes*: "I returned and I saw under the
> sun, that the race is not to the swift, nor battle to the strong, neither yet bread to
> the wise nor yet riches to men of understanding; but time and chance happeneth
> to them all."
>
> Here it is in modern English: "Objective considerations of contemporary
> phenomena compel the conclusion that success or failure in competitive activities
> exhibits no tendency to be commensurate with innate capacity but that a consid-
> erable element of the unpredictable must invariably be taken into account."
> (Orwell 1953c:163)

Orwell's dual attitude (adulation of plain speaking and the noble savages who
engage in it coupled with boundless contempt for gobbledygook and its purveyors) also informs Anglo-American anthropological practice since Malinowski
and thus provides the moral bedrock which underlies William Labov's eloquent
albeit scholarly and impeccably academic partisanship of "the [superior] logic
of non-standard English" (Labov 1972a). "Larry," Labov's "paradigmatic"
exemplar of a speaker of Black English Vernacular is emphatically a BAD boy,
"one of the loudest and roughest members of the Jets, one who gives the least
recognition to the conventional rules of politeness," one who "causes trouble
in and out of the classroom" (ibid.:214). On the other hand, he "can sum up a
complex argument in a few words, and the full force of his opinion comes
through without qualification or reservation. He is eminently quotable"
(ibid.:215). "He does not wander, or insert meaningless verbiage" (ibid.:216).
Here is Labov's fifteen-year-old juvenile delinquent "Larry" on heaven: "An'
when they be sayin' if you good, you goin't'heaven, tha's bullshit, 'cause you
ain't goin' to no heaven, 'cause it ain't no heaven for you to go to" (ibid.:215).
And on why God is a white man: "Cause the average whitey out here got
everything, you dig? And the nigger ain't got shit, y'know? Y'unnerstan'? So—

um—in order for *that* to happen, you know it ain't no black God that's doin' that bullshit" (ibid.:217).

Without laboring the point too much, I would like to suggest that Labov—who sees himself with admirable candor as a "lame" or social wallflower/outcast (ibid.:291)—stands to Larry in something of the same hero-worshipping posture as do the executives in the Norman Dog cartoon shown in figure 7.2. Many a starry-eyed schoolboy has similarly admired the working-class stud he dreams up, dreams of, but despairs of imitating. As the sickly and bespectacled Friedrich Nietzsche (also a linguist) stood to the blond (later also blue-eyed and Aryan) beast he invented in the *Genealogy of Morals*; as Dave Barry stood to the disadvantaged kids of Camp Sharparoon; as the shy bespectacled genius Isaac Babel stood to virile brigands like Benya Krik in his *Odessa Stories* and to beautiful Cossacks like Savitsky in his *Red Cavalry* tales; as Merle Miller stood to Harry Truman in his aptly titled best-selling biography *Plain Speaking*; as Woody Allen stood to his fantasy of Humphrey Bogart in *Play It Again, Sam*; as Leonard Bernstein stood to the Black Panthers in Tom Wolfe's devastating send-up of limousine liberals in *Radical Chic*; and as Bruce Feirstein stood to the ultravirile 225-pound truck driver "Flex Crush" in *Real Men Don't Eat Quiche*—so too, perhaps, does Labov stand to Larry. (And so, of course, do I.)

A more complex example, one in which anti-intellectualism is more clearly identified as a specifically manly or guy virtue and tightly associated with downright sexual hostility, is provided by a recent Ferris-Bueller-at-the-opera Pepsi commercial in which Michael J. Fox as a waggish lowbrow scamp deflates his prissy date by rushing out of the concert hall in mid-aria to grab a Pepsi and winds up as the star of the show. It is probably an only half-conscious and

Figure 7.2. Two Executives Get Down, *Norman Dog*. (Reprinted with permission.)

fully unintentional aspect of this brilliant commercial that it resonates with one of the central themes of American literature—Huck Finn's flight from *our* version of the "eternal feminine":

> The Widow Douglas she took me for her son, and allowed she would sivilize me; but it was rough living in the house all the time, considering how dismal decent and regular the widow was in all her ways; and so when I couldn't stand it no longer I lit out. I got into my old rags and my sugar-hogshead again, and was free and satisfied. (Twain 1960:2)

Unconscious it may be, but there is no mistaking the spiritual kinship of the blithe Michael J. Fox (hoisting his Pepsi to the astonished chorus) with Mark Twain's plain-speaking unlettered Huckleberry Finn or the American identification of the "eternal feminine" with the dessicated and censorious Widow Douglas (covering her face in humiliation). That this is a staple treatment of sexual relationships in a great deal of American literature has been cogently argued by Leslie Fiedler (1960).

Closely allied with this populist tradition, I believe, is our emphatically nonegalitarian obeisance to strong, silent stoics like those portrayed by the likes of Humphrey Bogart, Marlon Brando, Clint Eastwood, Sylvester Stallone, Arnold Schwarzenegger, and countless others, exponents of the tough and laconic "Me Tarzan," "Make my day," "Read my lips" school of understatement. In *The Godfather*, the inarticulate Don Corleone hardly says a word, and when he does, it is clear that the English language—in fact, language in general—is not his natural medium. ("Real men never settle with words what can be accomplished with a flamethrower" [Feirstein 1982:17].). In *The Last Action Hero*, a young boy trapped in Miss Gundy's Shakespeare class fantasizes Schwarzenegger as a cigar-chomping Hamlet who short-circuits most of the boring palaver of the actual play by blowing Claudius away with a Magnum and the memorable words "You killed my father: big mistake."

One-liners consisting of plain, blunt words of one syllable (and often no more than four letters) are prized in this tradition for their pungent eloquence as well as for their honesty. Labov contrasts them with what he derisively calls "OK words" (like "science," "culture," and "intoxicate"), which advertise their mealymouthed speakers to be people of the middle class (1972a:220).

It's only one step from the idealization of four-letter words to the worship of total silence and the concomitant disdain for fluency and language in general. Talk is cheap, actions speak louder than words, poetry is for old maid schoolmarms, and real men (action heroes, strong, silent hunks like Clint Eastwood and Sylvester Stallone) either "never settle with words what can be accomplished with a flamethrower" or like Harry Truman are reticent about their inner feelings. Like Francis Ford Coppola's Godfather, some of them may, if necessary, condescend to *buy* fast-talking (vaguely effeminate, too often typically Jewish) mouthpieces to do their talking for them and to deal with the likes of the IRS, but mere inconsequential chitchat—and this is underlined—is almost beneath their dignity. When talk fails, they say it with acts of memorable violence.

Real men will tolerate the jibberjabber of fluent wordsmiths—lawyers, pundits, spin doctors, poets, speech writers, admen, schoolmarms, journalists, politicians, therapists, highbrow academic nerds (in a word *wimps*)—only with contemptuous reluctance and always view them, if they view them at all, with the thinly veiled disdain which the salt of the earth reserve for "the croissant crowd": gigolos, maître d's, feminist performance artists, and Woody Allen. In the company of such men, it is a badge of virility to flout the rules of grammar of the only language you know; grammaticality (to say nothing of multilingualism) is for sissies. It is interesting to note in this connection the peculiar connotations of things European: "Over in Europe, the comic foreigners are gabbling and gesticulating" (Orwell 1953b:295). Thus Orwell captured the chauvinist mindset of British "Boys' weeklies" in 1939. How unlike the British stoicism of the explorer Stanley, who after finally tracking down the missionary-explorer Dr. Livingstone in the heart of darkest Africa, greeted him with only the immortal one-liner "Dr. Livingstone, I presume?"

"Throughout the depression, the movies [in America] implied that money was poison, that only regular folks knew how to have fun, that the rich and their lackeys seemed faintly European, or worse" (M. C. Miller 1988:205). But to see how this same mindset grips the *male* American imagination today, "imagine" Arnold Schwarzenegger speaking German (which, of course, he does). Imagine Johnny Weissmuller—politely?!—saying not "Me Tarzan, You Jane" but "My name is Tarzan." It spoils the effect. "As a general rule, Real men avoid foreign movies like, well, quiche.... 'And besides,' says Flex Crush, 'if the movie really had something important to say, they would have made it in English in the first place'" (Feirstein 1982:25). Let the tightlipped schoolmarms enunciate, let the eggheads simper over their Latin puns, and let the Woody Allens of this world spout their psychobabble; real men avoid the softness of lexical embellishment, to say nothing of foreign languages, like the poisonous taint of effeminacy itself.

However much Americans overtly value the articulate fluency of aristocrats like William F. Buckley, Jr., we also no less overtly (albeit unofficially) worship the eloquence of a laconic aristocracy of brutes. Trudgill (1972) provided a sober and scholarly demonstration of this disparity in his discussion of the phonetics of prestige dialects in Norwich. While women in general aspire to emulate the likes of Henry James and the proverbially asexual arbiters of grammaticality—like Mark Twain's Widow Douglas and James Thurber's schoolmarm Miss Groby (Thurber 1994a)—real men (at least the men of Norwich, England) aspire to imitate the rugged hood, who (as Dave Barry pictured him) dropped out of school and was romancing every girl on the block at about the same age they entered high school, and who now (as Bruce Feirstein pictures him) is a nuclear-waste truck driver. When Bismarck sneered at fluency in foreign languages as a "fine talent for headwaiters" and dismissed parliamentary majorities in favor of blood and iron, he anticipated not only the blond beast of Aryan mythologizing but also our own American versions of this figure; the Marlboro Man, Mike Hammer, and Rambo. (It is worth emphasizing the truism that each of these instantly recognizable stereotypes—cowboy, hardbitten private eye, and soldier of fortune—is utterly remote from the experience of contemporary Americans, if not totally fictional.)

7.1.2. The Cultural Specificity of the Cult

To show how constructed our ideologies are, it is enough to compare them with others. To begin with, there is already a difference between the stoicism of Clint Eastwood's personae on the one hand and the British ideal as exemplified by the explorer Stanley and Walter Mitty's fantasies on the other. Both are repressed and clipped, but if Eastwood is a noble savage, Stanley is more the civilized stoic who dresses for dinner in the jungle; his code derives from the playing fields of Eton and does not include four-letter words. So, too, are Walter Mitty's heroes: "Pandemonium broke loose in the courtroom. A woman's scream rose above the bedlam, and suddenly a lovely, dark-haired girl was in Walter Mitty's arms. The District Attorney struck at her savagely. Without rising from his chair, Mitty let the man have it on the point of the chin. '*You miserable cur!*'" (Thurber 1994b:50). It is almost impossible to imagine Clint Eastwood, Arnold Schwarzenegger or Feirstein's teamster hero Flex Crush uttering these words. They are, of course, too literary.

Again, the American obeisance to strong, silent Godfathers and urban samurai is overt but unofficial. There is a bit of Ferris Bueller and Huck Finn in Rambo and the Godfather, inasmuch as part of their appeal lies in the fact that—unlike Stanley and the gallant heroes of Walter Mitty—they are unambiguously portrayed as outlaws. Needless to say, hero-worship *could* be enforced both on the playground and in the classroom. Or it could be equally banished from both. Both variations indeed occur.

Among the Wolof of Senegal (as well as other societies in the Western Sahel), Judith Irvine has shown that a laconic and semi-articulate way of speaking (*waxu géér*) is *official*, being associated with *nobles*, while a verbose and fluent style (*waxu gewel*) is associated with *lower-caste* speakers. Like Don Corleone in *The Godfather*, the nobles mumble, stammer, and make mistakes: "Correctness would be an unnecessary frill, an emphasis on fluency of performance or performance for its own sake, which would not be *appropriate*—or perhaps even possible—for these highest nobles" (Irvine 1990:140, emphasis added). The nobility let glib lower-caste griots do their talking for them. The speech of these praise-singers and go-betweens is not only phonetically and syntactically correct to the point of prissiness but also "replete with emphatic devices, parallelisms, and ideophones" (ibid.) and gabbled at a rate of up to 300 syllables a minute (ibid.:137).

Since these mouthpieces are "expressive vehicles" (ibid.:135) and "message bearers" (ibid.:150), their lack of sincerity is axiomatic: "In the Wolof communicative system, the displayer of affect (or the person who expresses an idea) need not be the same person who possesses it. A griot may display emotion on behalf of a noble, to whom the emotion is attributed, but who sits by impassively" (ibid.). But if laconic mumbling is officially respected, neither is fluency unofficially despised. Apparently, Wolof griots are not treated with the same suspicion and contempt that real (American) men lavish on schoolmarms. The restraint of the nobles and the volubility of the griots are instead compared by Wolof speakers to "a good set of brakes" and " a strong engine," both of which are necessary for a working car (ibid.:153).

Because our cult of plain speaking is so familiar and because parallels and variations like the Anglo and the Wolof traditions are so easy to identify, it is still tempting to see our idealization as an unofficial expression (with admittedly local peculiarities) of a *universal* attitude which the Victorians and the Wolof happen to have ritualized in slightly different ways, but this is clearly not the case. The cult of plain speaking, although widespread, is without congeners in many other places.

To judge from the impressions of students of Javanese, for example (notably Mead, Bateson, C. Geertz, H. Geertz, Siegel, and Wolfowitz), etiquette, elaboration, insincerity, and alienation are seen not at all as the painful burdens of civilization but as the kind of good breeding that everyone aspires to in order to be fully human.

We plain-speaking buffs may despise sententiousness, but "one has arrived, in Javanese, when one has come to enjoy making the obvious comment at the proper time in an appropriate tone" (Keeler 1984:358 apud Wolfowitz 1991:58).

We PSB's regard alienation as a disability, but "this state of weakened emotional investment in one's immediate environment, of self-induced distance and disciplined aloofness from all events in the transient world of men . . . is among the most valued of Javanese feeling patterns, *iklas* (=‘detachment’)" (C. Geertz 1960:53 apud Wolfowitz 1991:59).

We may claim to despise playacting and hypocrisy, but "to the Javanese, ‘pretence’—etok-etok—is without any devaluing connotations and is positively valued as a good way to deal with troublesome situations" (H. Geertz 1961:134 apud Wolfowitz 1991:64).

Psychotherapy aims to liberate *us* from repression, but "It is . . . formal style that embodies the dominant cultural value, ‘refinement’ (*alus*), a consistent negation of the spontaneous, dramatic, and self-expressive elements in social interaction. Refinement, conventionally framed in opposition to the negative value *kasar* (‘coarse, rough, crude’) constitutes a cornerstone of Javanese personal philosophy and aesthetics" (Wolfowitz 1991:69). For similar observations on the acceptability of clichés and conversational routines among other groups, see Matisoff (1979) for Yiddish; Tannen and Oztek (1981) and Tannen (1982) for Greek and Turkish; and Coulmas (1981) for Japanese.

Plain speaking exists among the Javanese as well as among every other social group and is normal between siblings and spouses and between young children and other family members. It is characterized as laconic, elliptical, and abruptly intoned "almost as if the activities of speaking, moving, and interpreting constitute a burden to be avoided as far as possible" (Wolfowitz 1991:87). If plain speaking (PS) is a discipline of the playground in the United States and of the classroom in the Sahel, it is banished to the outhouse in Java.

7.1.3. The Incoherence of the Cult

Like every ideology, the cult of plain speaking is of interest not nearly so much for what it says about its alleged denotatum, "real men" or the "salt of the earth," as for what it reveals about ourselves, as the people who put it together and subscribe to it. In evaluating the validity of this cult, I will therefore pass over whether or not the blue-collar male happens to be anything like what Dave Barry or Isaac Babel imagine him to be and consider only whether the idealization of plain speaking is logically consistent on purely internal grounds.

I believe that it is logically invalid for two reasons, articulated by Mikhail Bakhtin and Ferdinand de Saussure. The first reason is that the very self-consciousness involved in choosing to employ PS and associating it with its appropriate context clearly marks it as an essentially arbitrary affectation no different from any other consciously chosen mode of behavior. Plain speaking is never plain; it is at best "plain." The second reason is that all language is already artificial, all speaking is unplain by design.

But before I develop these arguments, I should try to defend myself against the reasonable charge that I am flogging a dead horse. Surely in a thoroughly urban culture, worship of muscular brutes like Arnold Schwarzenegger is an anachronism. Indeed, Philip Slater suggests that their spiritual ancestor, the demigod Herakles, was already difficult for an urban people like the ancient Athenians to take altogether seriously for this very reason more than 2,000 years ago (Slater [1968] 1992:339). And surely in American popular culture, where self-reference, irony, and satire are virtually the mother tongue of everybody with a TV set, where every naive ideal exists virtually only as its caricatured representation in parody, there is no need to belabor such an unresisting imbecility as the superior virtue of the salt of the earth. Hasn't the destruction of the cult been consummated by experts already?

I would say that the answer is, surprisingly, no. To be sure, the cult of PS does figure in a very large number of satirical treatments by writers, filmmakers, and cartoonists—from James Thurber's "The Secret Life of Walter Mitty" to Woody Allen's *Play It Again, Sam*, from Norman Dog to Garry Trudeau—but when we look closely at these works, it is clear that what the satirist derides is always the nerd and never the validity of his dream of masculinity.

Bush is pathetic when he tries to talk country and western or use four-letter words. So are the two executives portrayed by Norman Dog, trying to talk Black English Vernacular. But country and western and BEV are still the language of real men. Walter Mitty is immortally pathetic in his daydreams of tightlipped manly valor, but what makes Thurber's story an enduring tragedy is the aching *reality* of the gap between Mitty's dream and the henpecked hubby that he is. And we can say the same of Woody Allen's persona contrasted with his vision of "Humphrey Bogart" in *Play It Again, Sam*.

With all our cynicism and hipness, the cult of PS is one of the very few things we (white-collar American males) seem to believe sincerely. Dagwood Bumstead, Woody Allen, Walter Mitty, George Bush, and all of the other wannabe heroes are clearly absurd. The actual action heroes are not; to the

Greeks, Herakles may have been portrayed as "a good-natured oaf" (Slater [1968] 1992), but his spiritual descendants, the hard-bitten types portrayed by countless actors from John Wayne to Bruce Willis, are not. They have not been demolished or at least not in any readily accessible or familiar work that I am aware of. And it is in the absence of such demolition that I offer the following remarks.

7.1.3.1. BAKHTIN'S REJOINDER

Some modes of speaking may be thought of as masks which disguise the speaker's true self; politeness and irony come to mind, as do affectations and playacting in general. We owe to Bakhtin a profound rhetorical question: What makes us so sure that there is any mode of speech which is truly a "face" and not just another "mask"? In particular, what makes us think that the brutal laconic style of the Godfathers of this world is not a freely chosen mask?

In fact, if we consider the strong, silent actors on our own cultural stage, it is apparent that the plain speech they utter (and which we so idealize) may be no less of an affectation than Javanese *alus* "refinement," Japanese *enryo* "reserve," or the most florid operatic performance. I have already suggested that the fictional Godfather embodies the virtues of the Wolof nobility. What about the genuine article? Here is Norman Lewis discoursing on the original Godfather, Don Calogero Vizzini, and the Sicilian cult of *omertà* which he so perfectly embodied:

> Don Calo never confused the shadow with the substance of power, and saw no reason why he should ever be compelled to speak an emasculated Italian rather than the vigorous local dialect. . . . He remained an illiterate all his life, a state of affairs from which he seemed to derive positive satisfaction. (Lewis [1964] 1984:46)

Always laconic—indeed almost incomprehensible to the barons and politicians (with whom he divided up postwar Italy), patricians who spoke standard Italian (ibid.:113)—Don Calo achieved a tremendous charisma at least in part by virtue of his silence:

> The Johnsonian pithiness of his rare but massive utterances, the majestic finality of his opinions, appealed to the human search for leadership. Even men of education and intellectuals admitted their susceptibility to a strange power of attraction not uncommonly possessed by a capo-mafia. (ibid.:21)

Up to this point, Lewis might well be lavishing on the Sicilian Mafioso the same almost familiar respect that Labov showered on his paradigmatic inner-city badass teen, Larry.

Yet Lewis matter-of-factly speaks of Don Calogero's brevity and peasant earthiness as on a par with his slovenly dress—"typical Mafia *affectations*" (ibid.:21) which are resolutely cultivated: "It was not done for a Mafia chieftain to show off in the matter of his clothing or any other way, and sometimes, in Don Calo's case, this lack of concern for appearances was carried to extremes" (ibid.:21). Most interesting, Lewis regards Don Calogero's "schlump chic" (the term is from Suzanne Fleischman) as akin to a stoical *suppression* of the self: "The mafioso . . . developed a kind of self-control closely resembling that quality known as *giri* [constraint] by the Japanese, and so much admired by them. A true man of honour never weakened his position or armed his enemy in advance by outbursts of passion or of fear" (ibid.:30).

At this point, we may turn to a famous Japanese exemplar of plain speaking, the poet-priest Ryookan (1758–1831), whose *Kaigo* (Prohibitions) is a collection of aphorisms concerning daily conversation. Among the things prohibited are: "an excess of words; glibness; speaking pretentiously; saying things in a kindly seeming manner; speech reeking of the scholar; speech reeking of elegance; speech reeking of Zen enlightenment; speech reekin⌐ of the tea master." In all things, words should be spoken with sincerity (Doi 1986:118–20). In other words, Ryookan's advice is: "*cultivate* simplicity and sincerity. It is very hard to do, and there are countless pitfalls to be avoided in the dedicated and conscious pursuit of it. That is why it is so rare. Incidentally, that is why I have written the *Kaigo*."

We have come all the way back from the artifice of *enryo* "self-control,"[1] via plain speaking, to *giri* "constraint, obligation."[2] *But we have never left artifice behind.*

And this same paradoxical juxtaposition of plain speaking with a stiff (Anglo-Javanese) upper lip occurs in Merle Miller's heroic plugger Harry Truman. On the one hand, he "spoke his mind": "Harry's words were never fancy, but they were never obscure either. You never had to try to figure out what Harry was up to; he told you what he was up to. . . . There was not a duplicitous bone in his body. He was without guile" (1973:15). But on the other hand, he was what we would call emotionally repressed to the point of practicing Javanese *alus*:

> Did he weep? Did he curse the fates? Did he shake his fist at the thunder? If he ever did, he did it in private. Lincoln was an outwardly melancholy man; Harry Truman was not. His melancholy, if any, was all buttoned up inside him. He never, to use a phrase several of his contemporaries used in describing him, wore his heart on his sleeve. How are you? I'm fine. And you? (ibid.:29)

Needless to say, Merle Miller, Truman's admiring biographer, finds both his salty language and his stoicism equally and totally admirable. But whatever else we can say or think, speaking your mind ("he *told* you what he was up to") and being buttoned up ("he did it in private") are clearly mutually contradictory. That the fact does not occur to Miller suggests that the virtue he worships is laconic machismo, not unbuttoned sincerity, and most emphatically, not the unrestrained self-revelation of psychobabble, the histrionics of which Miller possibly regards with as much contempt as Woody Allen's "Humphrey Bogart" did or as Bismarck regarded the fluency of headwaiters.

According to Doi, this suppression of the self—classic *enryo*—is also at the very heart of the Japanese sage Ryokan's charm. He never spoke about himself (Doi 1986:119), thus possessing one of the "essential qualities of the human being who has charm: an interior life that is indiscernible from the outside" (ibid.:120). But what is this if not an image?

Being a man (and it is always a man; we are dealing with another gender-based affectation here) of few pithy words is an artificial achievement: the noble savage achieves stoical nobility by the calculated suppression of self.

I would go further and contend against the extreme relativism of anthropologists like Michelle Rosaldo, Alessandro Duranti, and Kenneth Read (who claim to have rediscovered the noble savage living free and speaking from the heart among the Ilongot of the Philippines, the natives of Samoa, and the Gahuku-Gama of New Guinea) that the concept of artifice and etiquette is already implicit in the very notion of obligation itself. A human society in which there is never any tension between what one wants and what one does seems entirely unimaginable to me (although it may well be that "lighting out for the territory" with Huck Finn or the Marlboro Man represents a fantasy of total freedom from this constraint to the American viewer).

7.1.3.2. THE CULT AS A REACTION

Even a cursory reading of Feirstein (1982) will clearly show that the cult of real men (and its linguistic aspect) is not only the product of an identity crisis but also a reaction to gobbledygook (29), glamor (15, 32), high culture (25), political correctness (13), psychobabble (28), cosmopolitan sophistication (21), every kind of fakery (30), gimmickry (10, 14), the Industrial Revolution and automation (13), the decline of the American Empire (10), and finally language itself (17). How sincere and genuine can any such an anxious and self-conscious revivalism be which defines itself by reference to a disjointed list of the things it is trying to avoid?

The Canadian psychoanalyst George Zavitzianos (1972) discovered a new perversion which he called *homeovestism*: "dressing up in the clothes of the same-sex person." Naturally, the behavior is more difficult to detect than transvestism, since it is an imitation or an exaggeration of what society normally expects. What distinguishes it from the normal behavior of just plain getting dressed (the existence of which is, of course, increasingly problematic) is that it is engaged in self-consciously by people who assert most vehemently what they feel most insecure about. Plain speaking may be an example in language of what Zavitzianos claimed to have discovered in dress: the perversion of what might be called "homeo-phemism," dressing up our speech "normally."

The American advent of the postmodern age of hip quotation was perhaps recorded by Susan Sontag's "Notes on 'Camp'" of 1966, but there are plenty of signals that we have had a surfeit of cynicism and glitz and that the sensibility of the 1990s is reverting to the sincerity and authenticity of an earlier time. Our cult of plain speaking, like our fondness for "real people" and "real men," may be an expression of this sensibility.

Advertising Age named Ross Perot—artist of the clunky pie charts and the schoolmaster's pointer—"Adman of the Year 1992." The *Utne Reader*, in a feature story on postmodernism, calls for a return to "the good, the true, and the beautiful." Garrison Keillor made the heartland fashionable among the yuppies who read the *New Yorker* with his tales of smalltown life in Lake

Wobegon. Bob Garfield, the Pauline Kael of *Advertising Age*, excoriates a recent Doritos commercial for doing exactly what commercials have been doing for at least the last ten years—minding their own business and entertaining through self-referential jokes. "Why don't they tell us how good Doritos taste?" he complains. Real (doggedly unglamorous) people are everywhere, endorsing beef and beer. This is to say nothing of Ronald Reagan, who campaigned "as the incarnation of the cleancut simple values of small-town America" (Anderson 1990:165).

It is a commonplace among academic students of popular culture (cf. L. Marx 1964; Ewen 1988; Anderson 1990:245) that an escapist nostalgia for a mythical pastoral innocence is if not "profoundly reactionary" at least allied with a profound acquaintance with and dislike of the present and a fear of the future. And I think that the popularity of Lake Wobegon and the trendiness of bib overalls are connected with a sentimental restoration of the world of Norman Rockwell in reaction against brittle sophistication, phony glamor, and the irony epidemic of the present.

By the same token, our adulation of "real men" may be a long overdue consequence the Industrial Revolution, which has by now removed the raison d'être for traditional masculinity by making physical differences between the sexes totally irrelevant for almost every kind of work. Mechanization has emancipated gender roles from biological sex and, incidentally, made men as a gender largely superfluous in peacetime.

But failing an epidemic of amnesia or another good war, no restoration of the past can be genuine because we are only too aware of the intervening decades we have lived through. Maybe Garrison Keillor's Lake Wobegon is a replay of *Oklahoma!* But it is for us emphatically a *re*play, a parody which is enriched for being framed in heavy quotation marks. Lake Wobegon is to *Oklahoma!* (I would suggest) as Ronald Reagan was to the "straw-hatted, wisecracking, but hardworking, white, Protestant, and middle-class America[n] of the Norman Rockwell paintings" (Anderson 1990:165), as Marie Antoinette was to what she conceived to be a real milkmaid, or as Pierre Menard's *Quixote* is to Cervantes's in Borges's magnificent parable—"verbally identical," perhaps, but "infinitely richer." In the same way, the supermen of the action movies are only parodies of Hercules. There can be no restoration of the past, not because the past never existed as we imagine it to have been (an irrelevant issue) but because we know it is a restoration.

So when we speak of hick, we mean "hick," when we speak of real people, we mean "real people," and when we speak of real men, we mean "real men," whose muscles come from working out on the Nautilus rather than pitching bales of hay. However much passion we throw between our quotation marks, they are still emphatically framing everything we say, and quotation, of course, is a large part of what camp and hipness and un-plain speaking are all about in the first place.

7.1.3.3. SAUSSURE'S REJOINDER

Obligation and artifice are implicit in the act of quotation, as in all acts of repetition. But they are equally implicit in the very idea of a language as a system of *signs*. By this definition, all languages, however simple, offer their speakers the means to lie, and all speakers, no matter how disfluent, do so. If it's true, guaranteed power, sincerity, and spontaneity we're after, we can no more find them in familial speech among the Javanese, the disfluencies of Wolof nobility, the mumblings of Don Corleone, Larry's raps on God, Dirty Harry's one-liners, the aphorisms of Ryookan, or the wit and wisdom of Harry Truman than in the sayings of Joe Isuzu, Vladimir Nabokov, or Jacques Derrida. Nor can we find them in true confessions, whether these are addressed to one's priest or one's therapist. We can only find them in *symptomatic communication*: prelinguistic cries, moans, and grunts. Compared to these, all talk—even the "clear and effective" and "eminently quotable" speech of Labov's paradigm speakers of Black English Vernacular—is cheap or at least an affectation.

Speakers using language in general are *eo ipso* alienated from the emotions they describe. Once they control them sufficiently to use language, they are not merely expressing them but also describing them; no longer merely, or even primarily, participants, they have become observers and exorcists of their emotional turmoil. And this is true no matter how much sincerity they speak with. Not for nothing is displacement listed as one of the design features of human language.

In noting that "on eut dit que son sentiment s'en allait avec ses paroles," Gide echoed an oft-repeated insight (1966:66). In fact, it is the central idea of psychotherapeutic catharsis:

> The so-called fundamental rule of psychoanalysis—namely, that the patient *must* free associate—also springs from an earlier procedure. Josef Breuer discovered the etiology of hysteria and its cure by listening to the verbal productions of a young woman. He and Freud called this the "cathartic method" to designate the idea that the cure consists of a kind of "cleaning out" of traumatic memories. These noxa, conceived on the analogy of pus, are drained, not through the sinuses in the skin, but through words issuing from the patient's mouth. (Szasz 1965:34; cf. Storr 1990:26–7)

But the idea of getting some distance from your emotions by expressing them is older than this "discovery":

> In part it is the nature of Javanese that its speakers can practice the emotional detachment (*iklas*) they so much value by speaking of things in order to avoid being possessed by them. Thus, Javanese dislike being surprised, and consequently they exclaim *lho* indicating they are surprised, in order to avoid feeling it. (Siegel 1986:27 apud Wolfowitz 1991:60)

But there is a further way in which language differs from the simple catharsis of a scream or any other prelinguistic cry. Rather than external signs which the speaker chooses, uses, and searches among for the "mot juste" or the best "costume" in a kind of verbal dress-up game, autistic prelinguistic cries are internal signs which emanate from the speaker involuntarily. They are "literally expressive" (Fonagy 1971b:170) or "presentative" rather than re-presentative (Bolinger 1985:98) signals. Only in the case of expressive language can we assert that "what I do is me" and nothing else.

Expressions are not a sign of anything in the world other than the speaker's state. This is similar to the much-diluted claim made by Searle (1979) in his taxonomy of speech acts: expressive illocutionary acts neither fit the external world nor attempt to make the external world fit them. Searle's expressions, however, include linguistic expressions like "Congratulations!," all of which are capable of being uttered insincerely. I use the term "expression" only for involuntary symptoms.

It may be because of its private nature that an expression—even a conventionalized linguistic pseudo-expression—can be directly quoted but resists indirect quotation to varying degrees (cf. Banfield 1982):

1. a)   He cried "Yuk!"
    b)   *He cried that Yuk.

The contrast between (1a) and (1b) is, of course, very heavily grammaticalized in English. It is not only expressions but any fragment of discourse other than a conventional proposition which resists being introduced by the complementizer "that":

1. c)   *He said that yes.

Other languages like Spanish allow the equivalent of (1c) but not of (1b); yet others like Russian and Hebrew allow both (1b) and (1c). There may well be a universal hierarchy of complementizability, similar to the famous Keenan–Comrie accessibility hierarchy (Keenan & Comrie 1977), with propositional discourse at the top of the hierarchy (all languages allow complementizers) and ideophones like "Brrrr" and totally nonlinguistic expressions at the bottom (where no languages, or very few, allow complementizers to appear).

The contrast in acceptability between (1a) and (1b) indicates that, conventional grammar to the contrary, direct and indirect quotation are entirely different speech acts. Direct quotation is fundamentally an act of demonstration, mimicry, or playacting; the quoter steps out of character for a moment and pretends to be the person quoted. In this respect, direct quotes have many of the same properties as ideophones, inasmuch as they tend to offer scope for mimicry, are often isolated from the discourse within which they are embedded by a pause, and tend to resist morphophonological sandhi processes including declinability (cf. Childs 1995). Indirect quotation is an act of translation; the quoter translates the utterance of the original speaker into his or her own frame of reference, which may differ from that of the original speaker not only with respect to conventional shifters like tense and deixis but also concerning what these two people think they know about the world. An actor or mimic may put himself or herself in the speaker's place, but nobody can *translate* the speaker's private emotions into his or her own frame of reference.

In fact, expletives like "yuk," of which English has a large number, although they are in fact linguistic signs, are conceived as the expression of auditory gestures which are not linguistic. Such paralinguistic "unmonitored, purely physiological externalizations of an inner state" (Couper-Kuhlen 1986:174), including whimpers, moans, squeals, laughter, sobbing, yells, sighs, grunts, and hums, are not only available to speakers of all languages but also shared in large part by other animals. "Yuk" is already a language-specific verbalization (compare German "pfui," Russian "fuu," Dakota "xox") of a universal gesture of revulsion, which is only partially (and perhaps accidentally) auditory in expression. There seems to be a yawning chasm between *symptoms* such as screaming with pain, bellowing with rage, or howling with laughter on the one hand and *signs* (even nonindirect quotable "E" signs such as "Ouch," "Damn," or "God!") on the other (cf. Bühler 1934; Goffman 1983; Bolinger 1985). It seems likely to me, however, that the admittedly profound contrast between expression and description, like many other categorical distinctions in languages, could be replaced by some kind of hierarchy of possibilities (cf. Stankiewicz 1964). At its irreducibly animal base are paralinguistic purely expressive and involuntary signs like laughter, sobs, bellows of rage, squeals of pain, and so forth. Higher on the hierarchy are already totally staged and conventionalized epithets like "mmmm," "yuk," "ouch," "aha," "wow," "hurray," "bah," oaths and imprecations, and invocations of the deity. These betray their "expressive" status through their inability to occur as indirect quotations or translations and undoubtedly owe some of their expressive power to their violation of linguistic etiquette and convention at various levels. For example, negative grunts contain the glottal stop, "brrr," "it's cold" consists of a non-phoneme, and "mmm" violates constraints on canonical syllable structure in English. Oaths like "Fuck!" clearly owe their expressive power to the violation of purely social taboos against mention of the sacred or the polluted. Exclamations like "Jesus H. Christ!," "You idiot!," and "Lucky little Rupert!" are nonpropositional. Even higher in the hierarchy of expressive insincerity are very syntacticized constructions, charades of strong feeling like "—the hell" or "Ce que—," which can occur in utterances containing full propositions, and therefore *can* be indirectly quoted, such as

2. a) What *the hell* are you talking about?
    b) *Ce que* Pierre est intelligent! (Ducrot 1984:186)

It is notable, however, that these are of ambiguous origin. In the following indirect quotation, it is possible that the quoter is reproducing the original speaker's exasperation (in which case [3] is a translation of [2a]) or interpolating his own (in which case [3] is both a translation of and an editorial comment on [2a]):

3. She asked what the hell they were talking about.

Most verbal and most descriptive are thoroughly conventional declarative propositions with their grammatical shoelaces tied like:

4. a) You are a fool.
    b) I am angry.
    c) I am angry at you.
    d) I am proud of you.

    e)   I am very angry and impatient.
    f)   I think Irma is very lucky.
    g)   I think she is an amazing woman.

Or the conventional rendition of (2b):

5.   Pierre est tres intelligent.

I propose that a speaker negotiating the hierarchy between a gag reflex—
"Yuk!," "Gross!," or "That's gross!"—then, is moving between structures
meant to convey relatively spontaneous, sincere, and involuntary expression
on the one hand and cool, objective, detached, *alienated* description on the other.

Expletives and epithets in English often subsist at different stages of this
(ontogenetic and possibly phylogenetic) hierarchy of expressive sincerity. It
is notable, for example, that "ouch" and "ow" are on different rungs, the former
more conventionalized and therefore less expressive than the latter.

What is involved in the gradual taming of emotive expressions is their conversion from symptoms, which are part of the speaker, to consciously selected
signals, which are external to him or her. In expressing their emotions by means
of linguistic signs, objects of an alien origin, speakers are alienating themselves
from the emotions which they represent in the most iconic fashion possible.
(Compare Muecke's observation that "the concept of detachment seems to be
implicit in the concept of pretense, since the ironist's ability to pretend attests
a degree of control over more immediate responses" [1970:36]).

All humans with conventional language of one kind or another do this. This
much alienation and detachment and *enryo* is simply a unique and characteristic part of being human, no matter how plain the language we speak.

7.2. Plain Speaking in Linguistics

Throughout this chapter, I have been dealing with an attitude toward language
which regards plain speaking not as "neutral" but as heavily steeped in very
specific populist and macho virtues. I have therefore postponed discussing
arguments presented by commentators like Barthes (1977), Geertz (1960), or
Sontag (1966e) against the possibility of such a neutral mode of unmarked
"degree zero" discourse in general. I would like to turn to a consideration of
this more general topic now.

Plain speaking is an attempt to get back to "the thing in itself": an object
stripped of cultural baggage, which a distinguished colleague of mine, describing a distinguished journal of linguistic research, has called "metacrap." While
the impossibility of such a pursuit has been a commonplace in philosophy since
Kant's distinction between phenomena and noumena in his *Critique of Pure
Reason* and in sociology since at least Berger and Luckmann's *Social Construction of Reality*, there are two almost universally accepted constructs in
linguistic theory which still subscribe to the fallacy that such a thing not only
is possible but also must serve as the indispensable foundation for any linguistic thinking in general. These are the transcription of the International Phonetic

Alphabet (IPA) and Russell's "object language." In the following brief remarks, I cannot treat these subjects with the rigor and thoroughness they deserve. I do hope to show, however, that there are reasons for regarding the IPA as a virtually Platonic abstraction and that there are reasons for regarding the object language, as described by Bertrand Russell, as no more a language than the drooling of Pavlov's dogs. Since the authors of these theories are among the most distinguished members of their disciplines, I do not think that the easily discoverable problems in their formulations can be as easily remedied. Rather, they reflect a fundamental incoherence and impossibility in the very project of getting "back" to "the basics," at least as far as language is concerned.

7.2.1. The IPA as the Phonological Thing in Itself

Virtually every student of phonetics and phonology accepts that the phoneme and the distinctive feature are framed language-specific bits of socially constructed and psychological reality. Underlying these, however, there is the physical signal, whose existence is a biological and acoustic reality. This signal is captured on the sound spectrograph. Its written version is the narrow phonetic transcription, which is language-independent. The phoneme /t/ is only a psychological reality of English; the phone [t] is a fact of nature. We learn the phonology of a language through slow acquaintance with its sound pattern. On the other hand, a trained phonetician—like a sound spectrograph— can produce with equal facility and accuracy a phonetic transcription of a text in his or her own language or a text in any totally unknown language (cf. Laver 1994:29). Call this the naive version of the physical reality argument.

No sophisticated linguist believes in the naive version of this argument. All it takes to become a "sophisticated linguist" in this sense is five minutes of experience with a sound spectrograph, during which time the student can learn that there are no acoustic invariants for any single phone and in fact no strong evidence for the reality of a linguistic segment of any sort. Segmentation and the IPA are now universally believed to be abstractions of some kind. Most crudely, the IPA abstracts away from personal qualities in the human voice and aims to record only "linguistic qualities" (Ladefoged 1969). Nevertheless, the prevailing view is that an IPA transcription is somehow *an abstraction of a lower order than a phonemic transcription*, and it is this commonsense view which I wish first to present and then to challenge.

The idea that phones are language-independent and conceptually prior to phonemes (cf. Laver 1994) is most famously associated with the "cardinal vowel" theory of Daniel Jones. (Interestingly, no phonetician has ever proposed producing the same benchmark set of cardinal consonants.) Jones emphasized— almost *boasted*—that the eight cardinal vowels which he proposed (discovered? invented?) are not—any of them—precisely the same as the vowels of any specific language (see, for example, the frontispiece of his *English Pronouncing Dictionary* [(1917) 1946; cf. Catford [1988:138]) and that they were *radically* different from all of the vowels of English (although some of them were by a happy coincidence not too far from some of the vowels of French). They could only be learned directly from him and, subsequently, from students he had trained, from the students of those students, and so on (cf. Jones 1917 apud Ladefoged 1969:76; 1993:220). Other distinguished phoneticians have stepped back, somewhat uneasily, from this extreme position and maintained that by following instructions and with practice we can all learn the vowels at home (*Principles of the IPA* [1949] 1962:4–5; cf. Catford 1988:133–53), but the IPA account already equivocates between acoustic and articulatory characterizations of these vowels:

> Cardinal e, ɛ, a are selected so that the degrees of *acoustic* separation i - e, e - ɛ, ɛ - a, a - ɑ, are approximately equal. Cardinal ɔ, o, u are vowels of the back series continuing the same scale of equal degrees of *acoustic* separation. . . . The *tongue positions* of e and ɛ are intermediate between those of i and a, and the *tongue positions* of ɔ and o are intermediate between those of ɑ and u. (*Principles of the IPA* 1949:4–5; emphasis added)

A closer reading of Catford's superficially pedantic and pedestrian account reveals that the series can in any case only be constructed by self-contradiction. Between the reference vowels [i] and [ɑ] which are based on the idea of physical limits ([i] is the highest vowel we can make before uttering the glide [j]; [ɑ] is the lowest back vowel we can make before uttering the pharyngeal fricative [ʕ]), the intermediate vowels [e], [ɛ], and [a] are inserted at "equal articulatory intervals of tongue height" and then the series is continued to [u] through ascending in equal intervals through [ɑ] and [o]. As Catford acknowledges, the points are *neither articulatorily nor acoustically equidistant, the distance between [a] and [ɑ] being greater than that between any two contiguous front or back vowels.* "Partly because of this, it is desirable to learn the front series and the back series as two distinct, though related sets. *This helps to avoid the problem that arises if one is to produce* [i - e - ɛ - a - ɑ] *as a single set of equidistant vowels*" (1988:134). But *this* is a practice which he initially identified as the fundamental principle of construction for the Cardinal Vowel Series and then characterized as "an error to avoid" exactly one page further on.

Ladefoged (1969:71) is even more explicit in dispensing with the idea of equal intervals: "It seems that the tongue does not move in a series of even approximately equidistant steps when a set of cardinal vowels is pronounced. . . . [In fact] the tongue has such a different shape for the front and back vowels that it is meaningless to compare." What this means, of course, is that the cardinal vowels cannot be specified in purely articulatory terms. The crucial ingredient in the construction of such a series, *equal intervals of tongue height*, is a chimera.

Nor is there any hope of characterizing these cardinal vowels acoustically by precisely specifying their formants. As Ladefoged notes, even the select group of Jones's first-generation students whom he recorded under Jones's explicit supervision produced acoustically quite different sounds.

So it seems that if we want to learn the cardinal vowels, there is no alternative but to learn them from Jones or one of his students. The central idea of the cardinal vowels, which as a student I was disposed to view as hopelessly pedestrian, sort of like the directions for assembling a lawn mower, is actually wildly romantic: "I was taught the Cardinal Vowels by Jones himself, and it was a lengthy and painful process. CV number 1 ([i]) turned out to be the most difficult of all, rather unexpectedly, and it took a long time before Jones was satisfied with my version. I had trouble too with CV number 3" (Abercrombie 1991:40). Kafka could have written a marvellous parable about the incorruptible "language" which Jones's disciples maintained, chanting their mantra, keeping their heroic vigil while empires and their native languages rose and crumbled, resolutely unnoticed, all around them.

The full richness of the lunacy of the IPA becomes apparent when one attempts to use it as a point of reference in learning a foreign language. Here is Catford (1977:177) on French [o]: "The French [o] of *mot* is near CV number 7, but in modern Parisian is slightly centralized. CV 7 has somewhat closer endolabio-endolabial [*sic*] rounding."

Contrast this approach with the practice of any pedagogically naive textbook in a foreign language. Turkish /i/ is like the sound of English "pit" or when long as in "machine" (cf. Lewis 1953: 13). That is, one uses "as reference points, the vowels of a particular dialect of a language known to both teacher and student" (Ladefoged 1993:223). There is no question whom the naive language learner finds more *useful*, but my contention is that the flat-footed approach is also the only one which is theoretically sound. All linguistic phones (including the cardinal vowels) are in fact *inductively arrived at generalizations*: we arrive at [i] and [t] from learning /i/ and /t/ in human languages like French, Italian, Spanish, Turkish, and even English.

And there are no other linguistic sounds. When we learn a new language, we may try very hard to transcribe it in IPA, but what we are writing when we do this honestly and diligently (as we see when we look back after having learned some of the language) is almost totally unusable junk. (To avoid offending my fellow linguists, I should say that this has been my experience as a serious investigator of one language and as someone who has dabbled in a dozen others.) When we first transcribe utterances in a totally unfamiliar language, we are clambering out of one boat (the bilgewater on the bottom being the socially constructed reality of our native language) into another (which contains its own bilge, the socially constructed reality of whatever language we are trying to learn) and spending almost no time in the awful shark-infested abyss of "pure phonetics" in between. Not only is this abyss, I would maintain, unknowable, like Kant's object in itself. I would go further and claim that without the boats tossing on its surface (each with a little bilge inside), it would instantly *cease to exist*. There is an infinite realm of sounds and noises (car revving, dolphin squeals, bird songs, cricket chirping, brooks babbling, and the hum of my PC as I write this, to mention a few), but the phone [a] does not exist except as an abstraction based on "[a]-like sounds" in human languages.

Lest I should seem to be guilty of the effrontery of trying in three pages to debunk the august discipline of phonetics, I should point out that I am merely repeating what most phoneticians more or less casually agree on. See Pike ([1943] 1971:138), Heffner (1964:69–70), MacKay (1987:54), and, finally,

Ladefoged (1993:280), whose closing words in his textbook of phonetics are worth lingering over: "Most phonetic observations are made in terms of a phonological framework. . . . As soon as the data is segmented or described in any way, then phonological considerations are bound to be present." The IPA "thing in iself," it turns out, is a Frankenstein's monster, a compromise, an abstraction based on the *disjecta membra* of the socially constructed and *mutable* realities of different actual languages. The "rigor" of etic objectivity survives as well as it does because like many other kinds of "rigor" (like the distinction between linguistic and encyclopedic knowledge) it is happily ignored in actual practice.

Exactly the same objections could (and should) be leveled against the notion of "mentalese," a "fundamental alphabet of human thoughts," which is but translated into English, Urdu, or Mandarin.

7.2.2. The Object Language

Natural languages have a considerable array of lexical and other signs whose referents are language itself. For example, the English word "well" in examples like the following seems to function as a metalinguistic commentary on the inadequacy of the speaker's words (which are nevertheless the best words he or she can come up with) (cf. R. Lakoff 1973):

a) —What's up?
    —Well, Denise and I have just split.
b) Well, this is it, I guess.
c) Real men are, well, realistic.
d) It strikes us that lately there are a lot of relatively fortunate people who—how shall we say this?—well, who seem to have a wee bit of difficulty keeping their problems in perspective. (Tom Tomorrow, *This Modern World*)
e) —Did you or did you not pull the trigger?
    —Well, yes, but—
    —Just answer the question.

"Well" is what appears to be an extreme example of a purely metalinguistic word. Polite language in particular is awash in metalinguistic expressions in which the speaker characterizes not the purported referents of his or her message but rather himself or herself and the message with all appropriate deference to the addressee. In Japanese, Aoki and Okamoto (1988) provide explications of the following:

Chotto:	"I feel small in making this request." (51)
Nee, anoo:	"Excuse me for intruding on you with this." (58)
Sore ga:	"It's not easy for me to say this, but . . ."
	"What I am going to say is probably different from what you hoped or expected to hear from me, but . . ." (83)
Maa X:	"I wouldn't go so far as to say 'X', but . . ." (228)
Saa:	"I am sorry not to be able to answer your question." (230)
Soo desu nee:	"Well, let me think, I agree with what you say, but . . ." (230)

There are more or less adequate equivalents of these in English (albeit less conventionalized ones). But in addition to the familiar hedges and mitigators, there are many more basic-seeming metalinguistic words, including common words like "not." Horn (1985) gives a brilliant description of a contrast between "ordinary" and "metalinguistic" negation, as exemplified by the contrast between

6. a) I am un-happy.
    b) I am not "happy" (I am ecstatic).

The word "not" in (6b) is a characterization of the *mot juste* and thus eminently metalinguistic. The prefix *un-* creates a word which directly describes a state of mind; it is not about language at all. Fundamentally, however, all uses of the word "not" in any kind of assertion are at least metalinguistic, in the sense that they are not about the world at all but about the fit between propositions and the world. This has been accepted for some time.

Russell (1940) pointed out that an enormous number of apparently solid words like "true," "false," "or," and "some" are also metalinguistic words since they are commentaries on sentences rather than descriptions or labels of objects in the world. It is reasonable (and, to avoid the liar paradox, necessary) to keep them out of the most primitive language, the object language, whose existence does not presuppose any other language and wherein words relate only to objects. It is interesting to note that Russell's metaphorical idea of such a language reflected Orwell's ideal of "prose like a windowpane"; in the object language, "the words are transparent" (ibid.:66).

What does this "transparency" mean, exactly? Well, it seems to mean, unfortunately, "not being a language at all," as I will now try to show. To begin with "object words are defined logically as words having meaning in isolation, and psychologically as words which have been learnt without it being necessary to have learnt any other words" (ibid.:62). So far, this is plausible. It is possible to make assertions in the object language, but every assertion that is made in the object language is formally identical to an assertion that is made in the secondary language: "The assertion which is the antithesis of denial belongs in the secondary language; the assertion which belongs in the object language has no antithesis" (ibid.:61). This is curious and suspicious. Mindful, perhaps, of Occam sharpening his razor in the background, Russell proposed minimal contrast pairs like

a) This is cheese. (assertion)
b) This IS cheese. (antithesis of "this is not cheese")

Only (a) belongs in the object language, since by asserting (b), we are actually saying "as unpedantically as possible 'the statement "this is cheese" is true'" (ibid.). And this statement involves the metalinguistic notion of truth. Sentence (a) is somehow about *seeing* (with just the eye, I-am-a-camera style), but sentence (b) is about *judging* (with the mind) (ibid.:72). We are by now much more skeptical of the possibility of being nothing but a camera than Russell was. What does it mean, exactly, simply to "see"? Can it be expressed in language without an act of judgment? Russell clearly begs the question even more forthrightly when he says: "An object word is a *class* of *similar* noises or utterances such that from habit they have become associated with a *class* of *mutually similar* occurrences" (ibid., emphasis added). Of course, notions like "class" and "similar" are entirely dependent on acts of judgment (and entirely socially conditioned). In using category labels of any sort (and all words are category labels), we are as much reflective and selective of the *mot juste* as when we qualify our utterances with metalinguistic operators like "well."

Indeed, it is clear that Russell is (must be) entirely aware of this problem (which is equally devastating for any variety of behaviorism). It is worth repeating his exposition of the elusive difference between the object language and the formally indistinguishable secondary metalanguage in detail because it harkens back so clearly to the distinction between language and symptomatic signs, which I mentioned in the introduction:

> When the dog hears the word ["food"], he behaves very much as he would if you have a plate of food in your hand. . . . If you excite a dog by saying ["Food!"] when there is no [food], your speech belongs to a higher order since it is not caused by the presence of food, but *the dog's understanding belongs to the object language*. A heard word belongs to the object language, when it causes a reaction appropriate to what the word means. . . . Whenever you doubt or reject what you are told, your hearing does not belong to the object language, for in such a case you are lingering on the words, whereas in the object language the words are transparent, i.e., their effects upon your behaviour depend only on what they mean and are, up to a point, identical with the effects that would result from the sensible presence of what they designate. (ibid.:64–6)

For the dog—as for the villagers in Aesop's fable of the boy who cried "Wolf!"—words continue to be transparent until the dog learns that talk is cheap. So much for transparency for the *hearer*. This must be true for the *speaker* of the object language as well: words are transparent as long as they are responses to what they designate. They become *opaque*, part of the secondary language, when they are uttered (or can be uttered) in the absence of "the sensible presence of what they designate." But then what separates "secondary language" from "object language" for Russell is precisely what separates language (with its design feature of displacement) from symptoms. All language, then, is inescapably metalinguistic. The notion of an object language, like that of plain speaking itself, is an oxymoron or perhaps another case of homeophemism—that is to say, a masquerade disguised as normal clothing.

7.3. Style and Content in Art

In art, as in language, "cutting out the metacrap" means to get at the "core" meaning beneath the "superficial form" of a work; what it seems to *be* is different from what it *means*. I have tried to show that such a reductionist approach to language is misconceived. As long as signs are signs, they will be characterized by exactly this irreducible duality of form (*being*) and content (*meaning*). It would seem that the same irreducible duality is characteristic of the work of art as well.

The last and wisest words "against interpretation" that I have read are not from Susan Sontag's influential essay of that title but from an essay by Dave Barry, which deserves quotation *in extenso*:

> I was reading this James Bond book, and right away, I realized that, like most books, it had too many words. The plot was the same one that all James Bond novels have: An evil person tries to blow up the world, but James Bond kills him and his henchmen and makes love to several attractive women. There, that's it: twenty-four words. But the guy who wrote the book took *thousands* of words to say it. . . . And it's not just spy novels. Most books are too long. I remember in college when I had to read *The Brothers Karamazov*. . . . Our literature professor told us that Dostoyevsky wrote *The Brothers Karamazov* to raise the question of whether there is a God. So what I want to know is, why didn't Dostoevsky just come right out and *ask*? Why didn't he write:
> Dear reader:
> Is there a God? It sure beats the heck out of me.
>   Sincerely,
>   Fyodor Dostoevsky
> Here are some other famous works of literature that could easily be summarized in a few words:
> * *Moby Dick*—Don't mess around with large whales, because they symbolize nature and will kill you.
> * *A Tale of Two Cities*—French people are crazy.
> * Every poem ever written—Poets are extremely sensitive. (Barry 1987:178–9)

Like Susan Sontag, whose famous essay against interpretation preaches against the reductionist folly of "looking for the meaning" of the artwork, Barry points out that when the artistry is purged from the artwork, almost nothing is left. Sontag makes the same point when she notes that to interpret is to impoverish and deplete the world in order to set up a shadow world of "meanings" (1966e:7).

Incredibly, however, Susan Sontag lobbies for another kind of reductionism: "Transparence is the highest most liberating value in art—and in criticism—today. Transparence means experiencing the luminousness of the thing in itself, of things being what they are." (ibid.:12). What—again with the transparence and the thing in itself? Haven't we got beyond this with Kant? And isn't Sontag supposed to be campaigning *against* reductionism? She should be, but I think that maybe she has become so engrossed in the campaign against "searching for the core" that she proposes trashing the core itself—in exactly the same way that Whitman, Orwell, and the aficionados of plain speaking proposed trashing the "coating." The "thing in itself" which she invites us to once again appreciate is not the plain speaking core but the coating, the artistry, the metamessage, the outer form.

And in the course of this campaign, she has lost sight of the fundamental fact that, like the linguistic sign, the artwork is also ineluctably dualistic. A work of art is not a work of nature, like a mountain, a pig, a waterfall, or a virus. These are things in themselves. And here it seems to me that Barry the satirist is a little closer to the truth (if only by omission) than Sontag the philosopher. The message of an artwork may be minimal. Shorn of its artistry, it may seem unbelievably simpleminded. But the artwork does have both an ethical and an aesthetic component, and what distinguishes it from a natural object is the presence of this second dimension. Maybe the "message" of Moby Dick is trite, but *there is one*. A sunset or a waterfall has none.

7.4. Conclusion

I have attempted to sketch here the description of a metaphorical attitude toward language and some of its ramifications. The attitude is that language may be plain or fancy. Like architecture, it may be Dorian or Corinthian, Bauhaus or baroque. Like music, it may be plainsong or polyphonic, rap or grand opera. Honesty and sincerity, in all cases, are associated with the first choice—that of simplicity and brevity:

> Es trägt Verstand und rechter Sinn
> mit wenig Kunst sich selber vor.
> (Understanding and rightmindedness
> speak for themselves.) (Faust, I:550–1)

I have also tried to show, however, that the attitude (which, incidentally, I cannot talk myself out of sharing) is not only a homegrown artifact but also fundamentally invalid for two reasons. The first is the postmodernist reason that any mode of behavior—particularly, perhaps, the most simple one—which is freely chosen from a menu, as it were, is chosen with some degree of self-consciousness and is therefore necessarily artificial. (Not for nothing do languages like German etymologically confuse free will [*Willkür*] and arbitrariness [*Willkürlichkeit*].) The second reason is that all language consisting of "mere words" is essentially arbitrary and artificial. At this level of abstraction, Bakhtin and Saussure are saying exactly the same thing. Human language, in fact, may be the quintessential act of homeovestism. What makes us human (and perhaps what makes us appreciate dumb animals so much and invent noble savages) is our sad recognition of the duality of our symbols and therefore of ourselves: what they *mean* is not what they are. And, in the same way, what we *do* is not what we *are*.

NOTES

1. Offered food or drink, a guest may take only a little. The host may protest "Don't do *enryo*!" (example from S. Suzuki, personal communication). Hence *enryo* means politeness, suppression of one's inner wants. For a lengthy survey of much of the literature, see Wierzbicka (1991), and see the much fuller explication offered there (ibid.:352).

2. In modern Japan, girls give chocolate to their valentines. Recently, the custom has arisen of giving "*giri* chocolates" to co-workers for whom one has no sentimental feelings (example furnished by S. Suzuki, personal communication). Hence, we may deduce the meanings of etiquette, formality, insincerity. Again, Wierzbicka provides a sensitive survey of the changing definitions of *giri*, culminating in a comprehensive explication (1991:376). From Wierzbicka's careful summary, it seems that Lewis's use of Mafioso *giri* includes a meaning ("obligation to revenge") which is no longer current.

EIGHT

Zen Semantics

As an adolescent learning French, I was fascinated by the French expression for the verb "to mean," as in "Qu'est-ce que cela *veut dire*?" (freely, "What does that *mean*?"; literally, "What does that *want to say*?"). If you *want* to say something, after all, why don't you just come right out and *say* it? (The etymologies of English "mean" and German "bedeuten" prompt exactly the same question.) I now realize that this apparently pointless gap between "saying" and "meaning" is a necessary part of every language, as it is of every code, and presumably always will be until we evolve telepathy and eliminate the middle man. Moreover, the essence of understanding and interpreting every sign in a code lies in bridging the necessary yet perverse and ornery gap between the signifier and the signified. Another word for this peculiar decoupling in every human language is the design feature of displacement, and I have devoted the first chapters of this book to a survey of the inescapability of this feature. I would like now to yield to the temptation to inquire where and how this feature may have arisen in the course of human evolution.

There is always something suspiciously self-indulgent about speculating on Big Questions, and questions concerning the origin of displacement are perhaps even bigger than they seem. I have hinted in my preliminary discussion of insincerity and inconsequentiality that the design feature of displacement may be simply another name for what we call free will. Free will, after all, is what we could call the ability to say things we do not mean and to ignore messages we do not wish to heed.

From an objective point of view, it is no more or less disreputably self-indulgent to discuss the origin of language today than it was in 1867, when the Linguistic

Society of Paris declared this to be an illegitimate question. We have discovered
no incontrovertible missing linguistic link between ourselves and the nearest apes,
so our direct evidence for the genesis of language now is as sparse as it was then.
And I am unaware of any speculations in the biological literature, even disreputable ones, about the possible origins of intentionality or free will.

But I would argue that once we identify the fundamental process of the genesis of displacement, we will recognize that it has analogs in many other fields.
These analogs are more accessible to our present scrutiny than the conjectured
transformation of grunts and cries into words. If we simply adopt the common
sense of a uniformitarian hypothesis, we may hazard some respectable speculations about the origins of human language by investigating well-articulated
theories of similar processes in the development of other human cultural institutions, processes that go by names such as decontextualization, habituation,
aestheticization, reification, and ritualization. These, in turn, are cultural analogs of the biological process of emancipation, which has a substantial literature of its own.

To begin with, I would like to identify what seems to me the fundamentally
linguistic process of *semanticization*, which I regard as marking the true origin of language. And I will approach this by first comparing three familiar
theories of semantics: model theoretical semantics; the semiotic triangle of
language, thought, and reality; and the pragmatic "square" which includes language, thought, reality, and users of language (more exactly, the pragmatic
model is of a hexagon including language, speaker, hearer, and the communicative thoughts associated with each). I will not try to elaborate on or criticize
these models, but I will try to show how fundamentally they are talking about
the same thing (language), particularly in contrast to what I might call "Zen
semantics." It is the transition from Zen semantics to correspondence semantics (that is, semantics as described in any of the familiar models) which I will
identify as the origin of language, and I will try to give an account of a possible mechanism for this transition in the following pages.

8.1. Language and the World

Model theoretic semantics, as characterized by Emmon Bach in his lucid *Informal Lectures on Formal Semantics* (1989), provides the leanest and cleanest
account of conventional semantics and the one that corresponds most closely,
at least in its point of departure, with the average intelligent layperson's conception of meaning. That point of departure is that meaning is naming: a correspondence is established between words in a *language* and individual things
in (a model of) *the world*. Beyond this point of departure, things get harder for
the noninitiate to follow. All labels in model-theoretic semantics for "universals" (anything other than proper names, that is, labels such as common nouns,
verbs, adjectives, and prepositions for things, properties, or relations) correspond to *sets* (or sets of sets) of individual objects in the world. So, the word
"dog" corresponds to the set of {Lassie, Fido, Rin Tin Tin, White Fang}, and

so forth. Perhaps most disconcertingly for the intelligent layperson, *how* the membership of any of these sets is determined (e.g., how we decide that Rin Tin Tin is a member of the set of dogs) "is not a part of semantics" (ibid.:12). This seems to the layperson exasperatingly—even mind-bogglingly—counter-intuitive, but it is the price which model-theoretic semantics pays for being a correspondence theory that recognizes only two entities: names in a language and (sets of) things in the world.

8.2. Language, Thought, and Reality

A much more complex theory, the semiotic triangle (Ogden and Richards's symbol, thought, and referent; Whorf's language, thought, and reality), still includes names and (sets of) things in the world, referring to these as *symbol/language* and *referent/reality*, but enriches semantics by adding an ontologically questionable third entity: the notion of *thought*, conceived as being on a par with the other two. For Saussure in the *Cours* (1966), the thought corresponding to the formal sensible portion of the linguistic sign was a mental image reminiscent of Plato's ideal form. For Sapir, Whorf, and other linguistic relativists, thought was not only expressed through but also determined by linguistic form, while for universalists like the Port Royal grammarians, generative grammarians, and Anna Wierzbicka, thought or "mentalese" is largely independent of the linguistic expression (French, Turkish, etc.) in which it happens to be clothed. But the separate existence of language and the mental models of thought is recognized by both relativists and universalists. What is at issue is merely the distance and the direction of the causal connection between these two entities.

In practice, however, it turns out that the "thought" corresponding to a linguistic expression is always exactly the same thing as its *sense* or *definition*; it is just *another* linguistic expression, the "same thought" *in other words*. This move has its advantages. No longer does the analyst have to austerely and implausibly insist that how the membership of a set is determined (whether it be the set of individuals that are dogs, the set of objects that are white, or the set of individuals who snore) is "not a part of semantics." Rather, each of the concepts *dog*, *white*, and *snore* is defined ultimately in terms of a set of "semantic primitives," the rationale for which is extremely controversial (cf. Wierzbicka 1972). To a hardbitten model-theoretic semanticist, on the other hand, the semiotic triangle is immediately suspect because both thoughts about language and language *are* language (or they are represented, at least, as nothing but language). And if our thoughts (or, at least, the thoughts we clothe in language) are no different from language, why dignify them with a separate ontological status?

8.3. Pragmatic Theories

Even more complicated is the pragmatic square, which can be thought of as consisting of language, thought, reality, and user but which is probably best modeled as a transmission of a *message* from a *speaker* to a *hearer*. Each of these three entities is associated (in different ways) with a thought (hence the pragmatic hexagon). The speaker's thoughts are his or her intended message in producing the sign. The hearer's thoughts are his or her interpretation of the sign. And the thought connected with the sign itself is the conventional, inter-subjective meaning or concept of the sign, abstracted from the context in which it is presently employed by the speaker or interpreted by the hearer. This model allows us to detach sentence meaning from utterance meaning: sentence mean-ing is the conventional, intersubjective concept of the sign, while utterance meaning is the speaker's intention in producing it (and, perhaps, the hearer's interpretation). Such a model is necessary to accommodate not only common-places such as grammatical shifters like "I" and "now," polyphony, and all of the varieties of un-plain speaking we have surveyed but also a wide variety of related facts: the fact that the prototypical *lie* is defined primarily in terms of the speaker's intention to mislead his or her hearer rather than in terms of the utterance's noncorrespondence to reality (Coleman & Kay 1981); the fact that given the right circumstances, Disraeli's "at last, something warm" could qualify as a brilliant witticism; the fact that an apparently innocuous exclama-tion like "Now THIS is a house!" could be a mortal insult and an equally in-nocuous utterance like "the mouse is gonna have a good time" could be an outrageous obscenity, and so forth. But it is notable that in this model (in which what we are now calling "the message" incorporates Saussure's model of the sign), the sign is totally emancipated from any objects in the real world other than the speaker and the hearer who employ it:

| intention | intersubjective concept | interpretation |
| [speaker] | [message] | [hearer] |

8.4. The Duality of All Signs

It may seem difficult to imagine any theory of meaning more alien to the simple commonsense correspondence between words and things than the pragmatic theory. Yet the three theories of meaning summarized here (all of which I have vulgarized beyond belief) are essentially quite similar in the one sense which concerns us here. Each involves the crucial central notion of *some kind of cor-respondence*: in each, there is not only a correspondence but, more important, a *contrast* between what a sign *is* and what it *stands for*. (And the function of a sign is to *join* the two.) The word "dog," for example, *is* (when spoken) a series of noises or (when written) a series of marks on a surface, but it *stands for a dog*, which is something very different from either in any one of the theo-ries we've looked at. In this respect, a message is like a work of art which at best *portrays*, but *is* not, a hunk of reality. However much a statue may resemble a dog, it is not one. And this, as we have noted, is one of the strongest argu-ments in favor of the First Amendment (cf. F. S. Haiman 1972:31).

We take this alienation between a sign's outward appearance and its mean-ing so much for granted that it is difficult for us to conceive of any possible alternative. We do not seriously entertain a "theory of meaning," for example, which regards any such detachment of essence or value from existence, and thus the very idea of a sign, as possibly fundamentally pathological. In such an alternative "theory," *all signs are illegitimate*, and things are always exactly what they are: the "meaning" of an object is exactly what it is, and it cannot re-present anything else. From my understanding, this is precisely the theory of Zen: enlightenment and understanding are synonymous with getting past the symbols which intervene between the subject and reality and seeing that "mountains are mountains, and waters are waters" (Ch'ing Yuan apud D. T. Suzuki 1956:14; cf. Danto 1981:134). According to one of its most prominent Western expositors, Zen regards language itself as a kind of red herring across the path to enlightenment: "Words are not facts, but only *about* facts, whereas Zen is a vigorous attempt to come into direct contact with the truth itself without allowing theories and symbols to stand between the knower and the known" (Watts 1958:18).

The Zen idealization of the concrete (and the payoff for adhering to it) are stunningly intuited in J. L. Borges's beautiful short story "The God's Script." The Aztec priest Tzinacan has been tortured and imprisoned for life in a Spanish dungeon. He spends the decades of his captivity trying to discover and then decipher a secret magical incantation which he believes will set him free and restore him to his former power. At the very outset of his quest, he realizes the fundamental insight of conventional correspondence semantics—that anything can stand for anything: "A mountain could be the speech of the god, or a river or the empire, or the configuration of the stars" (Borges 1962c:170). In a moment of inspiration, he decides that the eternal script in which the incantation is written is the same as the markings on the jaguar imprisoned in the adjoining cell and attempts to commit to memory—and then decipher—this complex pattern, which he glimpses for only a moment every day. While pursuing his hopeless task, he dreams of a grain of sand, and it appears in his cell. He dreams of more and more grains of sand until he is suffocated beneath the weight of "the innumerable sand." With an immense effort, he wakes up, but a voice says to him: "You have not awakened to wakefulness, but to a previous dream. This dream is enclosed within another, and so on to infinity, which is the number of the grains of sand" (ibid.:172). He shouts out, "A sand of dreams cannot kill me, nor are there dreams within dreams" (ibid.), and he awakens (in every sense). It is as though his commonsense exit from his nightmare has cured him of the craziness of looking for meanings in correspondences at all. (Borges leaves his readers to ponder for themselves the possible logical incoherence of language-as-instrument [the spell] and language-as-sign [something to be deciphered]).

Tzinacan renounces his grandiose quest for meaning as he renounces the labyrinth of dreams, as he renounces an image of himself as avenger or decipherer or anything other than what he actually is—a prisoner. He accepts the squalid concrete reality of his harsh prison: "I blessed its dampness, I blessed its tiger, I blessed the crevice of light, I blessed my old suffering body, I blessed the darkness and the stone." And in this very instant, he achieves that mystical *connection* with the universe which is the common goal of all religion and philosophy:

> I saw an exceedingly high Wheel, which was not before my eyes, nor behind me, nor to the sides, but every place at one time. That Wheel was made of water, but also of fire, and it was (although the edge could be seen) infinite. Interlinked, all things that are, were, or shall be formed it, and I was one of the fibres of that total fabric and Pedro Alvarado who tortured me was another. . . . I saw the origins narrated in the Book of the Common. I saw the mountains that rose out of the water, I saw the first men of wood, the cisterns that turned against the men, the dogs that ravaged their faces. I saw the faceless god concealed behind the other gods. I saw infinite processes that formed one single felicity. (ibid.:172–3)

And, incidentally, "understanding all, I was able also to understand the script of the tiger" (ibid.:173)—which no longer interests him.

I think that Borges has imagined something like *satori*, or *prajna*, the Zen experience of illumination. Goffman might call it the dissolution of all "frames" or "laminations" which come between the subject and reality. His protagonist achieves this revelation precisely through the renunciation of the confusing alienation of signs and decipherment.

I am not prepared to defend *too* energetically my casual use of the label "Zen" for the kind of semantics which Borges has rendered with such power. Whether or not this attitude that "things are only what they are" is characteristic of Zen, however, it is definitely characteristic of a *prelinguistic* world in which there is as yet no bifurcation between the world and some language *about* the world, no distinction between things which are simply objects, and an artificially de-limited set of perceptually indiscernible things called *signs* which have acquired the new function of serving as labels or representations for objects (or thoughts or anything else).

As every student of semantics is well aware, the well-known arbitrariness of the linguistic sign means that anything may serve as a sign of anything; a mountain, for example, may be the speech of the god. The essence of a sign then lies not within its actual material form or substance but in the fact that it is *interpreted* (Goffman would say "framed"), or seen as standing for some-thing other than what it is. From an etic or objective point of view, there is no discernible difference between the mountain which is simply a mountain and a mountain which is a sign in "the god's script." That difference exists entirely in people's heads. The origin of language lies then not so much at the point where Neanderthals or our ancestors were capable of enunciating any particular sound like [i] but at the moment where the psychological dif-ference between [i] and /i/ came to exist, the point where the sound—any sound—ceased to be just a sound and also became a phoneme: an *interpreted* sound invested with a meaning (by virtue of a code). We must now ask where and how this dissociative (and from the Zen perspective, perhaps unwhole-some) split happened. And the answer from linguistic prehistory is, of course, that we simply don't know.

8.5. Semanticization and Aestheticization

An exactly comparable bifurcation, however, occurs in other contexts. It happens, for example, whenever a hunk of reality (say, an object like a vase with a practical function) becomes *aestheticized*: an object of use (without perhaps ceasing to be useful) becomes in addition an objet d'art. The theoretical point that there need be no discernible difference between the utilitarian implement and the object of beauty was famously made by Andy Warhol with his 1964 New York City "Brillo Box" exhibit which was indeed a Brillo box. The artist's philosophical point was appreciated and was treated with tremendous erudition and insight by Arthur Danto (1981), whose magisterial essay on the aestheticization process is the basis of my present discussion.

How does an object become a sign? The question is no different from the question asked by Danto: How does an object of use become an artwork? In both cases, a bifurcation or dissociation occurs in people's heads.

Danto begins by (perhaps mistakenly) disposing of Kant's theory of aestheticization in his *Critique of Aesthetic Judgment*. For Kant, the transformation of the object into an object of beauty was achieved when the viewer adopted a detached perspective on it. The vase from such a disinterested perspective is perceived not simply as a means to an end, a receptacle which can do work, but as an an end in itself, an object in its own right. Quite so, says Danto, but since it is possible to cultivate such an attitude of detachment toward *anything in the world* (for example, all of social life can be seen as "the human comedy," the universe can be seen as "the book of nature," and so forth), Kant's criterion provides us with no basis for making a distinction between an object of use and an objet d'art (Danto 1981:22). And with this, I totally agree.

But it seems to me that by repudiating Kant here, Danto still clings silently to some hope of finding an intrinsic absolute quality which sets a work of art apart from other objects, and it seems to me that he thereby commits—incredibly—the very fallacy which Warhol's artwork supposedly debunks and from which Danto's entire book is supposed to set us free. In the same way that anything can be a sign of anything, so too can any object whatever—even a Brillo box—be invested with aesthetic value. As Danto rightly points out, if Warhol's work is art, then no perceptual criterion for an artwork can be given (ibid.:61), and anything at all can be a work of art (ibid.:65), just as anything in a language can stand for anything else. Detachment is not a bad characterization for the attitude which permits the aesthetic appreciation of an artwork to occur just as it is the literal description of what semanticization entails, but how does this detachment itself come about? Kant is silent on this. (We should note that the detachment of which he speaks is the same, essentially, as the design feature of displacement which characterizes language [Hockett & Ascher 1964] or the feature of "objectivation" which characterizes social institutions in general [Berger & Luckman 1966:36]. All of them can be characterized as a kind of emancipation from functionality, from the practicality of dealing in a purely instrumental fashion with the here-and-now.)

Danto offers three answers of his own to this question. Neither of the first two are any worse than Kant's account, but it seems to me that neither of them are any less tautologous. According to one answer, aestheticization occurs in the mind of the producer when he or she intends it (1981:130) and in the mind of the beholder when he or she not only sees the object but also interprets it (ibid.:113, 125). According to the other, aestheticization depends on the existence of an "art world": a community with some knowledge of history which makes conventions of interpretation possible (ibid.:45). Both of these answers, for all the wit and elegance with which they are offered, merely restate the problem and beg similar questions. To say that aestheticization occurs by virtue of the speaker's intention and the hearer's interpretation is to say no more than we would say if we said that semanticization occurs by virtue of these things. But that is to say no more than that a sign is a sign when it is intended and interpreted, which is to say that a sign is a sign when it is a sign. To say that this can only happen when the viewer belongs to a community with common traditions of some kind is to restate what in linguistics is again a familiar truism—that a sign has its meaning by virtue of some kind of social contract or convention among the members of a community, be it the "artworld" or the "people who speak French." In other words, the sign is arbitrary. But we have not done more than to provide a common definition of art, which not too surprisingly recapitulates a common definition of language. We have still not answered the question: How does this change from object to sign/art happen in people's heads?

Danto cites with immense approval a historical conjecture of another German philosopher. In *The Birth of Tragedy*, Nietzsche speculated that tragedy, a symbolic narrative representation which has exactly the *aboutness* of both language and art, originated as something much closer to magic; it was not a story *about* gods and heroes any more than "Abracadabra," "Open Sesame," Tzinacan's magical incantation in "The God's Script," or "Shazam" are stories about anything. The narrative (like Sainte-Colombe's music in the movie *Tous les matins du monde*) originated not as a representation of anything else but as a totally practical instrument: for conjuring up the god, getting out of jail, or raising the dead.

Over time, the primitive enactive magical function was replaced by the symbolic representative function. How? *This* question Danto answers in a way that I think is entirely and absolutely on the money. Somehow, *in the course of innumerable repetitions*, the rite and its participants come to be perceived not as the real thing but as *imitations* of reality:

> [First], the god is actually invoked into re-presence by the appropriate religious technology. . . . And when this magical relationship of complex identity was dissolved, and rites and statues were interpreted merely as representations of the kings and gods, they did not have to undergo change in form to undergo change in semantic function. Or better, under the structures of magic, these figures and rites had no semantic structure; they only acquired that when they began to be representations in the sense of standing for what it was also believed they resembled. (ibid.:76–7)

Anything at all *becomes* language, or is appreciated as art, when it is seen no longer as a part of life or as having a magical power over life but as some kind of an *imitation* of life—in other words, a fake. This change in perception happens—but only for human beings—over time, as the sign/artwork becomes decontextualized *through repetition*. As an imitation, it can and does gradually become progressively more emancipated from what it represents: "And then, over time, standing for or denoting came to be less and less an important thing for artworks to do" (ibid.:77).

At the final familiar stage of abstraction and autonomization, when the original intended usefulness of the art object atrophies and the instrumental function is entirely forgotten, we have purely decontextualized and decorative "art for art's sake." Nor is art the only human institution which can be seen to have developed in this way.

The evolution of money has repeatedly followed precisely the same trajectory as the aestheticized work of art. In a subsistence economy, cattle (or gold) are objects of use and have a unitary use value; "repeated" (that is, extra or surplus) cattle or gold or other objects of use acquire an *additional* exchange value; as is well known, the original use value eventually becomes irrelevant and atrophied, and the formal substance of money becomes increasingly useless and immaterial.

A great deal has been written and is known about the latter change—how repetition gradually erodes an icon (one kind of sign) into a symbol (another kind of sign). This is essentially the process of grammaticalization. I would argue that a prior and infinitely more important transformation is semanticization—the conversion of an incarnation or enactment (which *is* something real in the world) into an icon (the most primitive kind of sign *of* something). For human beings, at least, *it is effected by exactly the same process of repetition*. Schematically:

Semanticization (=Symbolic Bifurcation)	*Grammaticalization* (=Material Atrophy)		
Object →	Object/Sign →	Sign	
Incarnation →	"Icon" (insofar as anything is an icon of itself) →	Icon →	Symbol
For example: cattle-as-food →	cattle-as-wealth →	coinage →	paper money

In the last several chapters, I noted that uttering words for the second (or third) time is one of the ways in which speakers may transform use into mention and distance themselves from what they mean by uttering words in an alienated fashion. And it is only in the course of repetition that stylization and exaggeration can occur. But repetition is of far greater importance in the development of linguistic structures than the weak words *stylization* and *exaggeration* can suggest. In fact, repetition may be the major instrument in both the construction and demolition of grammar and almost certainly played a major role in the origin of language. I will use the term "ritualization" in language as a cover term for all of the irreversible changes which are brought about by repetition. Unlike many linguists who insist on the uniqueness and autonomy of language, I find it profitable (at least for my approach to this discussion) to compare language not only with other human institutions like art but also with the development of languagelike behavior (including ritual and play) in other animals. Chapter 9 accordingly deals with emancipation, habituation, and automatization in both human and nonhuman nonlinguistic behavior. Chapter 10 deals with the linguistic analogs of these: habituation as grammaticalization, automatization as double articulation, and emancipation as codification. Chapter 11 deals with emancipation in metalanguage and with the possibility of reversing this process. Chapter 12 proposes that the biological analogs of all cultural processes of ritualization, besides proceeding in a genetic rather than a LaMarckian fashion, are parallel to these cultural processes.

NINE

Nonlinguistic Ritualization

Ritualization subsumes a number of distinct processes. In the following discussion, I will highlight three: habituation, automatization, and codification. The last of these, which itself subsumes several possibly unrelated processes (certainly processes that deserve more detailed examination than I can give them here), is treated as a unitary fact for one principal reason: all of the changes listed under this heading occur in human beings as a result of experience, while analogs among other animals seem to occur only through genetic evolution.

9.1. Habituation

One of the longest-running gags in the comic strip *Peanuts* features Lucy's repeated offer to hold a football for Charlie Brown to kick. She *always* snatches the ball away at the last instant, and Charlie always winds up flat on his back. Nevertheless, he *always* falls for this manipulation, thereby evincing—quite literally—an intelligence lower than that of several species of mollusk. Perhaps we can discern the first dim beginnings of one aspect of decontextualization, and possibly of free will in the animal kingdom, in our (by "our" here, I mean, of course, most multicelled animals other than Charlie Brown) diminished response to a repeated stimulus. If we're not Charlie Brown or a computer, our response to a stimulus is not (entirely) determined by the stimulus but by our recollection of how we responded to the same stimulus on earlier occasions. With this capacity to ignore what we have been exposed to before, we are perhaps at the beginning of the long road from manipulation (Dawkins [1982] believes all "animal communication" falls under this heading) to communication (cheap talk).

An often repeated ritual, in other words, can pall. With staleness very often comes a reduction of the ritual's formal manifestation and, although not always, a diminution of its meaning. (We express this familiar insight with idioms like "a ritual apology" or "an empty formality.") Almost any abbreviated or *token* gesture or verbal symbol of courtesy, greeting, or farewell, from a handshake to your signature to "goodbye" (cf. Firth 1972), is a ritual in this sense. For example, when a man opens a door for a woman, this may be viewed as a ritually reduced and almost entirely opaque and abbreviated version of "rescuing a damsel in distress" (Chris Orloski, personal communication). Any cliché is a ritual expression, as is the relatively illegible signing of one's own name. Ethologists sometimes use the term "ritualization" for this process of formal reduction. Thus, Plooij (1978:123) in his discussion of beckoning behavior among wild chimpanzees uses "ritualization" to describe the change whereby the token abbreviated gesture of leaning slightly backward comes to replace the original gesture of lying flat on one's back.

All of these are good examples of what psychologists call *habituation* or adaptation: a decline in the magnitude of the response, or the very tendency to respond, to stimuli that have become familiar due to repeated or persistent exposure (Bassett & Warne 1919; Karsten 1928; Lambert & Jakobovitz 1960; Smith & Raygor 1956; Peeke & Herz 1973; Gleitman 1986:88, 160, 200). These investigators have provided quantitative proof for the homely proverbs that "you can get used to anything," "familiarity breeds contempt," and "what we look at habitually, we overlook" (Mumford 1960:103). Repetition may lead to formal reduction (think of your satisfyingly cryptic signature), but independently of this, it may also drain meaning away. This may be the reason for the widespread practice in Zen and other spiritual exercises of repeating a mantra: "In order to lose themselves in God [or, perhaps, in order to destroy the pernicious doubleness of signs in general], the Sufis recite their own names, or the ninety-nine divine names, until they become meaningless" (Borges 1962f:164). As Mumford points out, a propos of the work of art in the era of mechanical reproduction, "there are paintings by Van Gogh and Matisse and Picasso that are descending the swift slippery slope to oblivion by reason of the fact that they are on view at all times and everywhere" (1960:102). Much the same trivialization has happened to musical masterpieces like the "William Tell Overture," of which a critic wrote that its very popularity (as the *Lone Ranger* theme tune) has successfully obscured its greatness. We have even done the same thing with the appalling mystery of death. Stalin once observed that while the death of one man is a tragedy, the death of several million is a statistic. And the main premise of the classical syllogism ("All men are mortal") is a cliché.

We should note that habituation is a learned behavior of many other animals besides ourselves. Aesop's villagers eventually learned to ignore the boy who repeatedly called "Wolf!" Cheney and Seyfarth (1991) showed that vervet monkeys are capable of learning to ignore persistently false alarm signals in the same way.

9.2. Automatization

But not only blasé habituation or boredom comes with repetition; so does skill. For example, the sequence of numbers 149162536496481100121144169196225 . . . may seem impossible to learn as long as the student relies on memory alone. But as the sequence 1, 4, 9, 16, 25, 36, 49, 64, 81, 100, 121, 144, 169, 196, 225, . . . it is learned in a moment. In the same way, while it is relatively difficult to learn a seven-digit telephone number, it *seems* easy to learn a seven-letter mnemonic like L-A-W-Y-E-R-S, or F-O-R C-A-R-S (or, even better, A-B-C-D-E-F-G) where each letter corresponds to a number. An expert telegraph operator receiving a coded message can keep six to twelve words behind the instrument when receiving. This means remembering, on an average, about 200 clicks—a truly amazing achievement. On the other hand, if the clicks represent disconnected numbers, the most skilled operators can hold only three or four numbers at a time—a maximum of about twenty clicks (Bryan & Harter 1899:353–4).

These are paradigm examples of *chunking* or *automatization*, the acquisition of what Bryan and Harter call "a hierarchy of habits" (Bryan & Harter 1899; Gleitman 1986:233, 270). Although, objectively, *learning seven digits involves less information processing than learning a sequence of seven letters*, and the digits in the ascending sequence of squares are identical with the digits in the seemingly random list prior to it, nevertheless, the work seems to be less when the "principle" which generates the sequence has been learned. Crucially, this is true whether the principle is a real generalization—one which can be expressed as a mathematical formula (as in the case of the sequence of squares)—or whether the "principle" is simply a painfully acquired skill (as in the case of reading, memorizing the order of letters in the alphabet, or reconstructing spelling from Morse). In either case, the computation which is done automatically "doesn't count" as a burden on the person who performs it. Mere repetition leads to automatization as effectively as possession of a formula: "Sheer plod makes plow down sillion / shine." Or as the social scientists point out, "any action that is repeated frequently becomes cast into a pattern, which can then be reproduced with an economy of effort" (Berger & Luckmann 1966:53).

9.3. Codification and the Notion of Emancipation

The R. D. Laing model of the divided self, as we have observed, implies the existence of three stages of selfhood: the natural real person, the divided self consisting of a true core and a false front, and a hollow shell consisting of the front alone. I want to propose that this model can be interpreted diachronically (and, in fact, the diachronic interpretation is all but explicit even in Laing). The transition from the ideal "thing in itself" to the bifurcated "sign" is semanticization; the transition from the bifurcated sign to hollow or empty ritual is grammaticalization. I will illustrate both of these developments with a spectacular allegorical example from the insect kingdom.

Wishing to copulate with the female dancing fly (which would just as soon eat him as copulate), the male signals his availability by giving her a remarkable "wedding present": a balloon of silk. While her attention is distracted in unbundling the package, he mounts her and then, if he is lucky, makes his getaway. (The package is empty, as it turns out.) On the basis of comparisons with closely related species which evince fragments of this extraordinary routine, Kessel (1955) has surmised that it became established in the following way. "Originally" (I use quotation marks to highlight the fact that the development occurred not over the lifetime of a single creature or community but as a result of random evolution), the male dancing fly distracted the predaceous female with the gift of a dead insect; at this point, the gift was purely instrumental. "Later," the gift was interpreted as a signal to the female, a signal whose message was something like "this fly is available for mating." Originally, the male partially wrapped his tiny prey up in silk exuded from his anal glands, probably in order to subdue it. The silk, like the dead insect, had an instrumental function, and its similarity to Christmas "gift-wrapping" was incidental. "Finally," however, the male achieved his original "purpose" by giving the female the elaborated wrapping alone, and it is the wrapping which serves as the mating signal (Kessel 1955). Kessel's conjectured development neatly reflects the stages of semantic development in the Laing metaphor: the dead insect is the thing in itself; the wrapped insect is a "divided self"; and the wrapping alone corresponds neatly to our notion of the husk of etiquette.

The mating behavior of these flies is an allegory for the development of languagelike behavior in animals generally. Among dancing flies, instrumental behavior "becomes" symbolic. In the same way, the searching behavior of bees at food sites (elements of which are attested in the behavior of a number of other nonsocial and emphatically noncommunicative insects) becomes stylized and evolves into the celebrated bee language (Frisch 1954; Bastock 1964; Dethier 1957).

These are paradigmatic examples of an evolutionary process that ethologists since Tinbergen have been calling *ritualization* (cf. Tinbergen 1952; Morris 1956; Blest 1963; J. Smith 1966:168; H. Gleitman 1986) and what sociobiologists (Wilson 1975:225) have called *semanticization*: "In the course of evolution, both locomotory movements and acts (concerned with comfort, with heat regulation, and with the capture of prey) have been selected and modified to produce signals" (Blest 1963:102). In other words, emancipation, ritualization, and semanticization are apparently synonymous expressions in biology, interchangeable labels for what amounts to *the creation of (a) language out of other kinds of behavior*.

Ethologists and anthropologists have noted, incidentally, that what they call ritual in many cases (though not all of the ones I have enumerated here) is akin to *play*. In both biological and cultural areas, we characterize as play an unconstrained and freely chosen activity that is found to occur *out of context*, when the animal is free of environmental and physiological pressures or in effect can take a holiday from the otherwise exceptionless rules of biological need and social hierarchy (Loizos 1966; S. Miller 1973). Structurally, play activity, like ritualized activity, differs from the phylogenetically prior act which gives rise to it in that it consists of both content and instrumentally useless "galumph-ing" (ibid.) or "style" (Sontag 1966b). That is, it is exaggerated, simplified, and repeated (cf. ibid.; Cosper 1983:410).

Both ethologists and anthropologists, then, have used the same word "rituali-zation" to describe the very general process whereby phylogenetically instru-mental actions are *emancipated* from their primary motivation and free to serve a communicative function instead (Tinbergen 1952; Morris 1956; Blest 1963; Manning 1967; Callan 1970; Koenig 1970:64; Jurgens & Ploog 1974:34). In this sense, ritualization (however it occurs) is the acquisition of meaning or the transformation of objects and activities into bifurcated signs. An action is identified as a ritual when it ceases to be purely instrumental and becomes an emblem of something else.

Codification, the creation of signs, is a dual transformation. On the one hand, the ritualized activity is routinized so that its form is relatively independent of (emancipated from) its original stimulus:

> It is a basic property of simple signals, when these are contrasted with other types of response, that they remain constant in form regardless of any change in the circumstances which cause them. (Morris 1956:1)

> Whereas stimuli of varying strength for the release of the unritualized precursors of display movements elicit responses of varying intensity and form, following ritualization, the derived responses acquire an almost constant form and intensity to a wide range of stimulus strengths. (Blest 1963:104)

A corollary to this *fixity of form* is *decontextualization*: the ritualized act not only does not vary in response to the intensity of the stimulus which provokes it but also does not necessarily occur in response to the same stimulus as the act which is presumed to be ancestral to it (ibid.:116).

On the other hand, the form (of the ritual or the play) may become stylized and (when viewed in purely instrumental terms) hypertrophied to the point where it is actually dysfunctional (Daanje 1950; Morris 1957, 1966; Blest 1963; Loizos 1966:7; Miller 1973:89, 92; Sontag 1966b:36). Hypertrophied styliza-tion or galumphing-for-the-hell-of-it is characteristic not only of ritual and play but also of art in general:

> [There is] a tendency on the part of human fantasy, once it is emancipated from the restraint of practical needs, to run riot. . . . In medieval cathedrals, this sometimes went so far that Ruskin even discovered carvings in places where no human eye but his own—if we except the original worker—had probably ever beheld it. (Mumford 1960:69)

It has been suggested that stylization (insofar as it involves standardization) is nevertheless functionally motivated in two ways: a stylized signal is easier to recognize (Morris 1957:1; Manning 1967:138) and easier to remember and reproduce (Coleridge & Valery apud Sontag 1966b:34; Fonagy et al. 1983:173–4; Bolinger 1986:231) than a spontaneous gesture. Lewis Mumford speculates that such standardization was an indispensable prerequisite for the related transition from handwriting to movable type:

> For the sake of legibility and universality, it was important that the human being who copied a book should achieve a certain kind of neutrality and impersonality, . . . making each letter conform to a common type, rigorously standardizing the product. . . . After a copyist repeated the same letter a thousand times, his letters would achieve that impersonal quality . . . at which [they] could be transferred into movable types. (Mumford 1960:69)

Two very homely and accessible examples of the connection between repetition and stylization are your signature and a mantra. *Compare your signature with your name written by someone else.* Beyond the personal differences of handwriting style (which can be controlled by making the exercise reciprocal), you will note that relative to the written name, the signature is typically opaque (tending to illegibility) as a consequence of formal reduction and characterized by some galumphing (exaggeration and stylization), particularly in the representation of the initial letter. The major difference between your signature and your name written by someone else, of course, is that you have repeated your signature many more times than someone else has repeated writing your name. Opacity is a kind of emancipation from instrumentality (that is, in this case, from legibility) and so is the galumphing flourish which defines your personal "style" (which is, of course, why signatures are conventionally used as guarantors of identity).

Note your behavior over a period of two minutes, during which you repeat any arbitrary word (preferably with your eyes shut). Most likely, after some initial playing around with different speeds, rhythms, word boundaries, and tunes, your repetitions will settle into a steady rhythm, so that you are repeating groups of two to five units characterized by a fixed melody and beat. You will also note that after a very short time, the word will entirely cease to conjure up an image of its referent and will become a pure form to be played with. Meaninglessness can be called again a kind of functional emancipation, and the liberty you exploit to play with form seems to be concomitant with this emancipation.

Emancipation of an activity from its instrumental functions, succinctly summed up in credos and slogans such as "art for art's sake" and "means replace ends" and even phrases like "taking on a life of its own," is a characteristic not only of humble forms like signatures, mantras, and the patter of flight attendants and auctioneers (cf. Justice 1985; Kuiper & Haggo 1964) but also of art, and it is as dependent on repetition in the case of artistic style as in these homely examples:

> Every style depends on, and can be analyzed in terms of, some principle of repetition or redundancy. . . . If one does not perceive how a work repeats itself, the work is literally not perceptible and therefore at the same time not intelligible. It is the perception of repetitions that makes a work of art intelligible. (Sontag 1966b:34–5)

Sontag is ascribing to mere repetition in this passage the same function of con-
ferring intelligibility that Goffman ascribes to the idea of a frame. I will return
to this deep identity of frame and repetition as creators of meaning in chapter
11, when I consider the relationship between messages and codes.

Stylization through repetition is a characteristic of almost every *cultural*
institution, including the institution of society itself, whose overarching metamessage, as Berger and Luckmann insightfully suggest, is "here we go again"
(1966:53, 57)—not all that different, we might recall, from the postmodernist
mantra "it's been done," noted by Rudnick and Andersen. Not only the university, government, the law, the stock market, and organized religion but also
any bureaucracy whatever affords a perfectly good illustration of an organization which has become "emancipated" through routinization from the original
purpose for which it was created.

The ritual nature of such institutional fixtures as the daily or 6 o'clock news
is familiar and has been searchingly analyzed by critics such as Boorstin (1962)
and Richardson (1975). Viewed from a purely pragmatic instrumental perspective, either there is news or there is nothing happening which is newsworthy.
Ritualized news "stories" such as photo opportunities, press conferences, human
interest stories, and puff pieces are called for *when the "news" must appear on
a regular basis (which is necessarily therefore decontextualized)*. So, too, are
pseudo-events like the American invasion of Grenada in 1984 (Anderson
1990:125) or Israel's *twenty-sixth* invasion of Lebanon in 1988 (timed to mark
the first anniversary of the Palestinian intifada [Chomsky 1989a:53]). These
are "politically motivated," which is to say purely symbolic, demonstrations
of strength (or whatever) rather than militarily motivated responses to an actual
threat.

The accelerating irrelevance of the vicissitudes of the stock market provides
a parallel example of emancipation. The market's original functions presumably included fundraising or providing a channel for investment in new production: a company or a government would issue stocks or bonds to finance
an enterprise. This instrumental function is now represented by less than
1 percent of transactions on the New York Stock Exchange, the other 99 percent being represented by simple changes of ownership of existing stocks and
by increasingly derivative and abstract transactions in futures, options, currency
and equity swaps, and other "instruments" which are not about production but
about other instruments which are about other instruments which are about . . .
(Baker, Pollin, & Schaberg 1994:622). The relative inconsequentiality of the
stock exchange as an indicator of productivity or an arbiter of the economic
state of the real world in general is stunningly demonstrated in purely self-
contained and autonomous events such as the utterly inconsequential crash of
October 19, 1987, which, as is well known, was greater than the famous crash
of 1929 that (at least in the popular mind) ushered in the Great Depression
(Krugman 1989).

In a similar vein, Heinz von Foerster (1984:46–8) starts with a definition of
cognition as "computing a reality" and then replaces this with successively more
displaced definitions: "computing descriptions of a reality," "computing de-

scriptions of descriptions of . . . ," and finally "computations of computations of. . . ." In cognition, as in the six o'clock news, literature, and the New York Stock Exchange, the elaboration and evolution of an institution go hand in hand with its increasing autonomy; in a mature system, "il n'y a pas de hors texte." Over and over again, we see this kind of emancipatory change occurring historically, *over time*.

For example, Greider (1987:68) notes exactly this change in the evolution of money: "Over the centuries, the evolution of money has been a long and halting progression in which human societies have hesitantly transferred their money faith from one object to another, at each step moving further away from real value and closer to pure abstraction." Anderson (1990:225–6) mentions as a parallel the transformation of the mystical personal religion of a charismatic leader into the doctrinal organized religion of Dostoevsky's Grand Inquisitor; in religion, as in politics, the revolutionary is succeeded by the apparatchik. Slater ([1968] 1992) speaks of an exactly comparable historical development for the expression of one human foible: narcissism. From relatively primitive beginnings (where it is naively and directly expressed by body adornment) to the "upper extreme" of the cultural continuum (where "self-denial becomes an end rather than the means" of achieving immediate bodily gratification), "we may conceptualize the change from ancient to modern narcissism," Slater writes, "as one involving greater detachment from the body . . . *a more elaborate circuitry of displacement and delay between the behaviour and its ultimate and original goal*" (ibid.:456; emphasis added).

The most deft and compact characterization of the end result of all of this ritualization and detachment and the resulting utter inconsequentiality of most things that are "purely academic" (note that the phrase is itself a virtual synonym for inconsequentiality) occurs in Nabokov's devastating send-up (in his novel *Pnin*) of my own discipline of linguistics, "that ascetic fraternity of phonemes, that temple wherein earnest young people are taught not the language itself but the method of teaching others to teach that method" (Nabokov 1966:10).

All of these human examples, of course, suggest the inevitable observation that repetition may lead to stylization and emancipation *for us*, but it does not do so for other animals. (Neither Kessel, nor Tinbergen, nor Wilson, nor any other student of animal behavior has ever argued that semanticization among balloon flies or whatever arose through acts of repetition.) Should we not then ascribe the semanticization which is at the heart of the origin of language to whatever uniquely human attribute it is which makes us stylize when we repeat the way we do? And if we do this, are we not then simply relabeling rather than accounting for the phenomenon we seek to explain?

I acknowledge that our tendency to stylize and emancipate repeated activities is peculiar to human beings. There is, however, a distinction between mimesis and the production of language. Both are perhaps predominantly human, but the first may be the indispensable foundation for the development of the second. The psychologist Merlin Donald (1991:163–99) speculates that the mimetic faculty—the ability to "produce conscious self-initiated representational acts" (ibid.:168)—is not to be found even among apes. But it is to be found in even prelinguistic children (cf. Sacks 1996 citing J. Bruner on the ontogenetic sequence of enactment and then iconic and symbolic representations), and Donald ascribes this mimetic "platform" to an evolutionary missing link. The mimetic faculty, he speculates, may have been characteristic of *Homo erectus* for a million years before the great linguistic revolution of the last quarter to half million years (ibid.:166). He argues, very plausibly, that the social consequences of this prelinguistic faculty included rehearsing and modeling (173), conformity (174), pedagogy (176), the uniquely human capacity for rhythm (186), and toolmaking (193). I am skeptical only of his claim that play is also to be included among the by-products of a specifically hominid mimetic system (ibid.:193), since play is widespread among mammals. But I would follow him in arguing that language *is* definitely a by-product of this faculty, however "dissociable" (ibid.) it may be from it in principle. Among the criterial characteristics of mimetic representation which he cites are intentionality (ibid.:171) and displacement (which he divides into two characteristics, reference [172] and autocuing [173]; by reference, he means that the mimetic act is distinct from what it refers to; by autocuing, that it is voluntarily produced without the aid of external cues).

I have sketchily reviewed three processes in evolution that are driven (at least in the world of human institutions) by repetition: the replacement of instrumental substance by "empty ritual," illustrated by phenomena as diverse as mantras, signatures, handshakes, and the trivialization of "the work of art in the age of mechanical reproduction"; automatization, illustrated by telephone mnemonics and the virtuosity of the experienced telegraph operator; and the creation of signs, illustrated most vividly by the mating language of the balloon fly. The first and second processes find familiar analogs in traditional linguistics, where they are known as grammaticalization and double articulation. The last, semanticization, although it is far more profound, will require more discussion.

Ritualization in Language

10.1. Grammaticalization as Habituation

> So common indeed was [the word "fuck"] in its adjectival form that after a short
> time the ear refused to acknowledge it and took in only the noun to which it was
> attached. . . . Far from being an intensive to express strong emotion, it became
> merely a conventional excrescence. By adding -ing and -ingwell, an adjective and
> an adverb were formed and thrown into every sentence. It became so common
> that an effective way for the soldier to express emotion was to omit this word.
> Thus, if a sergeant said "Get your —ing rifles!" it was understood as a matter of
> routine. But if he said "Get your rifles!" there was an immediate implication of
> emergency and danger. (Brophy & Partridge 1931:16–17)

The use of "fucking" in the British army, as Brophy and Partridge capture it, is
a paradigmatic example both of markedness reversal (in the country of the blind,
it is the seeing man who is a misfit; cf. Andersen 1972) and of ritualization in
the sense used by Plooij. Another paradigmatic case of grammaticalization, quite
parallel to the degeneration of "—ing," is the erosion of referential pronouns
with argument status to verbal agreement markers, the mechanics of which in
many languages and language families have been described (cf. Meinhof 1936;
Givon 1970, 1976, 1979; Haiman 1989b).

There have been a number of recent accounts in the literature on grammaticalization (Heine et al. 1992; Traugott & Heine 1991; Hopper & Traugott
1994), but the fundamental observations (Meillet [1912] 1958; Zipf 1935) still
remain: all of the outward and formal signs of grammaticalization (reduction

to the point of opacity, stylization, obligatorification) and all of the concomitant semantic changes (notably including abstraction to the point where all
meaning is lost) result when individual words and collocations are frequently
repeated.

10.2. Double Articulation as Automatization

> —My kid said his first word today!
> —Well, my kid can say half a word.
> —Oh yeah, what's that?
> —Mother.

In the end result of automatization, I contend, we can also recognize *double
articulation*—the smallest meaningful signs are made up of still smaller units
which are themselves meaningless. This is, of course, a language universal
whose origins are almost as disreputable a subject of study as are the origins of
human language itself (cf. Wescott 1967).

The standard model of erosion whereby morphemes are reduced first to bound
affixes, then to phonemes, and finally to silence (cf. Givon 1979:chap. 5) may
provide the observable mechanism whereby languages evolved the design feature of double articulation (cf. Wescott 1967; Hopper 1994). Sounds now
meaningless may have evolved originally from meaningful morphemes.

The physiologically mysterious process whereby, for example, the phone
number L-A-W-Y-E-R-S is easier to remember than the corresponding sequence of digits bears witness to automatization (cf. the well-known Stroop
effect in Gleitman 1986:17), chunking, and double articulation. A recognized
word like "lawyers," like the twenty-six letters of the alphabet, involves a
sequence of letters, but we consider remembering a phone number whose digits spell out "lawyers" a simpler act than remembering a sequence of seven random letters or a sequence of seven digits, and it is easier to reproduce the
alphabet than a sequence of some permutation thereof because the effort of
having learned the spelling of the word or the sequence of the letters of the
alphabet is taken as a given. Before chunking or automatization, learning the
spelling of "lawyers" (or of any other word) involves no less work than learning any sequence of random letters. Automatization, it need hardly be emphasized, is the result of repetition. Erosion through repetition may be the major
source of meaningless phonemes (and of "half-words" like "mother" from the
example) in all human languages.

But perhaps it is not the only source. In any discussion of this structural property, we must note the ubiquity of double articulation. The genetic code of DNA
and RNA, no less than English, is characterized by what we may call double
articulation: codons (or the "words" of DNA) are formed from sequences of
three bases. The codon UCU is "meaningful" in that it forms a neutral acid
called serine, and as such has "synonyms" like UCA, UCC, and UCG, but the
base U (Uracil) has no such restriction or significance (cf. Ayala 1978). The
origin of double articulation in the genetic code is unknown.

The genesis of double articulation can also be observed in the simplest artificial codes, however, like the Library of Congress classification system and the system of arithmetic; signs X, Y, Z (the minimal units in the code) have invariable meanings "x," "y," and "z." In principle, these are codes with single articulation, in which every sign is meaningful and has a single fixed denotation. But now consider the efflorescence of possibilities of meaning in the Library of Congress system for a single letter, say "B." "Word"-initially, it means "philosophy, religion," but following other letters, it has other specific meanings determined by the initial letter with which it occurs: CB is "civilization" (within "history," or in the context C—, B means "civilization"); GB is "physical geography" (within "geography"); HB is "economics" (within "social sciences"); LB is "theory and practice" (within "education"); NB is "sculpture" (within "fine arts"; QB is "astronomy" (within "science"); and so on. The end result, of course, is that the letter "B" in the Library of Congress code is every bit as meaningless as a phoneme. A parallel though greatly impoverished efflorescence is possible for the digits in the decimal system of notation, since the actual value of the quantity represented by any digit depends on its position relative to the decimal point. In both cases, the "grammar" of the code assigns a number of context-sensitive semantic rules:

sign X has meaning "x"/ _____A
sign X has meaning "y"/ _____B
    . . .
sign X has meaning "*"/ _____N

Even where the meaning of the sign is fixed by context, the more possibilities of meaning a sign has or the greater its degree of context-sensitivity, the less of a meaning it has "intrinsically." This is why the difference between the various meanings of a digit in arithmetic is smaller than the various meanings of a letter in the Library of Congress classification system. (The meanings of a digit in arithmetic are related by a single simple rule, while various meanings of a letter in Library of Congress classification are specified by a large number of rules.)

Cases of this sort, which I would like to call "creeping double articulation," may arise spontaneously in the context of any system of signs whose interpretation is determined by context-sensitive grammatical rules. On the origins of context-sensitivity in artificially legislated languages, I have nothing to say, other than that it offers an attractive economy of means to planners who are given a limited inventory of signs to play with. But I would like to venture a commonsense suggestion about its origin in natural languages: as signs become emancipated from, and autonomous relative to, their extralinguistic real-world referents, they may be free to become more sensitive to their linguistic context, that is, the other signs with which they co-occur. In Saussurean terms, there may be an inverse correlation between the signification of a sign (its relationship to something in the world) and its valeur (its relationship to other words in the same semantic field and in the syntagm). As this happens, grammatical categories become drained of intrinsic meaning in the same way,

although not as much, as morphemes which are reduced to phonemes. The ubiquity of creeping double articulation is part of the basis for my own objection to
ingenious attempts to provide coherent Gesamtbedeutungen for grammatical
categories like the plural (Wierzbicka 1985) or the feminine gender (Corbett
1991). Multiple motivations eventually become indistinguishable from pure
arbitrariness, as was illustrated in the second letters of Library of Congress labels
(cf. Bolinger 1975:110).

   It is also highly likely, however, that the converse of double articulation—
a kind of codification or sign creation—often arises through repetition. What I
have in mind is the creation of arbitrary phonaesthemes like English <gl->, or
<cr->, which are now associated with "a vague impression of light" or an equally
vague "impression of crushing" as a result not of onomatopoeia but of a number of coincidences. That is, <gl-> has the associations that it does because of
the prior existence of words like "gleam," "glare," "glow," "glisten," "glim-
mer." The productivity of such associations may be attested by phonetic changes
like the development of our word "glamor" (with its attendant associations of
*gl*itz) from "gramarye" (the source of humdrum "grammar") (cf. Skeat 1963).

   Barthes (1972:119 cited in Goffman 1974:34n.) notes that "chance is supposed to vary events; if it repeats them, it does so in order to signify something
through them: to repeat is to signify." More homely is the repeated aphorism
from the James Bond novels: "The first time it's coincidence; the second time
it's happenstance; the third time it's enemy action." Similar "promotion from
the ranks" of the originally meaningless is observed in innovative forms like
"tele-thon" and "pre-quel."

   Rather than accepting double articulation as an irreducible given, we might
get a handle on its origins by thinking of degrees of significance with signs
arranged in a hierarchy:

Biggest (most "wordlike"):	1.	Words, lexical morphemes
	2.	Affixes, grammatical morphemes
Intermediate signs:	3.	Submorphemic sounds with associations
Smallest (most "soundlike"):	4.	Phonemes

Through etymologically coincidental associations which are often repeated,
phoneme sequences (4) may become phonaesthemes (3), thus acquiring significance. Through frequent repetition, lexical morphemes (1) may become
grammatical affixes (2), thus losing significance. The first process corresponds
to codification, the second to habituation and automatization.

10.2.1. The Act of Direct Quotation

Part of the driving mechanism which reduces words to meaningless sounds is
erosion through repetition. In fact, *direct* quotation itself (essentially nothing
more than the repetition of an utterance) does this kind of work through a single
act. In saying "I quote" (or "I repeat"), the speaker at least in principle is dis-
avowing a personal interest in and possibly even comprehension of the mean-

ing of what he or she utters and *imitating* what may well be for him or her utterly meaningless sounds.

The same point is made by Quine in his many discussions of the use/mention distinction, among them the following:

> From the standpoint of logical analysis, each whole quotation must be regarded as a single word or sign, whose parts count for no more than serifs or syllables. A quotation is not a description but a hieroglyph: it designates its object not by describing it in terms of other objects, but by picturing it. *The meaning of the whole does not depend upon the meanings of the constituent words.* (Quine 1965:26, emphasis added)

Quine could easily have been describing double articulation in this passage. That the internal structure of a quotation is not in itself significant, since it is merely the accurate imitation of the original which counts, is also an implicit insight of all programming languages like Pascal and LISP which distinguish fixed strings (in quotes) from concatenations of *interpretable* and manipulable symbols.

10.2.2. Double Articulation in Clichés

The insight that repetition drains meaning from words, converting them into phonemes, is also implicit in the already noted use by many authors of hyphens to indicate *cliché phrases* which are reduced to the status of words (whose component words are thereby reduced to the status of Quine's "serifs or syllables" or phonemes):

> "Nuts with that *ruining-me-in-this-town* stuff" I said. (Schulberg [1941] 1971:245)

> Show business is a *dog-eat-dog* world. No, it's worse. It's a *dog-doesn't-return-the-other-dog's-phone-calls* world. (From the film *Crimes and Misdemeanors*, cited in *People*, September 1989)

But the essence of this orthographic insight is that all direct quotation (whether of a single utterance of fresh talk or of the oft-repeated cliché) is an act of *repetition*. It differs profoundly from the act of indirect quotation, which is essentially an intelligent act of *translation*, shifting from one code to another a message whose meaning is preserved. (A parrot may directly quote an utterance in an unkown language, but indirect quotation is beyond its powers.)

It is notable that the rather recherché practice of rendering clichés with hyphens parallels a more widespread practice encountered in written representations of the act of "spelling out"—one spells "lawyers" L-A-W-Y-E-R-S. To spell out a word, of course, is to represent it in its phonological articulation; again, the components between the hyphens are understood to be themselves meaningless. And what makes them meaningless (I contend) is that they, like the components of a cliché, have been repeated.

10.2.3. *Repetition within the Speech Act Itself*

There is clearly a pragmatic difference between repetition of a gesture within the same speech act (by a single speaker) and repetition of the speech act itself (by many people over time). Our discussion focuses on the second, the only one which is related to questions of diachrony. Still, there are both formal and semantic-pragmatic parallels between these kinds of repetition. Consider left-dislocation and sarcastic assent as exemplified by:

> The one-l lama, he's a priest.
> Yeah, yeah.

We note that in each case, there is a formal reduction in the second repetition of the same token. In the case of left-dislocation, the full noun phrase is replaced by a short and unstressed anaphor. In the case of sarcastic repetition, the second (and later) tokens of the denigrated message are uttered at a lower pitch and volume than the first.

10.3. Linguistic Emancipation as Codification

Codification involves such fundamental transformations as the bifurcation of objects into signs. Understandably, I have emphasized this aspect of the process, since it can without pomposity (I hope) be identified with the origin of language. But there are other less grandiloquent and less controversial aspects of the same process which are totally familiar.

10.3.1. *Phonologization*

In the sound articulation of language, *phonologization* is a well-understood example of codification. Originally automatic or random fluctuations become phonologized (that is, both distinctive and uniform) when they are *emancipated* from their conditioning environments.

   Because of some imprecision in their formulation, some of the classic discussions of phonologization leave the erroneous impression that the process is *caused* by the loss of the original conditioning environment. Thus a propos the phonologization of umlaut in Middle High German, Twaddell ([1938] 1957:87) states that "the phonetic differences are phonologized . . . when the environmental differentiation is eliminated." Jakobson ([1931] 1972:136) says that "the loss of the reduced vowels (weak 'jers') in the Slavic languages brought about a correlation of phonologization for consonants." A moment's reflection will show that the loss of the conditioning environment does not cause phonologization; it only demonstrates that phonologization has indeed occurred. Consider Twaddell's schematization of Old High German umlaut, for example, where "U" represents the original phoneme /u/, with allophones [u] and [y], "x" represents a consonant (cluster) over which the umlaut could occur, and "xx" represents a cluster over which the umlaut was inhibited. In OHG, the umlaut rule (U → y/ —xi) yielded the phonetic results of "stage 1," while in MHG, after the operation of a merger (a,i → ə), "we have" the phonetic results of "stage 2":

Inherited Form	Stage 1	Stage 2
Uxi	yxi	yxə
Uxxi	uxxi	uxxə
Uxa	uxa	uxxə

The question is how do "we have" the latter results? Obviously not by virtue of the umlaut rule, which by stage 2 has nothing to apply to. The inescapable conclusion is that already in stage 1, *before the conditioning environment has disappeared*, the contrast [u]≠[y] has been established as something that can be maintained. Emancipation from the phonetic stimulus precedes loss of the stimulus itself.

10.3.2. From Connotation to Denotation

In discussions of "cognitive" versus "emotive" meaning, the primacy of the former is generally agreed upon (cf. Lyons 1968:449). It is denotation, not connotation, which is the business of the grammarian (just as culture, not individual personality, is the business of the anthropologist). But ontologically, in the documented cases of ritualization, it seems to be connotation which came first. We might say that *denotation is emancipated connotation*.

Schematically: a symptomatic gesture or fidget (let us say a cry of pain like [aaaa]) accompanies a psychological state. That is, originally the gesture *co-occurs with* the state. It becomes a signal which *connotes* that state once it is recognized and responded to by some other animal. Finally, it becomes a sign (say the English word "ouch") which *denotes* the state only once it is emancipated both from the stimulus which produced it originally and from the motivated state of which it served as a signal. Denotation, like ritualization, occurs in consequence of this same process of emancipation. Recall the story of the dancing fly. Closer to home, recall Pavlov's dogs. Originally the buzzer connoted food; it came to denote food when the dogs drooled even in the absence of the referent. For somebody (not the dogs) at this point, the buzzer had achieved the design feature of displacement.

In fact, I maintain, denotation is what emancipates language from its bondage to the concrete, *to the point where it becomes metalinguistic in the sense made famous by Russell* (1940). In his drive to purge language of paradoxes like the Cretan liar, Russell tried to design an artificial "object language" from which all metalinguistic words like "true," "false," and "not" are excluded. I have already discussed in chapter 7 the fallacy involved here in my attack on the idea of "das Ding an sich," but it deserves repetition here: "If 'p' is a sentence of the primary language, 'not-p' is a sentence of the secondary language. *It is easy to fall into confusion, since 'p,' without verbal alteration, may express a sentence only possible in the secondary language*" (1940:61; emphasis added). That indiscernible sentence of the secondary metalanguage is "'p'

is true." The question arises how can we distinguish between the primary assertion *p*, "which has no antithesis" and belongs to the object language, and
the indiscernible secondary metalinguistic assertion whose antithesis "'p' is
false" belongs to the metalanguage? (The question, of course, is exactly reminiscent of the question posed by Danto: How can we distinguish between an
ordinary object and an indiscernible artwork?)

Russell followed Pavlov in arguing that the meaning of a primary word is
learned by association, so that a dog may be said to have learned it when it
"produces behavior similar to that which the sight or smell of a dinner out of
reach would produce" (ibid.:64). So far, we are following the classical model
of denotation as emancipated connotation: the bell or the word connotes food
and the dog drools at the smell of the food or at the sound of the sign, which
co-occurs with it. Remove the food, and the dog drools at the sound of the sign,
which now denotes an absent referent. *But "denotes" for whom?* The above
model does not distinguish between the point of view of the dog and that of
the relatively ominiscient experimenter. Russell, crucially, did (and in the process, as I have argued, unwittingly demolished the very possibility of an object
language): "If you excite a dog by saying 'rats!' when there are no rats [simply
put, if you are lying to the dog] your speech belongs to language of a higher
order, since it is not caused by rats, but the dog's understanding of it belongs
to the object language" (ibid.:65). So for the dog, to "understand the object
language" is to continue—Charlie Brown–like—to be deluded. It is to respond
with an involuntary response to a stimulus of whose emancipation from its
referent the dog is unaware. Any response other than a reflex knee-jerk reaction is therefore already metalinguistic:

> Whenever you doubt or reject what you are told, your hearing does not belong to
> the object language; for in such a case, you are *lingering on the words*, whereas
> in the object language the words are transparent . . . and are . . . identical with the
> effects that would result from the sensible presence of what they designate.
> (ibid.:66)

It is clear that for Russell denotation is the same thing as displacement. But
language which exhibits this fundamental design feature is already metalinguistic, and the object language in Russell's terms becomes an impossible fantasy
once language consisting of conventional denotative signs exists at all.

That emancipation from its referent or "abstractness" is a crucial and defining property of any linguistic sign is wittily illustrated in an essay by Umberto
Eco on mirrors. A reflection, he argues, cannot be a sign, for all of its iconicity,
because it is never emancipated from the stimulus which produces it. Since a
mirror can never show anything other than what is in front of it, a reflection
can never draw attention to itself. Not only can a reflection never attain the
immortality of a Brillo box, but also it is incapable of providing significance
through contrast with the reality it imitates. I owe to Lisa Miller (personal communication), the confirmatory counterexample: a reflection would be meaningful if vampires existed and had the miraculous property attributed to them
of not having reflections. The "mirror code" would then have two contrasting

signs, [+vampire] or [−vampire], and would exist only by virtue of the partial emancipation which vampires could afford it.

10.3.3. *Ritualization of Suprasegmental Signs*

10.3.3.1. STRESS

Consider the familiar contrast between *black bird* and *blackbird*. The latter, clearly a ritualized form (note that the incorporated morpheme *black-* has undergone the semantic bleaching characteristic of grammaticalized forms), is treated for stress purposes as a single word. The former is treated as two. It is misleadingly reductionist to characterize the difference as one between compound stress (stress on the first syllable) and nuclear stress (stress on the last syllable). The essential difference is between a single word whose predictable grammaticalized ictus is automatically on the first syllable and a string of two words either one of which may be stressed at the will of the speaker.

10.3.3.2. DIGITIZATION: THE RITUALIZATION OF INTONATION

A frequently observed property of ritual or play activity is its stylization: the originally instrumental act when ritualized is rhythmically repeated or its component parts exaggerated (Morris 1957; Blest 1963:110; Loizos 1966:7; Miller 1973:89; Moore & Myerhoff 1977:7). How do analogs look in human language?

Uncoded natural signs (or symptoms) of anger, boredom, disgust, or excitement are universal (cf. Fonagy 1962, 1971a, 1971b, 1971c for some pioneering studies), but they are not ritualized. Sebeok (1962:431) suggests that they are "codified" in analog terms, while other "rational" aspects of existence are codified in digital terms. What Jakobson called the *ars obligatoria* of grammar (ritual or codification in our sense) begins formally, as we all seem to agree, with quantization or digitization. Digitization is perhaps necessary for intersubjectivity and replicability; it may be what distinguishes movable type from personal handwriting or linguistic from paralinguistic verbal behavior or, more generally, what distinguishes culture from personality. It is certainly one of the features which distinguishes ritual from spontaneous instrumental behavior. A number of ethologists have commented on the feature of *typical intensity*, the tendency for a ritual gesture to remain constant irrespective of the force (or even the presence) of the stimulus which produced it: "Postures or movements which have a typical intensity are more easily recognized *but correspondingly convey less information about the signaller's motivational state*" (Manning 1967:138). The locus classicus is Morris (1957).

Conceptually, the ritualization of such symptoms occurs when the "exuded expressions" over which the speaker has no control (presentations) are replaced by re-presentations, "standardized vocal comments on circumstances that are not, or no longer, beyond emotional or physical control" (Goffman 1983:100, 107). It occurs, in other words, where the universal symptomatic expression of pain, for example, is replaced by language-specific digitized coded signs like "ouch." Language and ritual begin where etiquette begins, at the point where it becomes possible for the speaker to lie, for what is lying but a kind of emancipation from the external world? In associating ritual with lying, I take issue with Gombrich (1966:398), who declares that "animals lack that distinctively human achievement, the lie." Insofar as animal communication through ritualization of gestures with a typical intensity is possible, animals communicate something other than the way they feel. This is "lying" at a more fundamental and less controversial level than the evidence for conscious acts of deception among animals (cf. Cheney & Seyfarth 1991) or the even more tenuous anecdotal evidence that some animals respond angrily to being lied to (cf. Watzlawick 1977:163): "A sign of adulthood is the 'insincerity' of originally autonomous actions. A smile is no longer the betrayal of a feeling but a purposive act intended to please. The hollow laugh and the crocodile tear are instinctive gestures that have become part of etiquette" (Bolinger 1975:20). *Mutatis mutandis*, surely the same could be said of the courtship ritual of the male balloon fly.

As a theory of language origins, the historical change from the personal involuntary "aaaaargh" to the codified "ouch" seems suspect, if only because involuntary expressions are controlled by different portions of the brain than human language. Citing a recent dissertation, Bolinger suggests that

> whereas language and tool using are related in the brain, language and primitive cries are not. In man, an electrical stimulus on the cortex—the region of highest organization—will cause vocalization; in animals the stimulus generally has to be applied below the cortex. This makes it highly unlikely that there was any direct transition from emotional noises to propositional language. (Bolinger 1975:315 citing van Lancker 1974:chap. 5, p. 5).

Bolinger's hesitation may have been overcautious. Throughout the animal kingdom, ritualization is often marked precisely by "the transfer of the signal function from one set of effectors to another" (Blest 1963:110–1 enumerates some spectacular examples). More to the point, even higher-level and demonstrably recent functions such as *reading* in humans take place in different brain locations, depending on whether the act is one of processing unfamiliar letter strings or the ritualized one of recognizing familiar vocabulary (Sieroff & Posner 1988; Sieroff, Polatsek, & Posner 1988; Posner et al. 1989, all cited in Givon, Gernsbacher, & Yang 1990) Finally, there is an enormous body of evidence that lateralization assigns and reassigns different linguistic functions to different portions of the brain during individual development. Among adults, "aphasics with lesions in the left hemisphere who have trouble with speech in general may use ritualized politeness formulas, like the related hesitation forms, non-referential introducers, and conventionalized interjections, with impressive fluency" (Ferguson 1981:22–3).

Almost completely lacking a paleontology of language, as of most other behavior, we should treat comparative synchronic observations of this sort as some of the best data we can build our speculations on. But not the only data. With insignificant exceptions like "ouch" and "boo hoo," we cannot observe how words developed out of nonwords; however far back we go, it seems that all of our etymologies of words trace back to nothing but other older words. But we may be able to observe the genesis of codification in the stereotyping of intonation, which, as it has often been noted, lies at the border between paralinguistic and linguistic behavior. Although there is much stereotyping (codification) in this realm, it is inherently less digitally coded than morphosyntax, more inherently analogic and iconic (cf. Bolinger 1985), and more subject to personal variation.

The quintessentially ritualized or stereotyped intonation is the array of singsong chants (cf. Liberman's [M]HL in English [1979]), which signal clichés (cf. Ladd 1978a, b; Fonagy et al. 1983). For reasons we will get to in a moment, the ritual in the case of (M)HL is something uttered playfully or whose informative meaning is not attended to.

A good locus of singsong intonation cross-linguistically is in the self-conscious repetition of phrases that are felt to be clichés. Among these are the following:

a) stale proverbs which the speaker feels to be irrelevant or dull;
b) clichés of greeting and so forth (cf. Fonagy et al. 1983);
c) rote speeches of instruction, greeting, and so forth, uttered by those whose sad business it is to deliver them *repeatedly* (auctioneers, tour guides, bus drivers, receptionists, telephone operators, clerks, flight attendants)—mostly, as it happens, women (cf. Justice 1985 and Kuiper & Haggo 1984).

It also occurs (relatively infrequently but with impeccable semantic motivation) in utterances which are intended playfully or sarcastically. Examples of clichés so uttered with the (L)HM melody with which most of us are highly familiar include "too bad," "never mind," "thank you," "sorr-eee," or "oh boy" uttered to the tune of "ho-hum" (Bolinger 1986:230) or "bo-ring."

The (L)HM is not the only ritualized or stylized intonation in English, of course. Another is LH, which is similarly ironic when used for stylized expressions of congratulation:

L	H
Waita go,	dad
Good	job
Nice	going

What is most remarkable about singsong intonation not only in these examples but also in a variety of languages where I have observed it is that it correlates with much the same range of (meta-) messages. One of these is what Bolinger (1986:231) calls the metamessage that "everybody knows." Another is predictability or boredom, the metamessage "here we go again" (cf. Ladd 1978b:520; Kuiper & Haggo 1984:216), which for Berger and Luckmann characterizes every traditional behavior (1966:53, 57). Another is playfulness or sarcasm, the metamessage "I don't mean this" or "this is play" (cf. Bateson 1956; Fonagy et al. 1983:157, 178). It is playfulness, of course, which is signaled by the homicidal wife in *Married to the Mob*. Why is singsong never used to code anger, grief, shame, or ecstasy (to cite some paralinguistic and personal messages)? Why is it never used to code interrogation (to cite only the most impeccably "grammatical" message)?

Repetition alone is not enough to explain this restriction; people have been expressing emotions and asking questions forever. But *self-conscious and intentional* repetition is something else. What is common to each of the meta-messages which singsong intonation can be used to code is precisely this:

"I am repeating."
"I quote."
(That is why I am bored, insincere, playful.)

Perhaps singsong is one means of marking an oft-repeated cliché. But another may be the mimicry of the act of repetition itself. I suggest that a possible reason for the sarcastic flavor of repeated "yeah, yeah" is that speakers who repeat such expressions are themselves *mimicking the process* whereby these words, like any others, have lost their original meanings through repetition by other speakers. It is notable that sarcastic repetitions are uttered on a series of downstepped tones, mimicking a fading of intensity over time.

10.3.4. Analogy as Routinization

Max Weber used "routinization" to describe the transfer of the legitimation of government from charismatic leaders to a hereditary ruling class or a bureaucracy. I use it to signify the extension of a form or other behavior *beyond the area where it was originally motivated by external pressures*. It subsumes both analogy and the creation of grammatical categories.

All cases of grammatical analogy are the result of routinization: paradigm coherence *(*honos > honor)* (the term, if not the example, from Kiparsky 1972), hypercorrection *(to Jennifer and me > to Jennifer and I)* (Labov 1972b), drift *(whom > who)* (Sapir 1921), analogical leveling (the loss of minority patterns for the plural: *scipu > ship-s*; the loss of the distinction between the past tense and the perfect participle as formerly strong verbs join the weak majority: *have gone > have went*). In all cases, a pattern is extended to structures which did not inherit it.

All grammatical categories are routinized. If a category is overt, obligatory, and grammatical, I contend (in the company of linguists in general) that it is arbitrary at least to some extent, which is to say that a purely notional definition for any grammatical category is never entirely satisfactory. The literature on this assumption, which underlies every variation of every discussion of the linguistic relativity hypothesis known to me, is far too extensive to summarize here. Wierzbicka (1985) provides a survey of some of the expressions of the prevailing conventional wisdom (which I endorse) and a heroic attempt at a refutation, using one particularly arbitrary-seeming grammatical category, noun number, as her demonstration example.

Countless examples will serve to illustrate my point that ritualization *pace* Wierzbicka tends to create purely formal categories. I will confine myself to citing three before returning to Wierzbicka's study in particular.

For example, the category *subject* in English is a formally marked (sentence-initial, nominative, conditioning verb agreement) category which should represent the intersection of the semantically motivated agent and the pragmatically motivated topic. There is no recorded stage of English where this was entirely true (for example, weather verbs like "rain" have always been provided with dummy subjects even in Old English), but it was once more true at least than it is today. The category *subject* has been extended in the last 700 years to include the experiencer of psychological and physical states: *methinks > I think* (similar are "think," "long [for]," "hunger," "thirst," "happen," "repent," "wonder," "like," and a host of others [cf. Visser 1984:29–35]). With each expansion of the extension of a grammatical form, however motivated, the intension of the form becomes diluted. However, when the extension includes *experiencers* on top of *agents*, as in this case, the category totally loses semantic integrity and becomes a purely ritualized construct.

In some cases, the routinized category becomes semantically counterintuitive. Hyman (1979:79) discusses the ritualization of the category *focus* in Aghem, a Bantu language. Focus corresponds in principle to new and exciting information, which is typically marked in English by extra amplitude:

—What should I eat?
—Eat RICE!

Through routinization all imperatives are focused in Aghem, which seems reasonable enough in general but sometimes leads to counterintuitive patterns in Aghem like:

—What should I eat?
—EAT rice!

There exists in Hua, a Papuan language of New Guinea, a virtually meaningless suffix, the so-called connective particle *-mo*, the distribution of which can be syntactically specified as follows (cf. Haiman 1977): the suffix occurs on all "potential topics," that is, it occurs only on constituents which are immediately but not exhaustively dominated by the S-node. Hua is a verb-final language without a VP node. The first stricture therefore essentially eliminates *X-mo*, where X is any constituent which acts as a modifier of a noun (true adjectives, relative clauses, nouns in the genitive case, nouns qualifying other nouns) or any constituent which acts as the modifier of a verb (same-subject medial verbs which act as manner adverbs). The second eliminates *X-mo*, where X is any constituent which is capable of acting as a complete utterance by itself (finite "final" verbs and nouns in the vocative "case"). The particle thus occurs freely on noun phrases in all other cases and on all subordinate clauses other than relative clauses, notably nonfinal coordinate clauses in compound sentences and conditionals. Since not all constituents marked by the suffix are topics (there is in fact a distinct topic suffix *-ve*), the best notional nomenclature available is that of "potential" topic.

Comparative evidence makes it clear, however, that *-mo* almost certainly originated as a true topic marker. In a number of closely related languages like Alekano, the cognate etymon is glossed as the definite article (cf. Haiman 1991:73), while in other closely related languages like Gimi, the etymon cognate with *-ve* has the same distribution as Hua *-mo* (ibid.). Routinization has drained meaning from *-ve* in Gimi, as it has drained motivation from *-mo* in Hua.

Finally, I should point out that Wierzbicka's own discussion of the mass/count distinction is a wonderful example of creeping double articulation through extension. Although in every case she discusses, the mass/count noun distinction is motivated and upheld, every distinction she makes is context-specific. Peas are plural while rice is singular *because the individual particles of the former are larger.* On the other hand, garlic is singular while olives are plural *because the latter are eaten individually.* As foodstuffs, cabbage is singular while brussels sprouts are plural *because one can see several brussels sprouts but not several cabbages on one's plate.* Furniture and cutlery are singular *because they represent collections of heterogeneous objects.* Leftovers and groceries are plural, although they also represent heterogeneous collections, *"because some of them may not be separate things"* (Wierzbicka 1985:340). In the end, a two-way morphological distinction is burdened with so many semantic distinctions that from any objective standpoint, it comes to seem quite arbitrary. To be burdened with too many conflicting systems comes to the same thing as to be unsystematic (Bolinger 1975:110) or:

> Friendship, like love, is but a name
> Unless to one you stint the flame. (John Gay, *The Hare and Many Friends*)

Having been convinced by each of her arguments, I find myself once I am "out on the street again" thinking that the distinction between wheat and oats is as arbitrary as Bloomfield ever said it was.

There is perhaps a systematic distinction to be noted here between overt ritualized categories like those we have just dealt with and the covert categories which are more subject to conscious manipulation and part of the pragmatic mode. The latter invariably motivated or at least much more regularly motivated than the frozen forms of the grammar. Russian offers a particularly clear demonstration of the distinction in the realm of gender (cf. Comrie 1979).

Formally, nouns belong to three declension types:

1. a) masculine nouns in a final consonant, like *stakan* "glass" and *voron* "crow"
   b) neuter nouns in final *-o* or *-e*, like *boloto* "swamp"
2.   feminine nouns in final *-a*, like *ulitsa* "street" or *zhenshchina* "woman"
3.   nouns of mixed grammatical gender which end in a final palatalized consonant, like *dver'* "door" and *mat'* "mother"

As with other languages, there is no particularly striking coincidence between grammatical and natural gender. However, in the singular and in the plural number, nouns like *voron* "crow" have the accusative identical with the genitive case, while nouns like *stakan* "glass" have their accusative identical with the nominative. And in the plural number only, nouns like *zhenshchina* "woman" and *mat'* "mother" have their accusative identical with the genitive, while nouns like *ulitsa* "street" and *dver'* "door" have the accusative identical with the nominative. Cross-cutting the formal category of grammatical gender is a covert category of animacy. Inanimate nouns will tend to make the accusative identical with the nominative, while animate nouns will tend to make the accusative like the genitive. And the animacy, unlike the grammatical genders, is real and tends to correspond to facts in the speaker's perception of the world.

At a deeper level, however, any category whatsoever cannot help but admit some arbitrariness. This is because no two things are ever entirely alike. Once a label appropriate for one thing is extended to apply to any other thing, a choice has been made to emphasize some features of the things that are treated alike and to overlook other features that aren't. And this choice is always an arbitrary one, leading in the end to greater or lesser semantic opacity.

This point is implicit in a recent discussion of one such allegedly "transparent" set of categories, those that are marked by noun classifiers in the Mayan language Jacaltec (Craig 1986). Noun classifiers, like gender markers, are notoriously formal in general, but the twenty-four classes of the classifier system of Jacaltec, Craig argues, are exceptionally transparent because the system is *so incomplete* (ibid.:266). First, only concrete nouns (and not even all of those) are classified. Second, the system is blatantly nonproductive, in fact, ossified; no extensions have occurred to accommodate new artifacts such as beer, soft drinks, or things made of plastic. Finally, no semantic extensions seem to have occurred even traditionally in twenty-two of the twenty-four classes, and the extensions that have been admitted in the remaining two seem to be minimal: the *corn* classifier has been extended to include "wheat" (which is therefore not classed with other plants, for which a separate *plant* classifier exists), and the *rock* classifier has been extended to include "ice" (which is therefore not classed with *water*) (ibid.:275). The moral of Craig's discussion is that semantic transparency or a coherent Gesamtbedeutung *is* possible for a category but only if no generalization by extension occurs. Since the raison d'être for a category is precisely to generalize, this is to say that only freakish categories can be purely semantically motivated.

Motivation is not always semantic or pragmatic. It may be entirely syntactic. But this motivation may also become obscured through routinization. All cases where any grammatical structure or process has been generalized or extended beyond its functional (possibly merely syntactic) necessity are then also examples of routinization. A standard example (cf. Comrie 1983) is the paradigm of reflexive pronouns. To avoid ambiguity, they are needed in the third person, and in some languages, like Latin, French, and German, that is the only place where a distinctive reflexive pronoun exists. They are not needed in the first and second persons ("I saw me," after all, is unambiguous), but in English, a full reflexive paradigm exists (which, as we have seen, has been pressed into service to make some novel distinctions). In Old High German and Medieval French, the presence of personal pronoun subjects was motivated by a word-order rule: they occurred before an otherwise initial verb in order to avoid *V/1 and to ensure the satisfaction of the target structure V/2 (Thurneysen 1892; Eggenberger 1961). This motivation is still transparent in one modern Germanic language, Icelandic (Haiman 1974). In modern French and German, as in all Germanic languages with the exception of Icelandic, personal pronoun subjects now occur independently of this requirement, and the correlation between the retention of the personal pronoun and word order has become obscured.

The cultural analogy to grammatical routinization in any and all of these cases is any traditional ritual, the ancestor of which may have had a purely instrumental function but which is now engaged in without actual physical impetus or need. The pilgrims' first Thanksgiving dinner may have been very timely and appropriate, but for most of us today, Thanksgiving dinner will occur at the usual date and time whether or not anyone feels thankful, remembers to feel thankful, or even feels particularly hungry. It evokes the reaction "here we go again." The six o'clock news is a comparable ritual which happens every night (and lasts exactly the same thirty minutes) whether there's anything newsworthy going on in the world or not.

Emancipation from actual context renders the ritualized form more autonomous but also more apparently useless and therefore opaque both to its participants and to outside observers. The only explanation they can offer for its present form, often, is tradition. One component of the "actual context" to which particular attention should be drawn is the *original producers who created the ritual in the first place.* However frozen or stylized a manner of behavior, it remains "transparent" to its originators in a way that it will never be to participants who were not present at its creation. For these latter arrivals, the ritual or institution seems both given and opaque. As Berger and Luckmann put it in their classic discussion of reification, the original participants may say "here we go again," but their children (also) will say "this is how it's done" and will eventually find this explanation entirely sufficient (1966:58–9). They go on to say that "only with the transmission of *the social world* to a new generation (that is, internalization as effectuated by socialization) . . . can one properly speak of a social world [at all]" (ibid.:61). That is, as long as action is transparently motivated, we are not dealing with culture or the social world at all. But once the institutions of the social world are no longer transparent, they require legitimation in the form of myths and appeals to the sanctity of tradition.

What is most striking about this passage is that if we substitute "language" for "the social world" it perfectly describes the specific institution of a language, in particular, the evolution of a pidgin into a creole, with the rules of an autonomous reified grammar performing the "legitimation of the status quo." It does not take an enormous feat of extrapolation to go back one giant step and see in this same process the evolution of symptomatic cries into languages of the human sort.

10.3.5. Ritual Language

If language is action emancipated from an instrumental function, ritual language is language which has been emancipated from meaning. Its formal properties and development are both accessible and of the highest interest.

The fundamental insight of Goffman's classic *Frame Analysis* (1974) is not that codes and contexts determine our perception of "objective reality"—this is already familiar to linguists from Sapir and Whorf and to everybody else from the poets. Rather, it is the recognition that mutually exclusive languages or personal attitudes are not the only codes there are. Quite the contrary; in any situation, at the disposal of any person, there are simultaneously shimmering an indefinite number of overlapping, superimposed, alternative codes. And at the very heart of Goffman's discussion lies the important idea that any given event may be viewed through what he calls "successive laminations" or *codes within codes*. Ritualization may be thought of, in terms of this metaphor, as a repeated process of lamination or emancipation from brute reality.

As human acts (like expressive cries of rage and pain) become emancipated from the laws of nature, they become what Goffman calls stereotyped "willed doings"—cultural acts. As cultural acts become in their turn liberated from functional or instrumental purposes, they become "symbolic" or magical communicative gestures—of these, the most important are the gestures which comprise spoken language, and the most instrumental function of language is to make others do one's bidding. As language becomes liberated from its instrumental (magical) function, it becomes referential. As referential language becomes liberated from even this abstract communicative function of imparting referential meaning, it becomes ritual (either ludic or phatic). Grammaticalized as phatic communication or as ritual, language and culture reach their highest degree of playfulness, abstraction, or liberation from the natural world of brute reality (cf. Callan 1970; Tambiah 1968:179; Koenig 1970:64; Jurgens & Ploog 1974:34; Wheelock 1982:57). A marvelously compact demonstration of the transformation of the originally expressive language of obscenity into purely ritual or phatic communication is afforded by the interchange between Dilbert and the mechanic shown in figure 10.1.

How do these "successive laminations," this emancipation, this stereotyping occur in ritualized behavior? Margaret Mead (1973:90) suggests (to my mind, correctly) that "it is of the essence of ritual that those who participate in it have participated before." One may, of course, participate in a ritual for the first time. But it *is* essential that those who participate are following a model that has been established perhaps by others who *have* participated before—if not in that exact ritual, then in others that are similar. (This is true even of

Figure 10.1. Dilbert, by Scott Adams. (Reprinted with permission of United Feature Syndicate, Inc.)

invented rituals or rituals of "junction" [Moore & Myerhoff 1977:7] which celebrate unique events. It is arguably even true of unprecedented acts whose onlookers spontaneously realize that "something sacred has happened here," their recognition depending largely on whether they have rehearsed the ritual in their heads.)

Gombrich (1966:399) makes a similar point about the essentially repetitive nature of ritual but in a rather less respectful way which suggests the kinship between ritual and clichés: "It may have been liberating for Jackson Pollock to break all bonds and pour his paint on the canvas, but once everybody does it, it becomes a ritual in the modern sense of the term, a mere trick that can be learned and gone through without emotion."

So, too, does Chomsky, who satisfyingly echoes both Gombrich and Karl Marx in his description of another repetition: "The conventional 'God that failed' transition from Leninist enthusiasms to service to a state capitalism can, I believe, be explained in substantial measure. . . . Though there were authentic elements in the early stages, it has long since degenerated to ritualistic farce" (Chomsky 1989a:46).

That is, acts not only are *invested with* meaning through repetition but also may be *emancipated from* (among other things) meaning by the same process. Ritual is born (at least in part) through repetition. Gombrich's example is particularly telling insofar as Pollock and others were, according to Danto (1981), paragons of what I would now call "Zen painting"; rather than being *about* something, their paintings *were simply paint as paint*. Nothing escapes ritualization, not even the blatant thing-in-itself.

In the same way, ritual language is born from repetition of ordinary language. If ritual language develops from ordinary language through repetition of the latter, we can account for an unremarkable but really puzzling fact: ritual language does (often) resemble ordinary language (cf. Wheelock 1982:60, who remarks that this is "obvious"). The Lord's Prayer, for example, is made up of phrases in English that can be understood by speakers of English and translated into phrases of any other language. Previous investigators have understandably chosen to emphasize ways in which ritual speech is keyed to be understood as distinct from ordinary language, but the first fact which requires explanation is that ritual language in cases of this sort *is* recognizably pretty much the same as the "real life" language from which it so clearly stands apart. (So, too, ethologists like Tinbergen have typically succeeded in showing how ritualized communicative behavior can be recognized as deriving from similar autochthonous noncommunicative behavior.) In saying that ritualized language comes from repeated ordinary language, we have accounted for this (very familiar) similarity. Otherwise, this resemblance, which we can and should dismiss as both obvious and banal, would have to be treated as an intriguing and inexplicable coincidence.

Even more striking than the similarity between ritual and everyday language are some of the recurrent differences between them, admirably summarized in DuBois (1986). Two of the distinctive features of ritual or formulaic language which DuBois enumerates are already familiar from our earlier discussion of superficially unrelated speech genres. Among them are *stylized intonation* (for example, Quiche "stylized intonation contour"; Seneca "short staccato phrases with a final rising tone, followed by a closing phrase with a fixed falling melody"; Cuna "chanted intonation"; Kiriwina "singsong") and what DuBois calls *gestalt form* (for example, Kiriwinan magicians as a rule cannot repeat spells slowly or piecemeal; Mojave informants apparently experience great difficulty in slowing down the sequence of memorized texts). The latter we recognize as characteristic even of the orthography of the oft-repeated cliché.

Both Chafe (1981) and Kay (1977) point out that ritual language shares many properties with written language, among them decontextualization and stylization. While fully acknowledging the correctness of their observations, I will not devote any time to them since the basis of the similarity, from our present standpoint, is fortuitous. Ritual language is polished and stylized through repetition, but written language achieves the same properties through the fact that the writer may stop and ponder and revise in the course of writing only once. (This last sentence, for example, took me about two minutes to write; I spent a conversationally unforgivable length of time staring off into space in composing it.)

10.4. Emancipation Produces Arbitrariness

Are the signs of language arbitrary or motivated? Is knowledge of language distinct from knowledge of the world? We are all familiar with the traditional answers to these related questions. Structuralist linguistics asserts both that linguistic structures are arbitrary (the "autonomy of syntax") and that semantic knowledge of language is distinct from pragmatic knowledge of the world. In recent years it has become fashionable in the functionalist school to which I belong to challenge both of these views. Many functionalists argue that the structure of language is motivated by its function and/or its meaning, and a smaller number maintain that the dictionary (which codifies linguistic meanings) is conceptually no different from the encyclopedia (a compilation of what we know about the world). In this section, I would like to propose a synthesis of the structuralist and functionalist views, a synthesis that is suggested by the concept of emancipation itself.

Closely related to the question of the origin of the linguistic sign is the question of the origin of arbitrariness, its most remarkable property and the one which most clearly distinguishes it from the expressive symptom (cf. Bolinger 1985). How do we get from motivated /aaaaaa/ to arbitrary "ouch"? Emancipation from semantic motivation, I would like to suggest, may be only one aspect of the more general process of emancipation from motivation in general.

Given the contrast between motivated symptoms like cries of pain and largely arbitrary signs like "ouch," a plausible hypothesis is that there may be parallels between language *functions* (from expressive through directive and referential to phatic or ritual) and types of language *structure* (from motivated to largely arbitrary). The more iconic a structure, the more likely it is to be at the magical and "expressive" end of what I would like to consider the functional spectrum. The more arbitrary a structure, the more likely it is to be at the phatic end of the same functional spectrum.

Language in this respect is like a compost heap: only the recently added topmost layers still reflect the original shape of the objects they derive from and thus exhibit motivation. The more "compacted" layers betray their motivation less clearly. In my view, the compacting mechanism in language is repetition.

One indication of the correctness of this horticultural simile is the banal observation that tokens of ritual or cliché language, like the formulaic signs of greeting and farewell, are most emancipated from their original meanings. Hello, Good morning, How are you?, Bonjour, Ciao, Szervusz, Zdravstvujt'e, Shalom, Good-bye, So long, Adieu, 10-4, Arivederci, Do svidanja, Güle güle and their kind are a graveyard of forgotten or neglected meanings. Even the once-expressive F-word, ritualized by automatic repetition, is no more than a marker of blue-collar bonding in the *Dilbert* interchange shown in figure 10.1.

Another related fact is the inverse correlation between formulaicity and size, culminating in the phenomenon of "double" articulation itself: words have meanings; grammatical morphemes are semantically bleached; phonemes are meaningless. The inverse correlation between frequency and meaningfulness in this case is patent (cf. Zipf 1935 and his successors). One can propose (almost as a matter of definition) that a structure is ritualized to the extent that its vestigial meaning (if any) is not congruent with its (emancipated) use.

Given a structure:	Its meaning is probably:	As its probable function passes from:
X	motivated	expressive
		directive
	↓	
		referential
		ludic
	arbitrary	phatic
	↓	
	totally lost	submorphemic

Examples are legion. "How are you?" said by a doctor to a patient is a genuine question and as such is motivated by its directive function. Said by the same doctor or anyone else as a conventional greeting, it is purely phatic and so little a question that it requires no answer but the reciprocal question repeated back. "Why are we here?" as a genuine expression of anguish or wonder carries the intonational indices of emotion. The garden-variety question "What time is it?" is directive but is still informed by the questioner's genuine desire to know. The catechist's schoolmarmish repetition of any question is still directive but ritualized by repetition. The intonations of the schoolmarm's questions and phatic questions are such that an alien observer listening to their melody would probably not identify them as questions at all.

The relationship between the brute facts of the world and the institutional facts of a culture (Searle 1979) is like the relationship between the encyclopedia (ideally, a compendium of brute facts) and the dictionary (ideally, a compendium of institutional facts) (Haiman 1980a). This in turn is probably parallel to the structural relationship between motivated and arbitrary acts, between symptoms and signs. The last is paralleled by the functional relationship between expression and ritual. If so, the distinction may be neither immutable and absolute (as implied by Searle and argued by Wierzbicka) nor utterly without foundation (as argued by Quine, Langacker, and once by me).

Rather, it is possible that all cultural institutions, however variegated and arbitrary, derive ultimately from the brute facts of nature via processes of reification or emancipation in the course of repetition. Phonemes derive from phonetic facts; grammatical gender derives from natural gender; subject and predicate derive from motivated semantic and pragmatic categories like agent and topic.

Graphically, the transition between Searle's "brute facts" and "institutional facts" is one which corresponds to a number of other familiar distinctions, notably that between etic and emic categories. The following list indicates some of the oppositions which are similar to this one. I have included references to treatments of the distinction only in those cases where there are relatively few discussions known to me which deal with it directly.

Nature	*Culture*	*Reference*
brute facts	institutional facts	Searle 1979
objects	artworks	Danto 1981
[phones]	/phonemes/	Twadell 1957
symptoms	signs	Bolinger 1985
connotation	denotation	Russell 1940
encyclopedia	dictionary	Haiman 1980a
motivated structures	arbitrary structures	Givon 1979
context-conditioned behavior	emancipated behavior	Tinbergen 1952
instrumental instinctive behavior	communication	Nathanson 1992
pragmatic behavior	ritualized behavior	Givon 1979
affectations	norms	Fonagy 1956
covert categories	overt categories	Whorf 1956
natural signs	grammatical signs	Hopper 1976
expressive language	phatic language	Cosper 1983
attended processing	automated processing	Givon et al. 1990
performance	competence	Chomsky 1965
pidgins	creoles	Givon 1979
parole	langue	Hagège 1993

In each case, I suggest, the distinction is not absolute. Rather, a development is possible, but it is always unidirectional. Structures or behaviors from the left-hand "nature" column are gradually transformed into the corresponding structures or behaviors in the "culture" column. In each case, the transition is mediated by ritualization or emancipation.

That the process is gradual is best revealed by consideration of the famous typological cycle of Schlegel and Humboldt, in which not two but three stages of grammaticalization are recognized: isolating, agglutinating, and synthetic. I think more stages can be recognized: extreme synthesis is indistinguishable from suppletion, for example. The gradualness itself argues for the reality of repetition as the driving motor in this series of changes.

Clearly, the degree to which emancipation is unconstrained is crucial in a consideration of the relativity hypothesis. If emancipation is allowed to proceed unchecked, then the ritualized categories of any given language will be purely conventional and will need to bear no relationship to reality or to the categories of any other language.

It is an open question whether there are any limits in principle to the degree of emancipation which may occur. Hale's important work on "deep-surface canonical disparities" (1971a) suggested that language-acquisition data set bounds (at least in phonology) on the degree to which the language-particular institution of phonological "deep structures," however plausible, could be emancipated from the brute phonetic facts to which language learners are exposed. Haiman's claim (1974) that "targets go underground" and Lightfoot's (1979) "transparency principle" are explicitly acknowledged restatements of Hale's stricture on "deep-surface canonical disparities" in diachronic syntax. When surface structures deviate too much from deep syntactic structures, massive reanalysis and restructuring occurs to bring the deep structures into closer conformity with what people actually say.

Matters are similar in nature. While much of evolution seems to proceed on the basis of a random walk rather than Tennyson's "onwards sloping motions infinite / making for one sure goal," natural selection sets apparent limits to how much downright dysfunction the real world will tolerate in any of its creatures. That is perhaps one reason why the animals from the circus of Dr. Doolittle and the poems of Dr. Seuss do not exist in real life.

10.5. The Scope of Ritualization

Ritualization in language subsumes all of the processes enumerated in Givon's justly celebrated synthesis of the process of syntacticization (Givon 1979:chap. 5). Discourse becomes congealed as syntax; syntax as morphology; morphology becomes eroded to morphophonemics and phonology; and sounds erode to silence. Implicit in Givon's treatment is an observation which I would like to spell out now. Not only does ritualization boil things down, but also they become stylized and arbitrary in the process, and it is the smallest units which become the most stylized. In support of this contention, I submit the following observations, some of them controversial, some of them widely accepted and familiar.

10.5.1. Word Stress Is Congealed Sentence Stress

Following a suggestion of Hyman (1977), Sipple (1994) has demonstrated that in American English there is reason to regard word stress in general as a ritualized form of sentential emphasis. More specifically, she has shown that the characteristic melody of the word is a congealed and stylized version of the melody of the sentence. Irrespective of emphasis, the sentence tends to start loud, high, and short and end soft, low, and long. Irrespective of stress, the word has the same melody. (The phenomenon is known as declination.) *But emphasis perturbs sentence declination more than stress perturbs word declination.* This asymmetry is congruent with my hypothesis.

10.5.2. *Context Sensitivity Leads to Creeping Double Articulation.*

As Bolinger mentioned in passing (1975:110), to be burdened with conflicting systems is the same as to be unsystematic. I have made this point with respect to the draining away of meaning in context-sensitive but in principle singly articulated systems like that of the Library of Congress classification code. But it is also illustrated by the growth of arbitrariness whenever too many semantic dimensions are mapped onto a single formal opposition such as the distinction between mass and count nouns in English. The end result of extreme ritualization is double articulation, and it is the smallest units of language (not the largest ones) which are the most tightly organized and also the most meaningless.

10.5.3. *The Agreement Hierarchy Is a Distance Hierarchy*

Corbett's celebrated agreement hierarchy (1983; 1991:chap. 8) is a universal continuum which characterizes the likelihood of formal syntactic agreement between a controller (typically a noun) and its target (the word which agrees with it in person, gender, and number, typically an adjective or pronoun). Formal syntactic agreement is agreement with a grammatically unmotivated gender or number; it is ritualized in the sense that it is motivated not by meaning but by a language-specific convention. Ritualized agreement contrasts with semantic or motivated agreement, wherein the target agrees with its controller in natural features which reflect properties of the controller in the real world. Syntactic agreement is exemplified by the counterintuitive but grammatically impeccable agreement between article and head noun in German phrases like *das* (neuter singular) *Mädchen* "the girl." Semantic agreement is exemplified by the ungrammatical but motivated agreement between this noun and a later personal pronoun referring back to it, as in *Maedchen . . . sie* "she." Corbett proposed that the likelihood of semantic agreement increases monotonically from left to right for the following targets:

attrib. adj. → pred. adj. → rel. pron. → pers. pron.

There is a clear syntactic sense in which the attributive adjective is closer to the head noun than a predicate adjective is to a subject, and both are closer than a personal pronoun, which is not even in the same simple sentence as its antecedent:

1. [attributive adjective + noun]
2. [[noun] [copula predicate adjective]]
4. [... [noun] ...] [... [personal pronoun] ...]

But the situation with the relative pronoun seems anomalous:

3. [[noun][[relative pronoun] ...]]

The relative pronoun and the head noun belong to the same noun phrase, and thus the elements of the agreement chain (3) are presumably closer together than those of (2), the noun and the predicate adjective. Corbett adduces some further spectacular evidence, however, which makes the distance hypothesis so compelling that a slightly more abstract distance analysis for the relative pronoun becomes virtually irresistible.

He points out, first, that in some languages, like Serbo-Croatian and Chichewa, "stacked targets" of a given controller may appear in different agreement forms. When they do, the further target will show semantic agreement:

    njihov - i   stran   - e   vodje
    their   m. pl. foreign - f. pl. leaders
    "their foreign leaders" (1991:239)

Moreover, when parallel, conjoined targets appear in different agreement forms, again the further target will show semantic rather than purely formal syntactic agreement:

    Sarajlije   su igral - e   bolje i   gotovo potpuno   dominiral - i
    Sarajevans are played f. pl. better and almost completely dominated m. pl.
    terenom.
    field
    "The Sarajevans played better and almost completely dominated the field."
    (ibid.:240)

Finally, for any particular target type (say the personal pronoun), the further it is removed from its controller, the greater the likelihood of semantic agreement (ibid.).

So far from offering a counterexample to the distance hypothesis, the peculiar behavior of the relative pronoun now cries out for some analysis which will bring it into line with all of the other data which are consistent with this hypothesis. It has in fact been proposed that both restrictive and nonrestrictive relative clauses originate as clauses conjoined with the clause containing the head noun (Thompson 1971). The agreement hierarchy would seem to provide independent evidence for Thompson's analysis, for if it is adopted, then the agreement hierarchy regularly correlates with distance between the target and the controller.

10.5.4. Motivation Increases in Larger Syntactic Units

This observation, the converse of the correlation defended in the preceding paragraphs, is broadly accepted. Individual morphemes (e.g., "ten") are more semantically arbitrary than compounds (e.g., "nineteen"), compounds more arbitrary than collocations (e.g., "the more, the merrier"), collocations more than free syntactic constructions (Saussure 1966; Bolinger 1975:107; Fillmore, Kay, & O'Connor 1988). Iconic (onomatopoeic) words are infrequent. Iconic syntactic constructions are the general rule. Two further examples—the first from Hebrew, the second from Swahili—serve to show that Corbett's distance principle can be extended to more fine-grained data. In each case, arbitrariness drops off as the distance between the target and the controller increases.

An example from Hebrew is the behavior of attributive adjectives, compared with that of nouns, in the marking of gender. Typically, attributive adjectives agree in number and gender with the nouns they modify, so the following paradigms are normal:

sefer tov "a good book" (m. s. ending -ø)
sefer-im tov-im "good books" (m. pl. -im)
kit-a gdol-a "a big class" (f. s. ending -a)
kit-ot gdol-ot "big classes" (f. pl. -ot)

However, there are a large number of heteroclitic nouns in Hebrew. While the singular form signals the gender, the plural form is from the paradigm of the opposite gender. Thus, for example:

s. mil-a "word"
pl. mil-im "words" (not, as we might expect, *mil-ot)
s. luax "blackboard"
pl. lux-ot "blackboards" (not *lux-im)

The attributive adjective which agrees with these nouns, however, agrees with the actual gender of the noun, never with its irregular and misleading heteroclitic form. Thus:

mil-im tov-ot "good words" (f. pl. adjective)
lux-ot gdol-im "big blackboards" (m. pl. adjective)

Granted, grammatical gender in Hebrew (as in every language) is already arbitrary. But the further arbitrariness of heteroclisis subsists only within the nominal stem and does not extend to the noun phrase. The controller in each case is the nominal stem: the contrasting targets are gender affixes on the nominal stem versus gender affixes on the attributive adjective which is collocated with this stem.

The noun class system of Swahili provides an even more subtle example of the same principle. It is a widely acknowledged fact that "noun classes in Bantu are without semantic import" (Givon 1971:33). But Givon goes on to observe that "in their derivational use, for nominalizations, many noun classes reveal much greater correlation with various semantic features." While no Gesamtbedeutung can be provided for most gender classes of bare noun stems, the following regularities still hold:

All nouns of class 15 are "abstract infinitival nominalizers."
Most nouns of class 14 are "abstract (quality) nominalization from verbs, adjectives, or nouns."

Most nouns of classes 12 and 13 are "diminutive derivations of nouns originally belonging to other classes." (ibid.)

Schematically, the contrast is between

1. [Noun stem] + gender marker
2. [Noun stem + derivational affix] + gender marker

Arbitrariness rules where the target gender marker is directly affixed to the controlling nominal stem. Motivation picks up where the two are separated by a derivational morpheme.

All of these observations suggest that ritualization or formulaicity functions something like gravity: its effects are greatest at the closest ranges. In ordinary as in poetic language, it is within the smallest units that stylization or emancipation from extralinguistic reality (or, if you will, "emancipation from common sense") is the furthest advanced (cf. Kiparsky 1966). Part of the reason for this is that on a purely statistical level the smallest units that are the most frequently repeated (cf. Zipf 1935). But this reason is, of course, only valid if we acknowledge that ritualization no less than "erosion" (Givon 1979; Haiman 1985) is driven by repetition.

ELEVEN

Metalinguistic Ritualization

The more intricate a modern science becomes, and the better it understands itself methodologically, the more resolutely it will turn its back on the ontological problems of its own sphere of influence and eliminate them from the realm where it has achieved some insight. . . . It will then find that the world lying beyond its confines, and in particular the material basis which it is its task to understand, *its own concrete underlying reality*, lies, methodologically and in principle, *beyond its grasp*. (Lukács 1965:104)

The drive to ritualize, I maintain, is a human universal, as much as the law of gravity is a physical universal. And just as the law of gravity dictates the fall of Newton's apple, the motion of the tides, and the orbit of the comets and limits the expansion of the universe, so the principle of ritualization (emancipation, reification, routinization, decontextualization, grammaticalization) extends not only to culture and to language but also to activities which are parasitic on language, in particular to that class of discourses known as scientific theories. Most particularly, it extends to that class of scientific theories which are current in linguistics.

Provisionally, every theory may begin its career as an attempt to preserve the phenomena, but once the theory gets a good hold on life and becomes entrenched in the minds of its adherents, there ensues a drive to sacrifice the phenomena to preserve the theory. This is as true of folk theories (which are seldom recognized to be such, even by their adherents), as it is of academic theories published in the pages of technical journals. Linguistics offers examples of both.

173

11.1. The Emancipation of a Theoretical Category

> Once a tentative explanation has taken hold of our minds, information to the
> contrary may produce not corrections, but *elaborations* of the explanation. This
> means that the explanation becomes "self-sealing." (Watzlawick 1977:50)

As a quite typical example of emancipation in a *linguistic theory*, we may take
my own move in chapter 10 to make the Corbett agreement hierarchy conform
with a single principle of distance. (Recall that relative pronouns certainly
seemed to be closer to their antecedents than predicate adjectives to their subjects. This was an embarrassment to the theory that formal agreement declined
with greater distance between the controller and the target of agreement. So
appealing, however, was the generalization to which this awkward fact posed
a hindrance that I explained the awkwardness away by invoking Thompson's
theory of relative clauses.)

Another example, from phonology, is the analysis of stress and the phonological status of the vowel schwa in English, as presented in Chomsky and Halle
(1968:120). A large body of data bears witness to the nonphonological status
of schwa: it never contrasts with a "full" vowel since schwa occurs exclusively
in unstressed syllables and full vowels occur exclusively in syllables with some
degree of stress. To the elegant generalization that all unstressed vowels surface as schwa, the existence of minimal contrast pairs like *delegate* (N) and
delegate (V) poses a potentially troublesome counterexample. The solution
adopted by Chomsky and Halle, as is well known, was to claim that stress cycle
applied twice in derived nouns, reducing secondary stress of the final syllable
to tertiary. It is, however, a cold hard fact that there is no acoustic basis (pitch,
amplitude, or duration being indistinguishable) for claiming that the stress
pattern in the noun is any different from that of the verb. The stress-based analysis of the contrast between the members of pairs like *delegate* (N)/*delegate* (V)
is a classic example of sacrificing the phenomena in the cause of saving the
theory—and a very elegant theory it is.

A final example is the evolution of the inaudible syntactic category *PRO* in
Chomsky's influential theory of government and binding. The construct was
originally motivated by the need to explain certain data. Once created, it was
necessary to justify its presence in a consistent theory by demonstrating that it
differed from the other empty category (*trace*, with which it was, of course,
phonetically identical) in certain independently motivated respects. Once empirical evidence appeared which seemed to call the distinction into question,
however, it was necessary to do one of two things: either abandon the distinction and with it the theory of *PRO* or save the theory by relabeling the data.
Relabeling could take two forms: one could dismiss the evidence as "ungrammatical" or "marginal" performance data, thereby relabeling it as junk, or one
could recognize the validity of the data but create yet another category of
"inaudibilia" to conform with the theory.

As a phonetically empty category, *PRO* was indistinguishable from *trace*
but was required by the theory in order to account for Horn's observation that
want to → *wanna* contraction could not always apply. The solution: *want* +

trace + *to* did not allow contraction because of the inhibiting presence of *trace*. However, *want* + *PRO* + *to* did allow contraction because the contraction rule could not "see" *PRO* (Chomsky 1980). Hence, the famous minimal contrast pair noted by Horn could be represented as

1. a)   Who do you want + *trace* to succeed?
         (Answer: "I want Wellstone to succeed.")
   b)   Who do you want + *PRO* to succeed?
         (Answer: "I want to succeed Wellstone.")

Clearly, the *PRO versus trace* distinction as outlined here was embarrassingly ad hoc. It was necessary, given the theory of *GB*, to find some other feature which would serve to distinguish *trace* from *PRO*, and thus to motivate the latter as an entity in its own right. Such a feature was forthcoming in the notion of *government*.

A defining feature of the empty category *PRO* in *LGB*—in fact the defining distributional feature of this empty category—is that unlike trace it is "ungoverned" (e.g., it cannot occur as the subject of a tensed clause or the object of a transitive verb or a preposition).

The data which seem to call this distinction into question include examples with unspecified (PRO $_{arb}$) *objects* in English: sentences like

2.   John is eager to please —.

Parallels exist in many other European languages:

3. a)   Cela — fait un peu penser à un réseau. (French)
         "This is somewhat reminiscent of a network."
   b)   Wir müssen — darauf aufmerksam machen, dass S. (German)
         "It is necessary to draw attention to S."
   c)   Questo — induce a rivedere le proprie opinioni. (Italian)
         "This impels one to reconsider one's own opinions."
   d)   Uno — permite dormir de pie. (Spanish)
         "One (cubicle) permits one to sleep standing up."
   e)   Obshchestvo ne pomeshalo — sdelat' zlo. (Russian)
         "Society did not hinder anyone from doing evil."
   f)   Dergi Türkiye-Fransa iliskilerinin "Bahar havasï" girdiğini — bildirdi. (Turkish)
         "The journal informed — that Franco-Turkish relations had entered into a 'spring season.'"
   g)   Mr. Pickwickre emlékeztetett —. (Hungarian)
         "He reminded — of Mr. Pickwick."

To dismiss examples of this sort as "mere performance" would entail also dismissing sentences like (2) as mere performance. Given the yeoman's work done by this structure in the development of generative grammar, generative grammarians have not attempted to do this. Rather, they have treated the silent unspecified object in sentences like (2) and (3) as examples of another category, distinct from both *trace* and *PRO*: namely, *pro* (cf. Rizzi 1986; Koster 1987; Manzini & Brody 1988).

My reason for singling out *PRO* as an emancipated category here is not to attack it, for *LGB* is no more guilty of emancipation than any other theory (and I have nothing but admiration for Rizzi's careful and insightful discussion of implicit objects in Italian and English). Within the functionalist tradition, the attempt to bend the celebrated Keenan-Comrie accessibility hierarchy (1977) to accommodate phenomena in ergative languages leads to relabeling the ergative as an object case, a result which invites no less ridicule from outsiders than the generativists' creation of *pro* (cf. Cheng 1989). I am absolutely not interested in criticizing *GB* or any other theory for doing exactly what theories always do. On the contrary, I believe with Watzlawick and Lukács that any theory becomes "theoretical" precisely to the extent that it ceases to be "practical"— when it becomes emancipated from the data which provided its original functional motivation.

But I do wish to make the rather obvious point that the apparent arbitrariness of constructs such as *PRO* is not in itself an argument for the innate autonomy of syntax. It is only an argument for arbitrariness in linguistic theories, and nobody would deny that there's a lot of arbitrariness in every theory that has ever been proposed. But this arbitrariness argues, indirectly, for the universality of nothing more hardwired than emancipation or ritualization. In fact, it is worth asking whether emancipation may be entirely responsible for the most famous design feature in human language: the famous arbitrariness of the linguistic sign.

Total emancipation seems to be most attainable in the realm of human play (Miller 1973). There is no need for a game to resemble the conflicts of life or for a theory to bear any direct relationship whatever to the data it accounts for.

I should call attention at this point to one striking feature of ritual activity which is noted by ethologists and grammarians together. Ritual activity and grammatical categories are not only codified, stylized, and arbitrary but also obligatory. To say that the past tense or the plural number is a grammatical category in English—unlike the "sarcastive modality," for example—is to say (among other things) that it is almost impossible to avoid specifying tense on verbs, number on nouns.

Strangely, the more obligatory a given category, the more emancipated it seems to be even from the requirement that it have a meaning at all. Examples from grammar include the well-known arbitrariness of grammatical gender as opposed to natural gender, grammatical number as opposed to natural number, and so forth—an arbitrariness that characterizes every grammatical category in every natural language I have ever heard of: "Although attempts have been made to do away with syntax by trying to argue that everything can be accounted for in terms of either semantics or pragmatics, no such attempt strikes us as even nearly approaching success" (Comrie 1981:59–60). Hence the ultimate futility (or at least, to my mind, the limited success) of the repeated heroic efforts of some of the greatest grammarians in constructing absolutely leak-proof notional definitions for the parts of speech (Lyons 1973) or Gesamtbedeutungen for grammatical categories like case in Russian (Jakobson [1936] 1971; Wierzbicka 1980), gender in Dyirbal (Dixon 1969), or number in English (Wierzbicka 1985). Hence the deepest (though in my opinion still inadequate) justification of autonomous grammarians like Bloomfield and Chomsky for liberating syntax from semantics and doing linguistic analysis in purely formal distributional terms.

11.2. Emancipation of the Code from the Message

Having looked at what may be called the high culture of grammatical theory, I would like now to examine a case of "popular culture" in this same area: grammatical theory as shaped by naive speakers of human languages. Ritualization proceeds here also, as I hope to illustrate by considering one representative syntactic change in English.

In sentences like "A is (not) B," where "A" and "B" differ in person, gender, number, or some combination of these, the equative verb sometimes agrees not with its grammatical subject "A" but with the predicate complement "B" with which the identity of "A" is asserted or denied by the verb itself. For example, while in Modern English or French, we say "It's me," in medieval English and most other languages the structure of choice is more like the Spanish translation: *Soy yo*. The copula verb *soy* agrees with the predicate complement rather than with the subject. Révai (1995) surveys some of the formalist and functionalist theories which have been proposed to account for this intriguing irregularity. After careful consideration of a somewhat wider body of data than these theories have considered (including some cases of "agreement cop-outs" in languages like Hebrew and Surselvan where the copula verb fails to agree with either the subject or the predicate complement), he rejects all of them in favor of the following: asserted coreference is as good a basis as is presupposed coreference for triggering agreement phenomena (or coindexation) of various types.

This was once as true of English and French as it still is of other languages like Spanish, indicating that the *loss* of this principle is a possible syntactic change. Gradually, subjects acquired a monopoly over the right to trigger coindexation. Another way to look at this change is that coindexation ceased to be a speech act and became an impersonal grammatical rule.

By Révai's principle, it is the speaker himself or herself in uttering the message, rather than some autonomous rule of grammar or structural property of the inert grammatical items in the utterance, which performs the coindexation. In fact, it is not only *co*indexing but also indexing in general which is often (and still quite typically) performed by the speaker. Consider such mind-bogglingly trivial examples as "Our Father, who *art* in heaven," where it is only the speaker's use of an NP as a term of address or vocative which provides it with the feature 2sg.

Low-level grammatical machinery (and what could be lower than agreement?) is in general totally ritualized automatized behavior carried out by speakers beneath the level of conscious awareness and attention. In my opinion, this is a significant part of what grammaticization is all about.

Agreement should not be—and, in general, is not—sensitive to information in the message which it is used to convey, but in sentences like *soy yo*, it is.

And it seems to me that irregular agreement and agreement cop-outs are equally sensitive in this regard.

We are occasionally made aware of this kind of interplay between code and message in the clever manipulations of brilliant wordsmiths like Rimbaud, whose famous "Je est un autre" captures the very essence of alienation, or Frigyes Karinthy, whose "I dreamed I was two little kittens and I played with each other" both prefigures and outdoes Lakoff's "I dreamed I was Brigitte Bardot and I kissed me" (1970). But the humdrum examples discussed in Révai's article do not lend themselves to the ingenious counterparts solution that Lakoff proposed. In these sentences, where assertions of identity occur not in a dream or in the complement of a world-creating predicate, there is only one world, the world created by the act of discourse itself, which is continually being reshaped even as we speak of it. Ordinary language, then, in the mouths of ordinary speakers, comes close to Belsybabble, James Joyce's wonderful imaginary language which the devil "makes up as he goes along." The rigid distinction between message and code is so much a given in our grammatical tradition that we regard Joyce's description of Belsybabble as inspired non-sense. In fact, however, it is not only fallacious but doubly fallacious.

First, the code shapes the message. As a host of distinguished thinkers have emphasized, the code is itself a bundle of messages which, because they are presupposed, constitute our unquestioned ideology and set the limits of con-ceivable debate. In his political writings, at least, Noam Chomsky is a brilliant and utterly convincing proponent of this version of the Whorf hypothesis, which in his linguistic writings he has repudiated.

Second (and this may seem more controversial), the message may shape the code. Coindexation or agreement occurs between items about which the speaker makes assertions of identity, by virtue of those assertions alone. We take it for granted that there is a sharp and inviolable distinction between the code (con-tainer) and the messages we may transmit using the message (the thing con-tained). It is possible, however, that this apparently commonsensical and rigid separation of code and message is the outcome of exactly the familiar rituali-zation or emancipation process: the same process of grammaticalization which creates arbitrary grammatical categories creates a code distinct from the mes-sage it is used to convey. In such a rigid code, copula verbs will agree with their formal subjects, and pronouns will agree with their grammatical anteced-ents. What you say will not affect the way you say it. In a less ritualized sys-tem (the linguistic equivalent of cadi justice), copula verbs may agree with whatever is asserted to be identical with their subjects, and pronouns will agree with whatever phrases are asserted to be their antecedents.

If it is indeed true (as I wish to claim) that grammar is simply automatized (or ritualized or emanicipated) verbal behavior, then it should follow that all grammatical rules, categories, and distinctions—like the rule of subject agree-ment which I have looked at here—are (perhaps very marginally) capable of being resuscitated (or, if you prefer, recaptured) by the speaker so that they mean what the speaker means rather than something which he or she no longer attends to and has abdicated responsibility for (cf. Berger & Luckmann 1966:81,

"Institutionalization is not an irreversible process"). The difference between asserted and presupposed *coreference*, as I have argued here, can be blurred, and in the grammars of certain languages, it is blurred.

I would also argue that the distinction between presupposition and assertion *in general* can be blurred, since presupposition may be thought of as automatized assertion. It has been claimed in the literature since Bolinger (1968) and Kiparsky and Kiparsky (1970) that this distinction is grammaticalized in English and other languages in such things as the choice of different complementizers for factive and nonfactive verbs.

Suzuki (1994) argues that the choice of complementizers in Japanese is not determined by the factivity of the predicate (as argued by Kuno 1973) but by *the speaker's degree of conviction* in the truth of the complement clause. But grammatical factivity is perhaps nothing more than the social precipitate of many speakers' frozen or ritualized convictions. It is perfectly natural that the grammatical distinction between assertion and presupposition could then be replaced by the speaker's distinction between those things he or she strongly believes in and those which he or she does not. In just the same way, the grammatical distinction between asserted and presupposed identity can be blurred as speakers reclaim as theirs to make a distinction which has become all but frozen in the morphosyntax of agreement. In this view, the code comes into existence as the aggregate of repeated messages and has no other source.

11.3. Emancipation, Rationalization, and "Autonomy"

The "autonomy of syntax" is such a familiar slogan in generative linguistics that it may be useful to see how very similar claims of autonomy are ventured for social constructions in other fields for very similar reasons. A striking example is the code of law. In the schematic diachrony of Max Weber, cadi justice (where the individual judge made ad hoc decisions) gave way to common law (a code which is explicitly the aggregate of repeated decisions). Most recently, however, "the law wishes to have a formal existence." With these words, Stanley Fish (1993:141) begins a demolition of any claims the law might have to such an existence. What Fish calls "formal existence" is synonymous with the idea of an autonomous legal code, emancipated from the real-world muck of precedent and morality from which it arose and from the real-world particularity of interpretation, which reconnects the legal code with its users. Debates about the autonomy of the law (like similar debates about the autonomy of Jungian archetypes or the autonomy of abstract laws of economics, for example) will have an eerily familiar ring to students of linguistic debates. Here is Georg Lukács on the economic version of the performance/competence distinction: "In consequence of the rationalization of the work process, the human qualities and idiosyncrasies of the worker appear increasingly as mere sources of error when contrasted with these abstract special laws functioning according to rational predictions" (1965:89). Compare this with Henning Andersen on the distinction in linguistics: "Having accepted a theory that is powerless to describe the true complexity of a speaker's phonological competence, King bravely belittles as 'random fluctuations' the very facts of performance from which alone it is possible to infer a speaker's competence" (1972:14).

Why should the law want autonomy? For the same reasons, presumably, that syntax "wanted" autonomy from semantics and semantics "wanted" autonomy from pragmatics. Partially because ritualization really will emancipate any structure to some degree. And partially because its practitioners and students wished to secure for their subjects some respect and authority as systematic sciences. Why is this desire at least partially unrealistic? For the same reasons that phonological analysis without grammatical prerequisites, semantics-free syntax, and pragmatics-free semantics proved to be so. To read Fish or Lukács is to reread the generativists inveighing against the structuralist principle of "separation of levels" in the 1950s and 1960s, the antiformalist invectives of the generative semanticists of the 1960s, the natural generative phonologists of the 1970s, and the functionalists of the 1980s and 1990s. The issues are the same, although the medium can vary, as one can see by performing minimal substitutions in Fish's attack on the autonomy of the law.

For example, legal autonomists wish to deny that legality and morality are identical. If legal reasons were identical with moral reasons, not only would the law become superfluous, but it would also "lose its most saliently desirable properties: "generality and stability" (Fish 1994:142). Substitute for the identity of morality and law the identity of semantic representations and syntactic deep structure; substitute for "generality and stability" the notion of grammaticality itself: that is, intersubjective standards of grammatical well-formedness, distinct from whether or not a string of words "makes sense."

Legal formalism (perspicuity) is "the thesis that one can devise procedures that are self executing in the sense that their unfolding is independent of the differences between the agents who might set them in motion . . . free of all ethical-political value judgments" (ibid.:142–3). Compare Chomsky's withering contempt for the role of semantics in a grammar:

> A great deal of effort has been expended in attempting to answer the question: "How can you construct a grammar with no appeal to meaning?" The question itself, however, is wrongly put, since the implication that obviously one can construct a grammar *with* appeal to meaning is totally unsupported. One might with equal justification ask: "How can you construct a grammar with no knowledge of the hair color of speakers?" (1957:93)

In other words, the aim of an autonomous formal structure is to "let the (legal) grammar decide" (ibid.:14) the validity of a legal claim, independently of contextual accidents such as the meaning of the utterance (semantics), the identity of the speaker or the hearer, or the circumstances under which the utterance is produced (pragmatics).

The humanist response to a legal formalist is that the answers or legal decisions generated by a purely formal system will be empty of content. (Indeed, defenders of formalism must see this vacuity as a virtue.) The critical response to the formalist is that the slogan "no value judgments" in itself cannot help but be a value judgment, an unspoken commitment to the values and power relationships of the status quo. (It is ironic that in his political writings, at least, Chomsky has been among the earliest and most eloquent proponents of exactly this critical viewpoint [1968]. No one has ever spoken with more passionate contempt of "value-free social sciences" than he.) The autonomy of any formal system such as a code of laws crucially depends on "other things being equal." One could retort that other things never *are* equal, but the basic flaw lies deeper, in the very word "depends," which already subverts the essence of autonomy.

The dream of a formal autonomous system in language goes back at least to Leibniz: if we could define our terms and agree on our semantic primitives, there would be no room for misunderstandings in language, any more than there is room for "schools of thought" in addition or subtraction (Wierzbicka 1972). In the legal realm, this is a dream of a code of laws so perspicuous, so self-evident, that there is no room in it for interpretation, ambiguity, lawyers, or the practice of law itself. But there are no such laws, nor are there any such legal documents, nor can we eliminate lawyers and the practice of law, because it is not "feasible to determine the meanings the parties gave to the words from the instrument alone" (*Pacific Gas & Electric Co. v. G. W. Drayage & Rigging Co.* apud Fish 1994:146).

The law is "a signal example of the way in which human beings are able to construct the roadway on which they are traveling, even to the extent of 'demonstrating' in the course of building it that it was there all the while" (ibid.:156). The legal codes we build, however abstract, gleaming, and pure they may seem, arise from the rag and bone shop of ongoing social relationships. Just like Belsybabble, we make them up as we go along.

11.4. The Motivations for Emancipation

A phenomenon as widespread as emancipation must have a reason. A variety of causes for the process have been suggested from different fields.

11.4.1. Civilization Represses Direct Gratification

In writing of the emancipation of narcissism between the time of Ancient Greece and modern America, Slater invokes the historical fact of a "generalized increase of libidinal repressiveness" (defined by him as "any social interference with any kind of bodily gratification"), an increase that prevails because more repressive societies are more aggressive ([1968] 1992:457). In subscribing to this, Slater is presumably fully aware of following in the footsteps of the author of Genesis, of Rousseau (cf. Lukács 1965:136), and of Freud ([1930] 1989), and is also aware of the skepticism which some social scientists have voiced about the historical accuracy of any such conjectured "fall from grace" (cf. Berger & Luckmann 1966:90).

11.4.2. Deep Structures in Language Facilitate Parsing

The metaphor of core reality and superficial appearance surfaces with only a minor topological modification in the familiar Chomskyan contrast between deep and surface structure in both syntax and phonology.

In describing the emancipation of phonology from phonetic fact, Kaye (1989:41) correctly points out two seldom-discussed facts. First, although there is no logical necessity for phonological processes which map underlying structures onto distinct phonetic representations, there is no language in which phonological processes are absent; second, no work on theoretical phonology has addressed the question of why this emancipation of an abstract underlying phonological level should be universal. Why do grammars have "divided selves"? It is Kaye's tremendous virtue to ask this question and to propose a speculative answer. He suggests that phonological processes exist not by virtue of some principle of least effort but in order to facilitate parsing (ibid.:50).

11.4.3. Management Good, Gruntwork Bad

> I must study politics and war that my sons may have liberty to study mathematics and philosophy. My sons ought to study mathematics and philosophy, geography, natural history, naval architecture, navigation, commerce, and agriculture in order to give their children a right to study painting, poetry, music, architecture, statuary, tapestry, and porcelain. (John Adams, letter to Abigail Adams, May 12, 1780)

It is a truism of hierarchical social structures that the higher one ascends on the social ladder, the less one's fingers are soiled with the actual dirty work which the entire organization is devoted to. This is equally true of the personnel of armies, offices, schools, and factories, irrespective of the "product." Hitler, for example, never killed a Jew in his life. And in general, status is compromised by the taint of hands-on practicality:

> They were of a respectable family in the north of England, a circumstance more deeply impressed on their memories than that their brother's fortune and their own had been acquired by trade. (Austen [1813] 1985:15)

> To be admitted to military school he had had to prove that his family for several generations had "lived nobly": that is, had refrained from degrading commercial occupations. (Palmer [1941] 1973:8)

These quotations (which could be multiplied indefinitely) convey a very widely recognized attitude. Emancipation of an activity from a direct instrumental function very frequently confers social prestige on both the activity and its practitioners. This familiar inverse correlation between practical utility and high status was originally defended by Aristotle: a true gentleman should never defile himself by doing gruntwork or even learning how to do it. Banausic trades, such as cobbling and carpentry, were for the lowborn, while philosophy was for the aristocracy. (This attitude persists in our different attitudes

toward vocational schools and liberal arts colleges today [cf. Popper 1966]).
The same trade-off between (useful, plebeian) esoteric and (useless patrician)
esoteric knowledge was wryly noted though hardly defended some 2,400 years
later by Thorstein Veblen, and by the time the synonymy of promotion and
abstraction/uselessness is lampooned by Barbara Ehrenreich, it is a fundamental
cliché that one can allude to casually:

> We all know of the brilliant career of the young Yale-educated investment banker
> who started out as a humble broker of pollution rights, moved on to inside
> trading in pollution rights futures, and then redeemed himself by buying the *right*
> to be an inside trader. From there it was an obvious leap to *trading* inside trading
> rights, and finally to *inside* trading in the inside trading rights futures market!
> (1991:243)

Within the academy, pure mathematics is superior to applied; theoretical physics
to engineering; theoretical linguistics to teaching languages. The pattern is quite
solid, utilitarian and Marxist rhetoric about the dignity of labor and the incom-
petence of the elite to the contrary notwithstanding (those who can, do; those
who can't, teach; those who can't teach become administrators).

11.4.4. Innate Drive to Repeat

We have discussed a number of cases where ritualization seems to improve on
nature. For example, gayspeak or the caricature of effeminacy takes one biological given (higher fundamental frequency of the female adult voice) and
builds an effeminate stereotype by adding a number of phonetic and lexical
features to this base (Gaudio 1994).

Psychoanalysts like Nathanson (1992:206) suggest that the drive to ritualize and stylize is innately human (cf. Donald 1991 on our "mimetic faculty")
and that it is exercised through the conscious and intentional repetition and
hence imitation of originally instinctive behavior:

> The urge to improve on nature seems to be built into our very equipment! The
> hungry newborn will make sucking motions, and it is clear that these muscular
> activities are prewired reflexes—set in motion by a prewritten script. *Yet within a
> few hours of birth, the infant can be observed imitating its own previously
> reflexive sucking movements—taking over, as it were, cultivating happenstance
> into intentionality.* (emphasis added)

This emancipation is explicitly linked to the origin of languagelike (that is,
voluntary and hence arbitrary and insincere) behavior:

> As soon as the infant learns to recognize that crying brings mother, that infant is
> capable of using the vocal and facial display of cries and whimpers as a semiotic
> device to achieve contact with mother. Thus, the visible portion of an innate affect
> comes to be used intentionally *even when the conditions for the triggering of that
> behaviour as a true innate affect have not been met.* (ibid.:207; emphasis added)

Mark Twain makes the same by now familiar point in his story "My First Lie":
"I do not remember my first lie, but I told my second when I was nine days

old" (Twain 1904). He continues with a description of his having mendaciously cried for mother, an account that is virtually identical with Nathanson's.

Trivers (1974) suggests that the origin of such mendacity (and possibly of what we call free will) may be an evolutionary "arms race." Offspring are presumably the best judges of what they need, and natural selection may favor parents who respond to the demands of their offspring. However, "once such a system has evolved, the offspring can begin to employ it *out of context*. The offspring can cry not only when it is famished, but also when it merely wants more food than the parent is selected to give [hence the origin of insincerity]. . . . Selection will then of course favor parental ability to discriminate the two uses of the signals [hence inconsequentiality . . . but still subtler mimicry and deception by the offspring are always possible." (cited in Dawkins 1982:64; emphasis added).

I would like to suggest that explanations such as Slater's "increase in libidinal repression" or Kaye's "facilitation of parsing" or Veblen's "prestige in uselessness" (1934), for all of their satisfying crispness, are bound to be inadequate because they are insufficiently general to account for a single drive which underlies phenomena so diverse as mendacity, the sublimation of narcissism, the institutionalization of phonological structure, the stylization of a register like gayspeak, and the existence of liberal arts colleges. At its most general and basic level, it is this drive which improves on the brute facts of nature and converts them into culture. The manifestation of this drive as an ever more "elaborate circuitry of displacement and delay" (Slater [1968] 1992:456) is common to the seemingly disparate phenomena assembled here.

I would also like to repeat my claim that whatever the reason for this institutionalizing tendency, it constitutes part of the very essence of our capacity for human language itself. The latter insight is familiar not only to linguists, who consider displacement one of the fundamental design features of language, but also to First Amendment legal scholars and students of Zen, who repeatedly emphasize that "words are not facts, but only *about* facts" (Watts 1958:18; cf. F. S. Haiman 1972:31), that "all things are *abstracted* from experience by thinking and naming" (Watts 1958:13–4), that to seek the truth in words or ideas makes no more sense than expecting nourishment from a printed menu (ibid.:21). It is implicit in our own tradition, in Voltaire's dictum that language is given to us to conceal our thoughts, in Hamlet's contemptuous dismissal of "words, words, words," and in Goethe's "grau ist alle Theorie, grün des Lebens ewiger Baum," and it is explicit in the homely proverb I have chosen as the title for this book.

The closest thing to an unchallenged "explanation" for the drive to ritualize is Nathanson's observation that to repeat, to rehearse, and to imitate ourselves is perhaps a part of our nature from the time we are born. It could be a very important part of—and even, as Donald (1991) argues, a precondition for—our undeniably linguistic faculty.

The infinite creativity of language is so much a given of current theoretical approaches that paeans in its praise have become among the most often repeated aphorisms in the literature. There can be no denying the fundamental fact that finite linguistic codes are adapted for conveying an infinite number of possible messages. When, however, we look at what *makes* these codes finite—design features like digitization and double articulation—it seems likely that they arose precisely through repetition and the stylization of form and habituated response that repetition gives rise to. And when we look at what makes these codes change over time—and formal reduction through grammaticalization is certainly one of the universal changes which all languages undergo—then again it seems likely that repetition is the motor which drives this very basic process.

Unquestionably, the uniqueness of human language seems to call into doubt evolutionary *accounts* (if not evolutionary theories) of its origin. Nevertheless, the biological genesis, multiplication, and decay of signs in the animal kingdom exhibit intriguing formal parallels with codification and grammaticalization in humans (cf. Andersson 1980; Moynihan 1970). And while the physiology of ritualization in human beings is unknown (Donald, for example, acknowledges that "the subsystems underlying mimetic skill seem to be distributed through several brain regions" and that there are "no reports of generalized 'dysmimetic' syndromes in the literature" [1991:194], it seems overwhelmingly likely that repetition plays an important and insufficiently appreciated part in its development.

How much repetition is enough to establish a habit or a bureaucracy? Clearly, we do not need eons to establish institutions. Witness the development of full-fledged languages like American Sign Language from purely artificial creations over the last 200 years. But the transition from spontaneous, presumably iconic prelinguistic "gesticulation" via gestures, pantomimes, and emblems to a mature and stylized sign language characterized by arbitrariness and conventional standards of grammaticality (Kendon 1988; McNeill 1992) may occur in almost the twinkling of an eye. McNeill cites Bloom (1979), an experimental study in which nonsigners were forced to use spontaneous gestures to communicate a story to each other. Within *fifteen to twenty minutes*, a system began to emerge with "segmentation, compositionality, a lexicon, syntax, arbitrariness, distinctiveness, standards of wellformedness, fluency, and streamlining" (McNeill 1992:66). It may well be that a large part of our undeniable linguistic faculty consists of nothing other than our very instinct for self-imitation that Nathanson wrote about (1992:206–7), coupled with the incredible speed with which we can "nurture nature" and do the work of stylization and ritualization.

The strongest hypothesis about this "incredible speed" that one could hazard is this: *one repetition* is all it takes for humans to "see" a pattern and feel some habituation. As a purely anecdotal illustration of this hypothesis, I offer the well-known experience of the "return trip phenomenon," something which we have all experienced. *The way back from a new destination is invariably "shorter" than the way there.* We experience this on completing the first round-trip. This is habituation after one exposure.

TWELVE

Reification and Innateness

The "autonomization" of any human creation, or its reification, is described by Peter Berger and Thomas Luckmann as "the apprehension of human phenomena as if they were . . . facts of nature" (1966:89). But what about the facts of nature themselves?

Biologically innate features are often as arbitrary, but no more arbitrary, than cultural institutions. Proponents of the "radical autonomy" of syntax emphasize the sheer dysfunctionality of linguistic rules in order to validate their claims that language is not a functionally motivated structure. Koster (1987), one of the most eloquent of these proponents, compares syntactic structures with patterns on the wings of a butterfly—beautiful but functionally neutral. (Even the friendliest of critics would have to say that this may have been an unfortunate choice of biological analogies: one of the standard examples of functional motivation for extremely rapid evolutionary change is of changes in the wing coloring of moths [cf. Smith 1966:137].)

I have argued so far that dysfunctionality, far from pointing unambiguously at innateness, can have cultural as well as natural causes. Dysfunction is rife in culture, and it occurs in culture through emancipation. I now would like to go one logical step further and suggest that dysfunction has a similar origin even in nature.

Perhaps even *biological innateness* is the outcome of a kind of emancipation, reification, or ritualization. We can entertain this claim to the extent that any *genetic* "adaptation" (however dysfunctional it may now seem to be) can be traced back to a time when the mutation which produced it was a motivated or *environmental* adaption. An example cited by John Maynard Smith (1966:19) is of the flight patterns of storks in Europe. Their southerly migration paths from Europe to Africa avoid the Mediterranean and the Alps. Eastern storks fly southeast, while western storks fly southwest, until the Mediterranean obstacle has been circumnavigated. Both flight paths are therefore apparently functionally motivated by features of the external environment. But when storks from East Prussia, for example, are transported to the west and allowed to migrate southward, they automatically take off as though from East Prussia, flying in a south*easterly* direction, bumping into the Alps. Their behavior is now genetically innate or context-independent and in this sense emancipated from the geographical conditions which originally motivated it (and still would seem to motivate it if the storks were left alone). The only way in which we can tell that emancipation has occurred in this case is by the artifice of an experiment.

Motor patterns in general may be emancipated from external stimuli much more than common sense would lead us to expect. Take, for example, the action of picking up an apple. Common sense tells us that we respond to the immediate environmental stimulus of the weight of the apple and exert an upward force which counteracts the force of gravity. But if we pick up a doctored apple, one with a lead core, our response makes it clear that we have a prior expectation of what the apple will weigh; environmental feedback only *corrects* a prepared response. Or consider an experience we have all had of walking down a flight of stairs and reaching the bottom one step before or after we were expecting to. Our awkwardness and stumbling are testimony to the fact that "the brain gives orders for the next motor response" in advance of the actual environmental stimulus (cf. Terzuolo & Viviani 1979).

Such cases may be the rule in nature. Genetic adaptation is to environmental adaptation as ablaut to umlaut (or phonologized umlaut to automatic subphonemic variation). In both cases, the present structure or activity exists independently of the environment which originally motivated it, but we can't tell whether the adaptation is in fact emancipated from the conditioning stimulus until the environment is altered.

In language, we should try to distinguish between arbitrary and dysfunctional structures. As Comrie and Givón, among others, have rightly emphasized, languages are replete with grammatical rules and categories which are at best only partially motivated by semantics, with all kinds of irregularities and arbitrary, "crazy" rules. One of the most striking regularities of historical reconstruction, however, is that crazy rules and structures which seem unmotivated at one stage often turn out to have been motivated at an earlier time. And one of the most striking regularities of linguistic change is that irregularity is never allowed to "get out of hand" and become truly dysfunctional.

It would be interesting to find a really dysfunctional linguistic universal and speculate on what might once have been its original functional motivation. I am not the person to do this, however, as I do not know any such universals.

In arguing for the ubiquity of emancipation in culture, language, and metalanguage no less than in biology, I am aware of seeming to buttress the analogy between languages and biological organisms and thus proposing yet another biological metaphor in linguistics. Such metaphors in linguistics (family trees, reproduction, transmission, evolution, extinction) are pervasive, and there is at least one potent linguistic metaphor in biology—the grammar of DNA. Nevertheless there are important distinctions between them which I wish to acknowledge, partly to preempt possible rejoinders and partly because the similarities become even more remarkable in the face of these distinctions.

DNA is to the somatic phenotype, roughly speaking, as grammar is to speech: the first is the code which generates the second. The main distinction between the two "codes" is that language like culture in general is transmitted through learning and thus evolves by Lamarckian means (cf. Gould 1980:70–71, cited in Givón 1989:389; Lumsden & Wilson 1981:4–5). The grammar of generation two is inferred by its speakers from (and thus shaped by) the speech of generation one. Emancipation, like all other changes in language, occurs in the reciprocal interplay between grammar and speech, between the linguistic equivalents of genotype and phenotype. In particular, emancipation in grammar is very often, if not always, the result of a social fact, namely, *repetition in speech.*

The central dogma of genetics, however, is that the DNA of generation two is shaped entirely by the DNA of generation one (Smith 1966:64). The social history, personal experience, and acquired habitual behavior of the organism which functions as the gene's "survival machine" is of no account in this model. Emancipation in a species occurs only through the selection of *mutations* or *novel combinations* in the DNA. For example, an individual organism may become habituated to a stimulus and no longer respond to it, but its offspring will not therefore be born indifferent to this stimulus themselves.

What seems to me of particular interest is that although the mechanism of emancipation is very different in the two kingdoms of nature (where information is transmitted by the germ plasm) and culture (where information is learned), so many of the results are nevertheless exactly the same.

Is this similarity entirely fortuitous? It would seem that it must be. Yet the metaphor of language as a biological organism is so deep and the parallels between cultural and biological evolution are so striking that it seems the famous analogy must be right in some very deep ways.

And indeed a partial resolution of the dilemma is forthcoming. Recent scholarship in sociobiology and biological evolution (e.g., Mayr 1962; Wilson 1975; Lumsden & Wilson 1981) suggests that in biology no less than in culture, changes in the function or behavior of the phenotype (the biological analog of *parole*) do favor, and thus indirectly foster, changes in its biological structure (the biological *langue*). This is not (granted) a development one can observe in individuals but one that can be traced over time in populations. For example, Wilson (1975:18) observes that "the entire process of ritualization . . . typically involves a behavioral change followed by morphological alterations that [over generations] enhance the visibility and distinctiveness of the behavior." That is, a "watered down" Lamarckianism, wherein behavior serves as the pacemaker for changes in structure (Mayr 1962) may be valid. The mechanism of social drift which accomplishes this is the familiar one of natural selection, whereby a happy coincidence of biological structure and environmental adaptation in an individual leaves that individual and its progeny at a competitive advantage. To return to our example of habituation, an organism, let us say an inhabitant of New York City, may acquire indifference to a constant stimulus, say, constant noise, through habituation. No matter how useful such acquired indifference (or any acquired behavior) may be, the New Yorker will be unable to pass on to his or her offspring the ability to sleep through the night. But random individuals will also be born with this built-in indifference (congenital deafness at certain frequencies), and if the trait is on balance a positive one, they will thrive, flourish, and multiply, eventually supplanting the hearing population. Thus over time the population as a whole will come to possess the trait that individuals in earlier generations had to acquire individually.

It may be, then, that natural selection resulting in "inclusive fitness" of entire populations is nature's very leisurely analog to cultural transmission. Recognizing this, perhaps we can see in natural and cultural emancipation only one aspect of what Gregory Bateson (1979) called the "necessary unity" of mind and nature.

Postscript

I began this book with a description of sarcasm, a patently insincere speech genre in which sentence meaning and utterance meaning are diametrically opposed. Sarcasm is, of course, only one such genre, and an attempt to locate it led to a discussion of other varieties of un-plain speaking and a skeptical look at so-called plain speaking, to which all of these varieties of insincerity are presumably opposed. I concluded with the claim that the ritualization or emancipation process, which transforms sincere spontaneous acts and utterances into autonomous and meaningless formal codes, not only is responsible for apparent excrescences such as sarcasm, formal politeness, phatic communion, ritual speech, and affectation but also is a significant part of human nature and therefore of the very essence of culture itself and may have played a necessarily undocumented role in the origin of human language.

Human language is only one of a number of biological and cultural developments which have contributed to our emancipation from the brute reality of the world. Others include habituation, warmbloodedness, toolmaking, agriculture, and electricity. But it is the only one which is shared by all human beings and by no other species. I have focused in this book on one single property of human languages: their ability "to say the thing that is not." Gulliver's Houynyhms had a hard time conceiving of a language in which such a thing was possible. For my part, I believe that it was a singular stroke of genius for Swift to have imagined a language in which it was not. A code in which lying is impossible is no code at all—hence the very deep level at which the technical and vernacular meanings of this term (as synonyms for "language" and "doublespeak") are absolutely synonymous.

Although I believe that much of what I have just said here is possibly true, I am not so naive or pompous as to mistake this book for any variety of hard science, soft science, or social science. It is an idiosyncratic personal essay. Open any textbook on language, and you will encounter the healthy mainstream view not only that language is what makes us fully human, but also that it is the infinite creativity of language alone which makes social interaction and cooperation possible and provides us the means for the most sincere and intimate expression of every thought and feeling. Of course, language is capable of all of these achievements, and I am willing to assume that the vast majority of the time it is what almost all of language is all about. My apparent cynicism in choosing to focus on the remaining speck, the vast potential of language for affectation, prevarication, empty formality, and concealment, and my claim that it is precisely in this sliver that we may find the essence of language may strike the well-balanced reader as both threatening and repellent. And like all choices of subject matter and focus, it is very likely shaped by uninteresting accidents. But I suspect that I am not alone among my colleagues in regarding unreflecting unself-conscious conversation almost as something of a circus trick ("God, how do they DO that?") and that the views expressed in this book will be congenial not only to students of society in general but also to many linguists in particular.

Why? Because for all of our brave post-Malinowskian rhetoric about "participant observation," and in spite of heroic post-Marxian exhortations to "change the world," most students of society tend to be, like their informants, inconsequential and isolated outsiders or *lames* (Labov 1972a). Some self-consciousness, a certain degree of separation from the secular world, is probably true of all of the intelligentsia to some degree, as Labov argues, but I think it must be particularly true of linguists. For we not only have substituted talk for action but have gone one step further than artists and other academics and (along with critics, parodists, and philosophers) substituted *talk about talk* for talk itself. That is a perfectly neutral description of what we do. It is difficult to imagine a profession which by definition commits its practitioners to any greater degree of abstraction or detachment from the world. To people who have been drawn to such a profession, however practical and rugged they may be, the idea that language is an object in its own right rather than an utterly transparent and permeable window to the movements of the soul is a professional cliché. The natural consequence of this idea, that such an object is opaque or distorting, must strike a familiar chord in the heart of every student of language.

In his wonderful yarn about the origins of consciousness, Julian Jaynes (1976) draws attention to the ubiquity of nostalgia in Western accounts of the human condition. The Golden Age, the Garden of Eden, the noble savage, civilization and its discontents all are staples of our inventory of concepts for talking about the land of lost content. And in a poignant and moving moment (ibid.:378), he describes his own personal nostalgia for the conjectured state of bicameral unconscious grace for which his book attempts a genetic and historical justification.

It seems possible to me that I also am nostalgic. What I am mourning in this most humble contribution to the literature of nostalgia is not the innocence of the pre-state Gemeinschaft of Durkheim and Tönnies, the precivilized sexual Eden of Freud, or the unconscious bicameral mind of Julian Jaynes but what I imagine to be the unself-conscious sincerity of animals: the prelinguistic honks, grunts, and squeals of geese, pigs, and rabbits.

> Into my heart an air that kills
> From yon far country blows.
> What are those blue remembered hills?
> What spires, what farms, are those?
> That is the land of lost content.
> I see it shining plain:
> The happy highways where I went
> And cannot come again. (A. E. Housman)

Appendix

Questionnaire for Eliciting Sarcasm

Subjects are asked to say the same words first sincerely and second sarcastically by doing some playacting. The scenarios follow.

1. a) Your best friend, after years of toiling in obscurity, has finally been awarded the Nobel Prize in Literature. From the bottom of your heart, you rejoice in her success and say:

   b) Your friend has borrowed your car to do some grocery shopping and calls to tell you that she has sideswiped a delivery truck and it looks like your car is a total loss. You say the same words as in (1a):

2. a) Your best friend has just discovered that he has leukemia and has only eight months to live. You say:

   b) Your best friend has just had his latest manuscript accepted by Oxford University Press, but they are only bringing it out in hardcover. You say the same words as in (2a):

3. a) You have just discovered that you have truly lost your wallet, containing not only over $200 in cash but all of your credit cards, your driver's licence, and the only copy of a photograph of your mother, now dead. The phone rings: it's a stranger who has found your wallet and wants to return it to you. Overcome with relief and gratitude, you say:

   b) Your husband announces that he's been having an affair with a student half your age and that he wants a divorce. Magnanimously, he tells you that he doesn't entirely blame you for what has gone wrong. You say the same words as in (3a):

4. a) You are visiting your in-laws, with whom your relationship has never been entirely comfortable. They are making an effort to be agreeable, as are you,

and are showing off to you their most prized possession, a vase which has been in their family for over 100 years. You trip, and in recovering, knock the vase off the table; it lands on the parquet floor and shatters. Overcome with mortification, you apologize:

b)   Your ex-mother-in-law, whom you have never liked, is visiting you because she missed a plane connection. You owe her nothing, but you are a good sort, so you offer to put her up for the night. In the morning, she complains that you failed to wake her up when she is SURE she asked you to. This is the last straw. You say to her the same words as in (4a):

5. a)   In a stunning upset victory, your candidate, whom everybody had written off as a no-hoper, wins the election. You have been pounding the streets, knocking on doors, stuffing envelopes, phone-banking, and writing huge checks for this candidate. You are ecstatic:

b)   You have been looking forward to spending a weekend alone with your lover, whom you have not seen in six months. She calls to say that she will be accompanied by her little brother and that you will be expected to entertain him while she goes to a job interview. You say the same words as in (5a):

References

Abercrombie, D. 1991. "Daniel Jones' teaching." In D. Abercrombie, *Fifty years in phonetics*. Edinburgh: University of Edinburgh Press.

Adachi, T. 1996. Sarcasm in Japanese. *Studies in Language* 19:1–36.

Adams, D. 1979. *The hitchhiker's guide to the galaxy*. London: Pan.

Aksu-Koç, A., & D. Slobin. 1986. "Developments in the use of evidentials in Turkish." In Chafe & Nichols 1986:159–67.

Allan, K., & K. Burridge. 1991. *Euphemism and dysphemism*. Oxford: Oxford University Press.

Almansi, G. 1984. *Amica ironia*. Milan: Garzanti.

Andersen, H. 1972. Diphthongization. *Language* 48:11–50.

Anderson, W. 1990. *Reality isn't what it used to be*. San Francisco: Harper.

Andersson, M. 1980. Why are there so many threat displays? *Journal of Theoretical Biology* 86:773–81.

Aoki, H., & S. Okamoto. 1988. *Rules for conversational rituals in Japanese*. Tokyo: Taishukan.

Aretino, P. 1971. *The dialogs*. Trans. R. Rosenthal. New York: Ballantine.

Austen, J. [1813] 1985. *Pride and prejudice*. Harmondsworth: Penguin.

Austin, J. 1975. *How to do things with words*. (2nd ed.) Cambridge: Harvard University Press.

Awolaye, Y. 1986. "Reflexivization in Kwa languages." In *Current approaches to African linguistics*, ed. G. J. Dimmendaal. Dordrecht: Foris, 3:1–14.

Ayala, F. 1978. The mechanism of evolution. *Scientific American*, September, 56–69.

Babel, I. 1965. *Konarmiya; Odesskiye Rasskazy; P'esy*. Chicago: Bradda Books.

Bach, E. 1989. *Informal lectures on formal semantics*. Albany: State University of New York Press.

Baiter, J., & C. Keyser (eds.). 1864. *Ciceronis opera omnia.* (Vol. 7.) Leipzig: Tauchnitz.

Baker, D., P. Pollin, & M. Schaberg. 1994. Taxing the big casino. *The Nation,* May 9, 1994.

Bakhtin, M. 1986. "The problem of speech genres." In M. Bakhtin, *Speech genres and other late essays,* trans. V. McGhee. Austin: University of Texas Press, 60–102.

Banfield, A. 1973. Narrative style and the grammar of direct and indirect speech. *Foundations of Language* 10:1–39.

————. 1982. *Unspeakable sentences.* London: Routledge.

Barry, D. 1987. *Bad habits.* New York: Henry Holt.

————. 1988. *Dave Barry's greatest hits.* New York: Fawcett.

————. 1994. *Dave Barry is not making this up.* New York: Crown.

————. 1995. *Dave Barry's guide to guys.* New York: Fawcett.

Barthes, R. 1972. "Structure of the *fait-divers.*" In R. Barthes, *Critical Essays,* trans. R. Howard. Evanston: Northwestern University Press.

————. 1977. *Writing degree zero.* Trans. A. Lavers & C. Smith. New York: Hill and Wang.

Bassett, M., & L. Warne. 1919. On the lapse of verbal meaning with repetition. *American Journal of Psychology* 30:415–8.

Bastock, M. 1964. "Communication in bees." In *Penguin Science Survey B.* Harmondsworth: Penguin, 181–200.

Bateson, G. 1956. "The message 'this is play.'" In *Group Processes,* ed. B. Schaffner. New York: Josiah Macy Jr. Foundation, 145–242.

————. 1972. "A theory of play and fantasy." In *Steps to an ecology of mind.* New York: Ballantine, 177–93.

————. 1979. *Mind and nature: A necessary unity.* New York: Dutton.

Becker, E. 1971. *The birth and death of meaning.* (2nd ed.) New York: Free Press.

Becket, S. 1952. *En attendant Godot.* Paris: Editions de Minuit.

Beetham, D. 1987. *Bureaucracy.* Minneapolis: University of Minnesota Press.

Behaghel, O. 1932. *Deutsche Syntax.* (Vol. 4.) Heidelberg: Carl Winter.

Bellah, R., et al. 1985. *Habits of the heart.* New York: Free Press.

Benveniste, E. 1946. Structure des relations de personne dans le verbe. *Bulletin de la Société de Linguistique* 43:1–12.

Berger, P., & T. Luckmann. 1966. *The social construction of reality.* Garden City, NY: Doubleday.

Berger, T. 1975. *Sneaky people.* New York: Dell.

Bergson, H. 1911. *Laughter.* London: MacMillan.

Bird, C., & T. Shopen. 1979. "Maninka" In *Languages and their speakers,* ed. T. Shopen. Cambridge: Winthrop, 59–112.

Blest, A. 1963. "The concept of 'ritualization.'" In *Current problems in animal behaviour,* ed. W. Thorpe & O. Zangwill. Cambridge: Cambridge University Press, 102–25.

Blinkenberg, A. 1950. *Le problème de l'accord en français contemporain: essai d'une typologie.* Copenhagen: Munksgaard.

Bloom, H. 1973. *Anxiety of influence.* New York: Oxford University Press.

Bloom, R. 1979. "Language creation in the manual modality." B.S. thesis, University of Chicago.

Bloomfield, L. 1930. *Sacred stories of the Sweet Grass Cree.* National Museums of Canada, Bulletin 60. Ottawa: The King's Printer.

Bolinger, D. 1968. Entailment and the meaning of structures. *Glossa* 2:119–27.

———. 1975. *Aspects of language.* (2nd ed.) New York: Harcourt Brace Jovanovich.

———. 1985. "The inherent iconism of intonation." In *Iconicity in syntax*, ed. J. Haiman. Amsterdam: Benjamins, 97–108.

———. 1986. *Intonation and its parts.* Stanford: Stanford University Press.

Boorstin, D. 1962. *The image.* New York: Atheneum.

Booth, W. 1974. *A rhetoric of irony.* Chicago: University of Chicago Press.

Borges, J. L. 1962a. "Averroes' search." In Borges 1962d:148–55.

———. 1962b. "Funes the memorious." In Borges 1962d:59–66.

———. 1962c. "The god's script." In Borges 1962d:169–73.

———. 1962d. *Labyrinths.* New York: New Directions.

———. 1962e. "Pierre Menard, author of the Quixote." In Borges 1962d:36–44.

———. 1962f. "The Zahir." In Borges 1962d:156–64.

Brackman, J. 1967. The put-on. *New Yorker*, June 24, 34–73.

Bramah, E. [1900] 1926. *The wallet of Kai Lung.* London: Jonathan Cape.

Brody, M., & R. Manzini. 1988. "On implicit arguments." In *Mental representations*, ed. R. Kempson. Cambridge: Cambridge University Press, 105–30.

Brophy, J., & E. Partridge. 1931. *Songs and slang of the British soldier, 1914–1918.* (3rd ed.) London: Routledge & Kegan Paul.

Brown, P. 1979. "Language, interaction, and sex roles in a Mayan community: A study of politeness and the position of women." Ph.D. dissertation, University of California, Berkeley.

Brown, P., & S. Levinson. 1987. *Politeness: Some universals in language usage.* Cambridge: Cambridge University Press.

Brown, R., & A. Gilman. 1960. "The pronouns of power and solidarity." In *Style in language*, ed. T. Sebeok. Cambridge: MIT Press, 253–76.

Bruce, L. 1984. *The Alamblak language of Papua New Guinea (East Sepik).* Pacific Linguistics C-81. Canberra: Linguistic Circle of Canberra, Research School of Pacific Studies.

Bruyère, J. de la. [1688] 1951. "Les caractères." In *Oeuvres complètes*, ed. J. Benda. 1951. Paris: Gallimard.

Bryan, W., & N. Harter. 1899. Studies on the telegraphic language: The acquisition of a hierarchy of habits. *Psychological Review* 6(4):345–75.

Buehler, K. 1934. *Sprachtheorie: Die Darstellungsfunktion der Sprache.* Stuttgart: Fischer.

Burckhardt, J. 1960. *Civilization of the Renaissance in Italy.* London: Phaidon.

Burroughs, W. 1968. *The naked lunch.* London: Corgi.

Burton, R. [1621] 1932. *The anatomy of melancholy.* London: J. M. Dent & Sons.

Caillois, R. 1967. *Les jeux et les hommes.* (2nd ed.) Paris: Gallimard.

Callan, H. 1970. *Ethology and Society.* Oxford: Oxford University Press.

Catford, J. 1977. *Fundamental problems in phonetics.* Bloomington: Indiana University Press.

———. 1988. *A practical introduction to phonetics.* Oxford: Oxford University Press.

Chafe, W. 1981. Differences between colloquial and ritual Seneca: Or how oral literature is literary. *Survey of California and other Indian languages.* Berkeley: University of California Press 131–45.

Chafe, W., & J. Nichols (eds.). 1986. *Evidentiality: The linguistic coding of epistemology.* Norwood, NJ: Ablex.

Chandler, M. 1990. *A healing art: Regeneration through autobiography*. New York: Garland.

Chaucer, G. 1940. *The Canterbury tales*. Chicago: University of Chicago Press.

Chekhov, A. 1963a. "Chelovek v futljare" (The man in a case). In Chekhov 1963b:168–82.

———. 1963b. *Rasskazy*. Moscow: Izdatel'stvo Xudozhestvennoj Literatury.

Chen, L. 1994. "Syntacticization of affect." In *21st Forum*, ed. M. Powell. Linguistic Association of Canada and the United States, 174–82.

Cheney, D., & R. Seyfarth. 1991. "Truth and deception in animal communication." In *Cognitive ethology*, ed. C. Ristau. Hillsdale, NJ: Lawrence Erlbaum Associates, 127–51.

Cheng, L. 1989. "Prosodic markedness of irony and sarcasm in spoken Mandarin." Unpublished manuscript, University of Manitoba.

———. 1990. "Clefting and the Keenan-Comrie hierarchy." Unpublished manuscript, Brock University.

Childs, G. T. 1995. "African ideophones." In *Studies in Sound Symbolism*, ed. L. Hinton, J. Nichols, & J. Ohala. Cambridge: Cambridge: University Press.

Chomsky, N. 1957. *Syntactic structures*. The Hague: Mouton.

———. 1965. *Aspects of the theory of syntax*. Cambridge: MIT Press.

———. 1968. *American power and the new Mandarins*. New York: Pantheon.

———. 1980. *Rules and representations*. New York: Columbia University Press.

———. 1982. *Lectures on government and binding*. Dordrecht: Foris.

———. 1989a. *Necessary illusions*. Boston: South End Press.

———. 1989b. The tasks ahead: II. *Zeta*, July/August:15–22.

Chomsky, N., & M. Halle. 1968. *The sound pattern of English*. New York: Harper and Row.

Clark, H., and R. Gerrig. 1984. On the pretense theory of irony. *Journal of Experimental Psychology: General* 113:121–6.

Coleman, L., & P. Kay. 1981. Prototype semantics. *Language* 57:26–44.

Comrie, B. 1975. Polite plurals and predicate agreement. *Language* 51:406–18.

———. 1979. "Russian." *Languages and their status*, ed. T. Shopen. Cambridge: Winthrop, 91–151.

———. 1981. *Language universals and linguistic typology*. Chicago: University of Chicago Press.

———. 1983. "Switch reference in Huchol: A typological study." In *Switch reference and universal grammar*, ed. J. Haiman & P. Munro. Amsterdam: Benjamins, 17–38.

Corbett, G. 1979. The agreement hierarchy. *Journal of Linguistics* 15:203–24.

———. 1983. *Hierarchies, targets, and controllers*. London: Croom Helm.

———. 1988. "Agreement: A partial specification based on Slavonic data." In *Agreement in natural languages*, ed. M. Barlow & C. Ferguson. Chicago: University of Chicago Press/Center for the Study of Language and Information.

———. 1991. *Gender*. Cambridge: Cambridge University Press.

Corbett, G., & A. Mtenje. 1987. Gender agreement in Chichewa. *Studies in African Linguistics* 18(1):1–38.

Corn, D. 1989. The S&L bailout: Sticking it to the taxpayers. *The Nation*, September 4/11, 238.

Cornish, F. 1986. *Anaphoric relations in English and French*. London: Croom Helm.

Cosper, R. 1983. "Language as ritual: An ethological perspective." In *Essays in honor of Charles F. Hockett*, ed. F. Agard et al. Leiden: E. J. Brill, 405–29.

Coulmas, F. 1981. "Poison to your soul." In Coulmas (ed.) 1981:69–91.

———. (ed.). 1981. *Conversational routine*. The Hague: Mouton.

Couper-Kuhlen, E. 1986. *An introduction to English prosody*. London: Edward Arnold.

Craig, C. 1986. "Jacaltec noun classifiers: A study of language and culture." In *Noun classes and categorization*, ed. C. Craig. Amsterdam: Benjamins, 263–93.

Crisp, Q. 1978. *The naked civil servant*. New York: Signet.

Crowley, M. 1968. *The boys in the band*. New York: Farrar, Straus & Giroux.

Crowley, T., & B. Rigsby. 1979. "Cape York Creole." In *Languages and their status*, ed. T. Shopen. Cambridge: Winthrop, 153–207.

Cruttenden, A. 1984. "Intonational misfits." In *Intonation, accent and rhythm*, ed. D. Gibbon & H. Richter. Berlin: de Gruyter, 67–76.

Daanje, A. 1950. On locomotory movements in birds. *Behaviour* 3:48–98.

Danto, A. 1981. *The transfiguration of the commonplace*. Cambridge: Harvard University Press.

Darwin, C. 1873. *The expression of the emotions in man and animals*. New York: Appleton & Co.

Davidson, D. 1968/9. On saying "that." *Synthese* 19:130–46.

Dawkins, R. 1978. *The selfish gene*. London: Granada.

———. 1982. *The extended phenotype*. New York: Oxford University Press.

de Groot, A. 1949. Structural linguistics and syntactic laws. *Word* 5:1–12.

Deighton, L. 1965. *Funeral in Berlin*. New York: Dutton.

DeLancey, S. 1986. "Evidentiality and volitionality in Tibetan." In *Evidentials: The linguistic coding of epistemology*, ed. W. Chafe & J. Nichols. Norwood, NJ: Ablex.

De Lillo, Don. 1977. *Players*. New York: Vintage.

DeMott, B. 1990. *The imperial middle*. New York: William Morrow.

Derber, C. 1983. *The pursuit of attention*. New York: Oxford University Press.

Descartes, R. [1637] 1912. *Discourse on method*. Trans. J. Veitch. London: J. M. Dent & Sons.

Dethier, V. 1957. Communication by insects. *Science* 125:331–36.

Dieterlen, G. 1973. *La notion de la personne en Afrique noire*. Paris: Centre National de la Recherche Scientifique.

Dill, H. 1989. Romantic irony in the works of Robert Schumann. *Musical Quarterly* 73(2):172–95.

Dixon, R. 1969. Noun classes. *Lingua* 21:104–25.

Doi, T. 1973. *The anatomy of dependence*. Tokyo: Kodansha.

———. 1986. *The anatomy of self*. Trans. M. Harbison. Tokyo: Kodansha.

Donald, M. 1991. *Origins of the modern mind*. Cambridge: Harvard University Press.

Duckworth, G. (ed.) 1961. *The complete Roman drama*. (Vol. 2.) New York: Random House.

DuBois, J. 1986. "Self-evidence and ritual speech." In *Evidentials: The linguistic coding of epistemology*, ed. W. Chafe & J. Nichols. Norwood, NJ: Ablex, 313–33.

———. 1993. "Meaning without intention: Lessons from divination." In *Responsibility and evidence in oral discourse*, ed. J. Irivine & J. Hill. Cambridge: Cambridge University Press, 48–71.

Ducrot, O. 1984. *Le dire et le dit*. Paris: Les Editions de Minuit.

Dundes, A., et al. 1972. "The strategy of Turkish boys' duelling rhymes." In *Directions in sociolinguistics*, ed. J. Gumperz & D. Hymes. New York: Holt, 130–60.

Duranti, A. 1985. Famous theories and local theories: The Samoans and Wittgenstein. *Quarterly Newsletter of the Laboratory of Comparative Human Cognition* 7(2):46–51.

Eco, U. 1984. *Postille a il nome della rose*. Milan: Bompiani.

Eggenberger, J. 1961. *Das Subjektspronomen im Althochdeutsch: Ein syntaktischer Beitrag zur Frühgeschichte des deutschen Schrifttums*. Chur: S. Sulser.

Ehrenreich, B. 1991. *The worst years of our lives*. New York: Harper.

Elias, N. 1978. *The civilizing process*. New York: Pantheon.

Enright, D. 1985. *Fair of speech: The uses of euphemism*. Oxford: Oxford University Press.

———. 1986. *The alluring problem*. New York: Oxford University Press.

Essien, O. 1982. The so-called reflexive pronouns and reflexivization in Ibibio. *Studies in African Linguistics* 13:93–108.

Ewen, S. 1988. *All consuming images*. New York: Basic Books.

Faltz, L. 1977. "Reflexivization in universal grammar." Ph.D. dissertation, University of California, Berkeley.

Feirstein, B. 1982. *Real men don't eat quiche*. New York: Pocket Books.

Ferguson, C. 1959. Diglossia. *Word* 15:325–40.

———. 1981. "The structure and use of politeness formulas." In Coulmas (ed.) 1981:21–35.

Fiedler, L. 1960. *Love and death in the American novel*. New York: Dell.

Fierstein, H. 1979. *Torch song trilogy*. New York: Villard.

Fillmore, C., P. Kay, & M. O'Connor. 1988. Regularity and idiomaticity in grammatical constructions. *Language* 64:501–38.

Firth, R. 1972. "Verbal and bodily rituals of greeting." In *The interpretation of ritual*, ed. J. LaFontaine. London: Tavistock, 1–38.

Fischer, J. L. 1958. Social influences on the choice of a linguistic variant. *Word* 14:47–56.

Fish, S. 1994. *There's no such thing as free speech—and it's a good thing, too*. Oxford: Oxford University Press.

Fitzgerald, D. 1975. "The language of ritual events among the Ga." In *Sociocultural dimensions of language use*, ed. M. Sanches & R. Blount. New York: Academic Press.

Fonagy, I. 1956. Die Eigenart des sprachlichen Zeichens. *Lingua* 6:67–88.

———. 1962. Mimik auf glottaler Ebene. *Phonetica* 8:209–19.

———. 1971a. Double coding in speech. *Semiotica* 3:189–222.

———. 1971b. "The functions of vocal style." In *Literary style: A symposium*, ed. S. Chatman. London: Oxford University Press, 159–76.

———. 1971c. Synthèse de l'ironie. *Phonetica* 23:42–51.

———. 1980. "Preverbal communication and linguistic evolution." In *The relationship of verbal and non-verbal communication*, ed. M. R. Key. The Hague: Mouton, 167–84.

Fonagy, I., et al. 1983. Clichés mélodiques. *Folia Linguistica* 17:153–85.

Fortes, M. 1959. *Oedipus and Job in West African religion*. Cambridge: Cambridge University Press.

Foulet, L. 1920. Comment on est passé de "ce suis je" á "c'est moi." *Romania* 46:46–83.

Freud, S. [1930] 1989. *Civilization and its discontents.* Trans. J. Strachey. New York: Norton.

Friedman, V. 1986. "Evidentiality in the Balkans: Bulgarian, Macedonian, and Albanian." In Chafe & Nichols 1986:168–87.

Friedrich, P. 1972. "Social context and semantic feature." In *Directions in sociolinguistics*, ed. J. Gumperz & D. Hymes. New York: Holt, 270–300.

Frisch, K. 1954. *The dancing bees.* London: Methuen.

Gaudio, R. 1994. "Sounding gay: Pitch properties in the speech of gay and straight men." *American Speech* 69:30–57.

Geertz, C. 1960. *The religion of Java.* Glencoe: Free Press.

———. 1983. *Local knowledge.* New York: Basic Books.

Geertz, H. 1959. The vocabulary of emotion: A study of Javanese socialization processes. *Psychiatry* 22:225–37.

———. 1961. *The Javanese family.* Glencoe: Free Press.

Gibbon, E. N.d. *Decline and fall of the Roman Empire.* (Vol. 1.) New York: Modern Library.

Gide, A. 1966. *Les Faux-Monnayeurs.* Paris: Editions de Poche.

Givón, T. 1970. The resolution of gender conflicts in Bantu conjunction. *Chicago Linguistics Society* 6:250–61.

———. 1971. Some historical changes in the noun-class system of Bantu, their probable causes, and wider implications. In *Papers in African Linguistics*, ed. W.-C. Kim & H. Stahlke. Edmonton: Linguistic Research, 33–54.

———. 1976. "Topic, pronoun, and grammatical agreement." In *Subject and topic*, ed. C. Li. New York: Academic Press.

———. 1979. *On understanding grammar.* New York: Academic Press.

———. 1989. *Mind, code, and context.* Hillsdale, NJ: Lawrence Erlbaum.

———. 1990. *Syntax.* (Vol. II.) Amsterdam: John Benjamins.

Givon, T., M. Gernsbacher, & L. Yang. 1990. "The processing of second language vocabulary: From attended to automated word-recognition." In *Proceedings of the tenth meeting of the second language research forum*, ed. H. Burmeister & P. Rounds. Eugene: University of Oregon.

Gleitman, H. 1986. *Psychology.* (2nd ed.) New York: Norton.

Goffman, E. 1967. *Interaction ritual.* New York: Doubleday.

———. 1974. *Frame analysis.* New York: Harper.

———. 1983. "Response cries." In E. Goffman, *Forms of talk.* Philadelphia: University of Pennsylvania Press, 78–123.

Goldman, W. 1974. *The princess bride.* New York: Dell.

Gombrich, E. H. 1966. "Ritualized gesture and expression in art." In *A discussion on ritualization of behaviour in animals and men*, ed. Julian Huxley. Philosophical Transactions of the Royal Society of London, series B, 251:393–401.

Gould, S. 1980. *The panda's thumb.* New York: Pelican.

Grave, R. (ed.). N.d. *English and Scottish ballads.* New York: Macmillan.

Greider, W. 1987. "Annals of finance: The Fed, part II." *New Yorker*, November 16, 1987.

Grice, H. 1957. Meaning. *Philosophical Review* 66:377–88.

———. 1968. Utterance meaning, sentence meaning, and word meaning. *Foundations of Language* 4:225–42.

————. 1975. "Logic and conversation." In *Speech acts*, ed. P. Cole & J. Morgan. New York: Academic Press, 45–57.

Haas, M., & H. Subhanka. 1945. *Spoken Thai*. New York: Holt.

Hagège, C. 1993. *The language builder*. Amsterdam: John Benjamins.

Haiman, F. S. 1972. *Speech and law in a free society*. Chicago: University of Chicago Press.

Haiman, J. 1974. *Targets and syntactic change*. The Hague: Mouton.

————. 1977. Connective particles in Hua: An essay on the parts of speech. *Oceanic Linguistics* 16:53–107.

————. 1978. Conditionals are topics. *Language* 54:565–89.

————. 1980a. Dictionaries and encyclopedias. *Lingua* 50:329–57.

————. 1980b. *Hua: A Papuan language of the Eastern Highlands of New Guinea*. Amsterdam: John Benjamins.

————. 1980c. The iconicity of grammar. *Language* 56:515–40.

————. 1982. "High transitivity in Hua." In *Studies in transitivity*, ed. P. Hopper & S. Thompson. New York: Academic Press, 177–94.

————. 1985. *Natural syntax*. Cambridge: Cambridge University Press.

————. 1988. "Incorporation, parallelism, and focus." In *Linguistic typology and universals*, ed. E. Moravcsik et al. Amsterdam: John Benjamins, 303–20.

————. 1989a. Alienation in grammar. *Studies in Language* 13:129–70.

————. 1989b. "From V/2 to subject clitics." In *Approaches to grammaticalization*, ed. B. Heine & E. Traugott. Amsterdam: John Benjamins, 2:135–58.

————. 1990. Sarcasm as theater. *Cognitive Linguistics* 2:186–209.

————. 1991a. "The bureaucratisation of language." In *Linguistic studies presented to John Finlay*, ed. H. C. Wolfart. Winnipeg: Algonquian and Iroquoian Linguistics, 45–70.

————. 1991b. *Hua-English dictionary*. Wiesbaden: Otto Harrassowitz.

————. 1993. Life, the universe, and human language. *Language Sciences* 15(4):293–322.

Haiman, J., & P. Benincà. 1991. *The Rhaeto-Romance languages*. London: Routledge.

Hale, K. 1971a. "Deep-surface canonical disparities in relation to analysis and change." In *Current trends in linguistics* (vol. 2), ed. T. Sebeok. The Hague: Mouton.

————. 1971b. "A note on a Walbiri tradition of antonymy." In *Semantics: An interdisciplinary reader*, ed. D. Steinberg & L. Jakobovitz. Cambridge: Cambridge University Press.

Hatcher, A. G. 1948. From *ce suis je* to *C'est moi*. *Publications of the Modern Language Association* 63:1053–1100.

Haviland, J. 1989. Sure, sure: Evidence and affect. *Text* 9:27–68.

Hayes, J. 1976. Gayspeak. *Quarterly Journal of Speech* 62:256–66.

Healey, P. 1964. Quotative sentences in Teleefool. In *Pacific Linguistics*. Canberra: Department of Linguistics, Research School of Pacific Studies, Australian National University, A3:27–34.

Heath, J. 1984. *Functional grammar of Nunggubuyu*. Canberra: Australian Institute of Aboriginal Studies.

Heelas, P., & A. Lock (eds.). 1981. *Indigenous psychologies*. New York: Academic Press.

Heffner, R.-M. S. 1964. *General phonetics*. Madison: University of Wisconsin Press.

Heine, B., et al. 1992. *Grammaticalization.* Chicago: University of Chicago Press.

Hemingway, E. 1940. *For whom the bell tolls.* New York: Scribner's Sons.

Henry, J. 1973. *Pathways to madness.* New York: Vintage.

Highet, G. 1962. *The anatomy of satire.* Princeton: Princeton University Press.

Hockett, C., & R. Ascher. 1964. The human revolution. *American Scientist* 52:71–92.

Hofstadter, R. 1963. *Antiintellectualism in American life.* New York: Alfred Knopf.

Hole, G., & D. Einon. 1984. "Play in rodents." In P. Smith (ed.) 1984:95–118.

Hopper, P. 1976. "The expressive continuum." Unpublished manuscript, Linguistic Institute, Oswego.

———. 1994. "Phonogenesis." In *Perspectives on grammaticalization,* ed. W. Pagliuca. Amsterdam: John Benjamins, 29–46.

Hopper, P., & E. Traugott. 1994. *Grammaticalization.* Cambridge: Cambridge University Press.

Horn, L. 1985. Metalinguistic negation and pragmatic ambiguity. *Language* 61:121–74.

Howe, N., & B. Strauss. 1993. *13th Gen.* New York: Vintage.

Howell, S. 1981. "Rules, not words." In Heelas & Lock 1981:133–43.

Huizinga, J. 1955. *Homo ludens.* Boston: Beacon.

Hyman, L. 1977. On the nature of linguistic stress. *Southern California Occasional Papers in Linguistics* 6:37–82.

———. 1979. *Aghem grammatical structure.* (Southern California Occasional Papers in Linguistics 9.) Los Angeles: Linguistics Department, University of Southern California.

Hymes, D. 1987. "A theory of irony and a Chinookan pattern of verbal exchange." In *The pragmatic perspective,* ed. J. Verschueren and M. Bertucelli-Papi. Amsterdam: John Benjamins, 293–337.

Irvine, J. 1990. "Registering affect: Heteroglossia in the linguistic expression of emotion." In *Language and the politics of emotion,* ed. C. Lutz and L. Abu-Lughod. Cambridge: Cambridge University Press, 126–61.

———. 1993. "Insult and responsibility: verbal abuse in a Wolof village." In *Responsibility and evidence in oral discourse,* ed. J. Hill & J. Irvine. Cambridge: Cambridge University Press, 105–34.

Israel, J. 1971. *Alienation.* Boston: Allyn & Bacon.

Jackendoff, R. 1983. *Semantics and cognition.* Cambridge: MIT Press.

Jakobson, R. [1931] 1972. "Principles of historical phonology." In *A reader in historical linguistics,* ed. A. Keiler. New York: Holt, 121–38.

———. [1936] 1971. "Beitrag zur allgemeinen Kasuslehre." In *Selected writings of Roman Jakobson.* Berlin: Mouton–de Gruyter, 2:23–71.

———. 1965. Quest for the essence of language. *Diogenes* 51:21–37.

James, W. 1890. *Principles of psychology.* (Vol. 1.) New York: Holt.

Jaynes, J. 1976. *The origins of consciousness in the breakdown of the bicameral mind.* Boston: Houghton Mifflin.

Jespersen, O. 1927. *A modern English grammar on historical principles.* (Vol. 3.) London: Allen and Unwin.

Jhally, S. 1986. *The codes of advertising.* New York: St. Martins.

Johnson, F. 1985. "The Western concept of self." In *Culture and self: Asian and Western perspectives,* ed. A. J. Marsella et al. New York: Tavistock, 91–138.

Jones, D. [1917] 1946. *An English pronouncing dictionary.* (7th ed.) New York: E. P. Dutton.

Jonsson, L. 1995. "Sarcasm in German." Honor's thesis, Macalester College.

Joos, M. (ed.). 1957. *Readings in linguistics*. (Vol. 1.) Chicago: University of Chicago Press.

Jurgens, U., & D. Ploog. 1974. *Von der Ethologie zur Psychologie*. München: Beck.

Justice, D. 1985. "Etiology of a prosodic shift: Enallage Ictus." Unpublished manuscript, University of California, Berkeley.

Karsten, A. 1928. Psychische Sättigung. *Psychologische Forschungen* 10:142–254.

Kaufer, D. 1981. Understanding ironic communication. *Journal of Pragmatics* 5:495–510.

Kay, P. 1977. "Language evolution and speech style." In *Sociocultural dimensions of language change*, ed. B. Blount & M. Sanches. New York: Academic Press, 21–33.

Kaye, J. 1989. *Phonology: A cognitive view*. Hillsdale, NJ: Lawrence Erlbaum.

Keeler, W. 1984. *Javanese: A cultural approach*. Athens: Ohio University Press.

Keenan, E., & B. Comrie. 1977. Noun phrase accessibility and universal grammar. *Linguistic Inquiry* 8:63–99.

Kemmer, S. 1993. *The middle voice: A typological and diachronic study*. Amsterdam: John Benjamins.

Kendon, A. 1988. "Gestures into words." In *Cross-cultural perspectives in non-verbal communication*, ed. E. Poyatos. Toronto: Hogrefe, 131–41.

Kessel, E. 1955. The mating activity of balloon flies. *Journal of Systematic Zoology* 4:97–104.

Kiparsky, P. 1966. "Oral poetry: Some linguistic and typological considerations." In *Oral literature and the formula*, ed. B. A. Stolz & R. Shannon. Ann Arbor: University of Michigan Press.

———. 1972. *Explanation in phonology*. Dordrecht: Foris.

Kiparsky, P., & C. Kiparsky. 1970. "Fact." In *Progress in linguistics*, ed. M. Bierwisch & K. Heidolph. The Hague: Mouton

Klapp, O. 1969. *Collective search for identity*. New York: Holt.

Kodama, Y. 1995. "Hypocrisy, politeness, and Rokakuka." Unpublished manuscript, University of New Mexico.

Koenig, 1970. *Kultur und Verhaltensforschung: Einführung in die Kulturtheorie*. Munich: Deutscher Taschenbuch Verlag.

Kononov, A. N. 1956. *Grammatika Sovremennogo Turetskogo Literaturnogo Jazyka* (Grammar of contemporary literary Turkish). Liningrad: Akademia Nauk.

Koster, J. 1987. *Domains and dynasties*. Dordrecht: Foris.

Kris, E., & E. Gombrich. 1938. The principles of caricature. *British Journal of Medical Psychology*. 17:319–42.

Krugman, P. 1989. *The age of diminished expectations*. Cambridge: MIT Press.

Kuiper, K., and D. Haggo. 1984. Livestock auctions, oral poetry, and ordinary language. *Language in Society* 13:205–34.

Kuno, S. 1973. *The structure of the Japanese language*. Cambridge: MIT Press.

———. 1987. *Functional syntax*. Chicago: University of Chicago Press.

Labov, W. 1966. *The social stratification of English in New York City*. Washington, DC: Center for Applied Linguistics.

———. 1972a. *Language in the inner city*. Philadelphia: University of Pennsylvania Press.

———. 1972b. *Sociolinguistic patterns*. Philadelphia: University of Philadelphia Press.

————. 1984. "Intensity." In *Meaning, form, and use in context: Linguistic applications*, ed. D. Schiffrin. Washington, DC: Georgetown University Press, 43–70.

Ladd, R. 1978a. *The structure of intonational meaning: Evidence from English.* Bloomington: Indiana University Linguistics Club.

————. 1978b. Stylized intonation. *Language* 54:517–40.

Ladefoged, P. 1969. "The nature of vowel quality." In *Three areas of experimental phonetics.* Oxford: Oxford University Press.

————. 1993. *A course in phonetics.* (3rd ed.) New York: Harcourt Brace Jovanovich.

Laing, R. 1965. *The divided self.* London: Penguin.

Lakoff, G. 1970. "Counterparts and the problem of reference in transformational grammar." In *Report # NSF-24 to the National Science Foundation*, ed. S. Kuno. Cambridge: Harvard Computation Laboratory, 23–37.

Lakoff, R. 1973. "Questionable answers and answerable questions." In *Papers in honor of Henry and Renee Kahane*, ed. B. Kachru et al. Urbana: University of Illinois Press, 453–67.

————. 1990. *Talking power.* New York: Basic Books.

Lambert, W., & L. Jakobovitz. 1960. Verbal satiation and changes in the intensity of meaning. *Journal of Experimental Psychology* 60:376–83.

Langacker, R. 1985. "Observations and speculations on subjectivity." In *Iconicity in syntax*, ed. J. Haiman. Amsterdam: John Benjamins, 109–50.

Laver, J. 1994. *Principles of phonetics.* Cambridge: Cambridge University Press.

Lejeune, P. 1980. *Je est un autre.* Paris: Editions du Seuil.

Lentricchia, F. 1980. *After the New Criticism.* Chicago: University of Chicago Press.

Levinson, C. 1991. Pragmatic reduction of the binding conditions revisited. *Journal of Linguistics* 27:107–62.

Lewis, G. 1953. *Teach yourself Turkish.* London: English Universities Press.

————. 1967. *Turkish grammar.* Oxford: Oxford University Press.

Lewis, N. [1964] 1984. *The honoured society: The Sicilian Mafia observed.* London: Eland/Hippocrene.

Liberman, M. 1979. *The intonational system of English.* Bloomington: Indiana University Linguistics Club.

Lightfoot, D. 1979. *Principles of diachronic syntax.* Cambridge: Cambridge University Press.

Lipmann, W. 1923. *Public opinion.* New York: Harcourt, Brace.

Loizos, C. 1966. "Play in mammals." In *Play, exploration, and territoriality in mammals*, ed. P. A. Jewell & C. Loizos. Symposia of the Zoological Society of London, 18. London: Academic Press, 1–9.

Lukács, G. 1965. *History and class consciousness.* Cambridge: MIT Press.

Lumsden, C., & E. O. Wilson. 1981. *Genes, mind, and culture.* Cambridge: Harvard University Press.

Lyons, J. 1968. *An introduction to theoretical linguistics.* Cambridge: Cambridge University Press.

————. 1973. Towards a "notional" theory of the "parts of speech." *Journal of Linguistics* 11:209–36.

————. 1977. *Semantics.* (Vol. 1.) Cambridge: Cambridge University Press.

Lyons, J. O. 1978. *The invention of the self.* Carbondale: Southern Illinois University Press.

MacDonald, D. [1941] 1958. "Kulturbolshevismus and Mr. Van Wyck Borrks." In
    D. MacDonald, *Memoirs of a revolutionist*. Cleveland: Meridian, 203–14.

MacDonald, L. 1990. Evidentials in Tauya. *Language and Linguistics in Melanesia*
    21(1/2):31–46.

MacKay, I. 1987. *Phonetics*. (2nd ed.) Boston: Little, Brown.

Malinowski, B. 1923. "The problem of meaning in primitive languages." In *The
    meaning of meaning*, ed. C. K. Ogden & I. A. Richards. New York:
    Harcourt, Brace, & World, 296–336.

Mallinson, G. 1986. *Rumanian*. London: Croom Helm.

Manning, A. 1967. *An introduction to animal behaviour*. New York: Addison-
    Wesley.

Marlowe, C. 1972. *Hero and Leander*. New York: Johnson Reprint Corporation.

Marx, L. 1964. *The machine in the garden*. New York: Oxford University Press.

Masson, J., & S. McCarthy. 1995. *When elephants weep*. New York: Delacorte.

Matisoff, J. 1979. *Psycho-ostensive expressions in Yiddish*. Philadelphia: ISHI
    Publications.

Matthews, B. 1995. "Gay speech: A preliminary investigaiton." Honor's thesis,
    Macalester College.

Mayr, E. 1962. "Accident or design: The paradox of evolution." In *Evolution and
    the diversity of life*, ed. E. Mayr. Cambridge: Harvard University Press.

McInerney, J. 1984. *Bright lights, big city*. New York: Vintage.

McNeill, D. 1992. *Hand and mind*. Chicago: University of Chicago Press.

Mead, G. 1934. *Mind, self, and society*. Chicago: University of Chicago Press.

———. 1973. "Ritual and social crisis." In Shaughnessy 1973:87–101.

Mehta, V. 1971. John is easy to please. *New Yorker*, May 1, 1971.

Meinhof, C. 1936. *Die Entstehung flektierender Sprachen*. Berlin: Reimer.

Merton, R. 1968. *Social theory and social structure*. New York: Free Press.

Miller, Mark. 1988. *Boxed in*. Evanston: Northwestern University Press.

Miller, Merle. 1973. *Plain speaking*. New York: Berkley Publishing Corporation.

Miller, S. 1973. Ends, means, and galumphing. *American Anthropologist* 75:87–98.

Minami, H. 1971. *Psychology of the Japanese people*. Toronto: University of
    Toronto Press.

Mitchell, B. 1987. *Old English syntax*. (Vol. 1.) Oxford: Oxford University Press.

Moore, S., & B. Myerhoff. 1977a. "Introduction." In *Secular ritual*, ed. S. Moore &
    B. Meyerhoff. Amsterdam: Van Gorcum, 3–24.

———. 1977b. *Secular ritual*. Amsterdam: Van Gorcum.

Moravcsik, E. 1978. "Agreement." In *Universals of human language* (vol. 4), ed.
    J. Greenberg et al. Stanford: Stanford University Press, 331–74.

Morgan, J. 1972. Verb agreement in English. *Chicago Linguistics Society* 8:278–86.

Morris, C. 1972. *The discovery of the individual, 1050–1200*. New York: Harper &
    Row.

Morris, D. 1957. Typical intensity and its relation to the problem of ritualization.
    Behaviour 11:1–12.

———. 1966. The rigidification of behaviour. *Philosophical Transactions of the
    Royal Society of London* (Series B, Biological Sciences), 251:327–30.

Moynihan, M. 1970. Control, suppression, decay, disappearance, and replacement
    of displays. *Journal of Theoretical Biology* 29:85–112.

Muecke, D. 1969. *The compass of irony*. London: Methuen.

———. 1970. *Irony*. London: Methuen.

Mumford, L. 1960. *Art and technics*. New York: Columbia University Press.

Munro, P. 1982. "On the transitivity of 'say' verbs." In *Studies in transitivity*, ed. P. Hopper & S. Thompson. New York: Academic Press, 301–18.

Mustanoja, T. 1960. *A Middle English syntax, part 1*. Helsinki: Mémoires de la société finougrienne, 22.

Nabokov, V. 1966. *Pnin*. New York: Atheneum.

Naipaul, V. S. 1959. *The mystic masseur*. New York: Vanguard.

Nash, J. 1980. Lying about running: The functions of talk in a scene. *Qualitative Sociology* 3(2):83–99.

Nathanson, D. 1992. *Shame and pride: Affect, sex, and the birth of the self*. New York: Norton.

Nietzsche, F. [1872] 1967. *The birth of tragedy*. Trans. W. Kaufmann. New York: Vintage.

Ochs, E. 1983. "Making it last." In *Acquiring conversational competence*, ed. E. Ochs & B. Schieffelin. London: Routledge & Kegan Paul.

Ogura, M. 1989. *Verbs with the reflexive pronoun and constructions with self in Old and early Middle English*. Cambridge: Brewer.

Orwell, G. 1953a. "Boys' weeklies." In Orwell 1953b:279–308.

———. 1953b. *A collection of essays*. New York: Harcourt, Brace, Jovanovich.

———. 1953c. "Politics and the English language." In Orwell 1953b:156–71.

———. 1953d. "Why I write." In Orwell 1953b:309–16.

Palmer, F. 1986. *Mood and modality*. Cambridge: Cambridge University Press.

Palmer, R. [1941] 1973. *Twelve who ruled: The year of the terror in the French Revolution*. Princeton: Princeton University Press.

Partee, B. 1973. "The syntax and semantics of quotation." In *Festschrift for Morris Halle*, ed. S. Anderson & P. Kiparsky. New York: Harper and Row, 410–18.

Paul, H. [1880] 1968. *Prinzipien der Sprachgeschichte*. (8th ed.) Tubingen: Niemeyer.

Piaget, J. 1951. *Play, dreams, and imitation in childhood*. Trans. F. M. Hodgson. London: Heinemann.

Pike, K. [1943] 1971. *Phonetics*. Ann Arbor: University of Michigan Press.

Plato. 1926. *Cratylus*. Trans. H. N. Fowler. Loeb Classical Library, 167. Cambridge: Harvard University Press.

Plooij, F. X. 1978. "Traits of language in wild chimpanzees?" In *Action, gesture, and symbol*, ed. A. Lock. London: Academic Press, 111–32.

Popper, K. 1966. *The open society and its enemies*. (Vol. 2.) (5th ed.) Princeton: Princeton University Press.

Postal, P. 1971. "The method of universal grammar." In *The place of method in linguistics*, ed. P. Garvin. The Hague: Mouton.

Postman, N. 1987. "The teachings of the media curriculum." In *American media and mass culture*, ed. P. Lazere. Berkeley: University of California Press, 421–30.

Principles of the International Phonetic Association. [1949] 1962. London: Department of Phonetics, University College.

Quine, W. [1953] 1963. "Reference and modality." In *From a logical point of view*. New York: Harper, 139–59.

———. 1965. *Mathematical logic*. Cambridge: Harvard University Press.

Read, K. 1959. Morality and the concept of the person among the Gahuku-Gama. *Oceania* 25:233–82.

Reid, W. 1991. *Verb and noun number in English*. London: Longman.

Révai, J. 1995. "Asserting identity." In *Alternative linguistics*, ed. P. Davis. Amsterdam: John Benjamins, 135–52.

Richardson, J. 1975. Six o'clock prayers. *Harpers*, 34–38.

Riesman, D. 1950. *The lonely crowd.* Yale University Press.

Rigsby, B., & T. Crowley. 1979. "Cape York Creole." In *Languages and their status*, ed. T. Shopen. Cambridge: Winthrop, 153–207.

Rizzi, L. 1986. Null objects in Italian and the theory of pro. *Linguistic Inquiry* 17:501–57.

Roberts, J. 1987. *Amele.* London: Croom Helm.

Rohlfs, G. [1949] 1972. *Historische Grammatik der italienischen Sprache.* (Vol. 2.) Bern: Francke.

Rosaldo, M. 1984. "Toward an anthropology of self and feeling." In Shweder & Levine 1984:137–57.

Roth, P. 1969. *Portnoy's complaint.* New York: Bantam.

———. 1972. *Our gang.* London: Corgi Books.

Rudnick, P., & K. Andersen. 1989. The irony epidemic. *Spy*, March 1989. (Reprinted in *Utne Reader*, May/June 1989:34–40.)

Russell, B. 1940. *An inquiry into meaning and truth.* Harmondsworth: Penguin.

———. 1950. "The superior virtue of the oppressed." In B. Russell, *Unpopular essays.* New York: Simon & Schuster, 58–64.

Sacks, O. 1996. *An anthropologist on Mars.* New York: Random House.

Sapir, E. 1921. *Language.* New York: Harvest Books.

———. 1925. Sound patterns in language. *Language* 1:37–51.

———. 1949. "The psychological reality of phonemes." In *Selected Writings of Edward Sapir*, ed. D. Mandelbaum. Berkeley: University of California Press, 46–60.

Sartre, J.-P. 1947. *La P . . . respectueuse (suivi de La mort sans sepulture).* Paris: Gallimard.

Saussure, F. de. 1966. *Course in general linguistics.* Trans. W. Baskin. New York: McGraw-Hill.

Savage-Rumbaugh, S. 1986. *Ape language: From conditioned response to symbol.* New York: Columbia University Press.

Schauer, F. 1982. *Free speech: A philosophical enquiry.* Cambridge: Cambridge University Press.

Schulberg, B. [1941] 1971. *What makes Sammy run?* London: Sphere.

Searle, J. 1976. A taxonomy of illocutionary acts. *Language in Society* 5:1–23.

———. 1979. *Expression and meaning.* Cambridge: Cambridge University Press.

Sebeok, T. 1962. Coding in the evolution of signalling behavior. *Behavioral Science* 7(4):30–42.

Sells, P. 1987. Aspects of logophoricity. *Linguistic Inquiry* 18: 445–79.

Shakespeare, W. 1956. *Troilus and Cressida.* New Haven: Yale University Press.

Shapiro, M. 1985. Signs, marks, and diacritics. *International Journal of Slavic Linguistics and Poetics* 31(2):375–84.

Shaughnessy, J. (ed.). 1973. *The roots of ritual.* Grand Rapids: Eerdmans.

Shweder, R., & R. Levine (eds.). 1984. *Culture theory.* Cambridge: Cambridge University Press.

Siegel, J. 1986. *Solo in the new order: Language and hierarchy in an Indonesian city.* Princeton: Princeton University Press.

Sieroff, E., A. Polatsek, & M. Posner. 1988. Recognition of visual letter strings following injury to the posterior visual attention system. *Cognitive Neuropsychology* 5(4):427–49.

Sieroff, E., & M. Posner. 1988. Cueing spatial attention during processing of words and letter strings in normals. *Cognitive Neuropsychology* 5(4):450–72.

Sipple, L. 1994a. "Ritualizaiton of sentence stress in English." Unpublished manuscript, Macalester College.

———. 1994b. "Word stress as grammaticalized sentence emphasis in American English." Unpublished manuscript, Macalester College.

Skeat, W. 1963. *A concise etymological dictionary of the English language.* New York: Capricorn.

Slater, P. [1968] 1992. *The glory of Hera.* Princeton: Princeton University Press.

———. 1970. *The pursuit of loneliness.* Boston: Beacon.

Smith, D., & A. Raygor. 1956. Verbal satiation and personality. *Journal of Abnormal and Social Psychology* 52:323–6.

Smith, J. 1966. *The theory of evolution.* (2nd ed.) Harmondsworth: Penguin.

Smith, P. (ed.). 1984. *Play in animals and humans.* Oxford: Blackwell.

Sontag, S. 1966a. *Against interpretation.* New York: Farrar, Straus, & Giroux.

———. 1966b. "Against interpretation." In Sontag 1966a:3–14.

———. 1966c. "The death of tragedy." In Sontag 1966a:132–9.

———. 1966d. "Notes on 'camp.'" In Sontag 1966a:275–92.

———. 1966e. "On style." In Sontag 1966a:15–36.

Sperber, D., and D. Wilson. 1981. "Irony and the use-mention distinction." In *Radical pragmatics*, ed. P. Cole. New York: Academic Press, 295–318.

Spitzer, L. 1922. *Italienische Umgangssprache.* Leipzig: K. Schroeder.

Stankiewicz, E. 1964. "Problems of emotive language." In *Approaches to semiotics*, ed. T. Sebeok et al. The Hague: Mouton, 239–64.

Steiner, G. 1975. *After Babel: Aspects of language and translation.* New York: Oxford University Press.

Stimm, H. 1976. "Über einigen syntaktischen Eigenheiten des Surselvischen." In *Rätoromanisches Colloquium, Mainz*, ed. T. Elwert. Innsbruck: Institut für Romanische Philologie der Leopold-Franzens-Universität, 31–58.

Stone, R. 1987. *A hall of mirrors.* New York: Viking.

Storr, A. 1990. *The art of psychotherapy.* (2nd ed.) New York: Routledge.

Suzuki, D. T. 1956. *Zen Buddhism: Selected writings.* Ed. W. Barrett. New York: Doubleday Anchor.

Suzuki, S. 1994. Is that a fact? *Berkeley Linguistics Society* 20:521–31.

Suzuki, T. 1976. Language and behavior in Japan. *Japan Quarterly* 23:255–66.

Sweet, A., & N. Davis. 1953. *Sweet's Anglo-Saxon primer.* (9th ed.) Oxford: Oxford University Press.

Szasz, T. 1965. *The ethics of psychoanalysis.* New York: MacMillan.

Tambiah, E. S. 1968. The magical power of words. *Man*, n.s. 3(2):175–208.

Tannen, D. 1982. "The oral-literate continuuum in discourse." In *Spoken and written language*, ed. D. Tannen. Norwood, NJ: Ablex, 1–16.

Tannen, D., & P. Oztek. 1981. "Health to our mouths." In Coulmas (ed.) 1981:37–54.

Terzuolo, C., & P. Viviani. 1979. "The central representation of learned motor patterns." In *Posture and movement*, ed. R. Talbott & D. Humphrey. New York: Raven Press, 113–22.

Test, M. (1989) "Uttering banalities with conviction." Unpublished, Macalester College.

Thompson, S. A. 1971. "The deep structure of relative clauses." In *Studies in linguistic semantics*, ed. C. Fillmore & T. Langendoen. New York: Holt, Rinehart and Winston, 79–96.

Thorpe, W. 1956. *Learning and instinct in animals*. London: Methuen.

Thurber, James. [1945] 1994a. "Here lies Miss Groby." In Thurber [1945] 1994c:69–72.

———. [1945] 1994b. "The secret life of Walter Mitty." In Thurber [1945] 1994c:62–68.

———. [1945] 1994c. *The Thurber carnival*. New York: Modern Library.

Thurneysen, R. 1892. Zur Stellung des Verbums im Althochdeutschen. *Zeitschrift für romanische Philologie* 16:289–307.

Tinbergen, N. 1952. "Derived" activities: Their causation, biological significance, origin, and emancipation during evolution. *Quarterly Review of Biology* 27:1–32.

Toulmin, S. 1977. "Self-knowledge and knowledge of the 'Self.'" In *The Self*, ed. T. Mischel. Totonaw, NJ: Rowman & Littlefield, 291–317.

Traugott, E., & B. Heine (eds.). 1991. *Approaches to grammaticalization*. Amsterdam: John Benjamins.

Trilling, L. 1972. *Sincerity and authenticity*. Cambridge: Harvard University Press.

Trivers, R. 1974. Parent-offspring conflict. *American Zoologist* 14:249–64.

Trudgill, P. 1972. Sex, covert prestige, and linguistic change in the urban British dialect of Norwich. *Language in Society* 1:179–95.

Tuan, Yi-Fu. 1982. *Segmented worlds and self*. Minneapolis: University of Minnesota Press.

Twaddell, W. [1938] 1957. "A note on Old High German umlaut." In *Readings in linguistics* (vol. 1), ed. M. Joos. Chicago: University of Chicago Press, 85–8.

Twain, M. [1884] 1960. *Huckleberry Finn*. New York: Washington Square Press.

———. 1904. "My first lie and how I got out of it." In *The man who corrupted Hadleyburg and other essays and stories*. New York: Harper, 145–56.

van Gelderen, E. 1992. Arguments without number: The case of *it* and *het*. *Linguistics* 30:381–7.

van Lancker, D. 1974. "Heterogeneity in language and speech: Neurolinguistic studies." Ph.D. dissertation, Brown University.

Veblen, T. [1899] 1953. *Theory of the leisure class*. New York: New American Library.

Visser, T. 1984. *Historical syntax of English*. (Vol. 1.) Leiden: E. J. Brill.

Voloshinov, V. N. 1973. *Marxism and the philosophy of language*. Trans. L. Matejka & I. Titunik. New York: Seminar Press.

von Foerster, H. 1984. "On constructing a reality." In *The invented reality*, ed. P. Watzlawick. New York: Norton, 41–61.

Vonnegut, K. 1970. *Cat's cradle*. New York: Dell.

von Rezzori, G. 1981. *Memoirs of an Anti-Semite*. New York: Viking.

Wald, B. 1987. Spanish-English grammatical contact in Los Angeles. *Linguistics* 25:53–80.

Watkins, C. 1962. *Indo-European origins of the celtic verb: Part I, The sigmatic aorist*. Dublin: Institute of Advanced Studies.

Watts, A. 1958. *The spirit of Zen*. New York: Grove Press.

Watzlawick, P. 1977. *How real is real?* New York: Vintage Books.

Weller, T. 1987. *Culture made stupid*. Boston: Houghton Mifflin.

Werner, H., & B. Kaplan. 1963. *Symbol formation: An organismic-developmental approach to language and the expression of thought*. New York: Wiley.

Wescott, R. 1967. The evolution of language: Reopening a closed subject. *Studies in Linguistics* 19:67–81.

Wheelock, W. 1982. The problem of ritual language: From information to situation. *Journal of the American Academy of Religion* 50:49–71.

Whorf, B. 1956. "Grammatical categories." In *Language, thought, and reality: Selected writings of Benjamin Lee Whorf*, ed. J. Carroll. Cambridge: MIT Press, 87–101.

Wierzbicka, A. 1969. Problems of expression: Their place in the semantic theory. *WDN Zam.* 146:1–27.

———. 1972. *Semantic primitives*. Frankfurt: Athenaeum.

———. 1974. The semantics of direct and indirect discourse. *Papers in Linguistics* 7:267–307.

———. 1980. *The case for surface case*. Ann Arbor: Karoma Publishers.

———. 1985. "Oats and wheat: The fallacy of arbitrariness." In *Iconicity in syntax*, ed. J. Haiman. Amsterdam: Benjamins, 311–42.

———. 1991. Key words and core values in Japanese. *Language in Society* 20:333–85.

Wilson, E. O. 1975. *Sociobiology*. Cambridge: Belknap Press of Harvard University.

Winner, E. 1988. *The point of words*. Cambridge: Harvard University Press.

Wolfowitz, C. 1991. *Language style and social space: Stylistic choice in Suriname Javanese*. Urbana: University of Illinois Press.

Wotton, H. 1949. "The character of a happy life." In *Elizabethan lyrics*, ed. N. Ault. New York: William Sloane Associates, 459–60.

Xiao, H. 1989. "Sarcastic intonations in Mandarin Chinese." Unpublished manuscript, University of Manitoba.

Zavitzianos, G. 1972. Homeovestism: Perverse form of behaviour involving wearing clothes of the same sex. *International Journal of Psycho-Analysis* 53:471–7.

Zipf, G. K. 1935. *The psychobiology of language*. Boston: Houghton.

Index